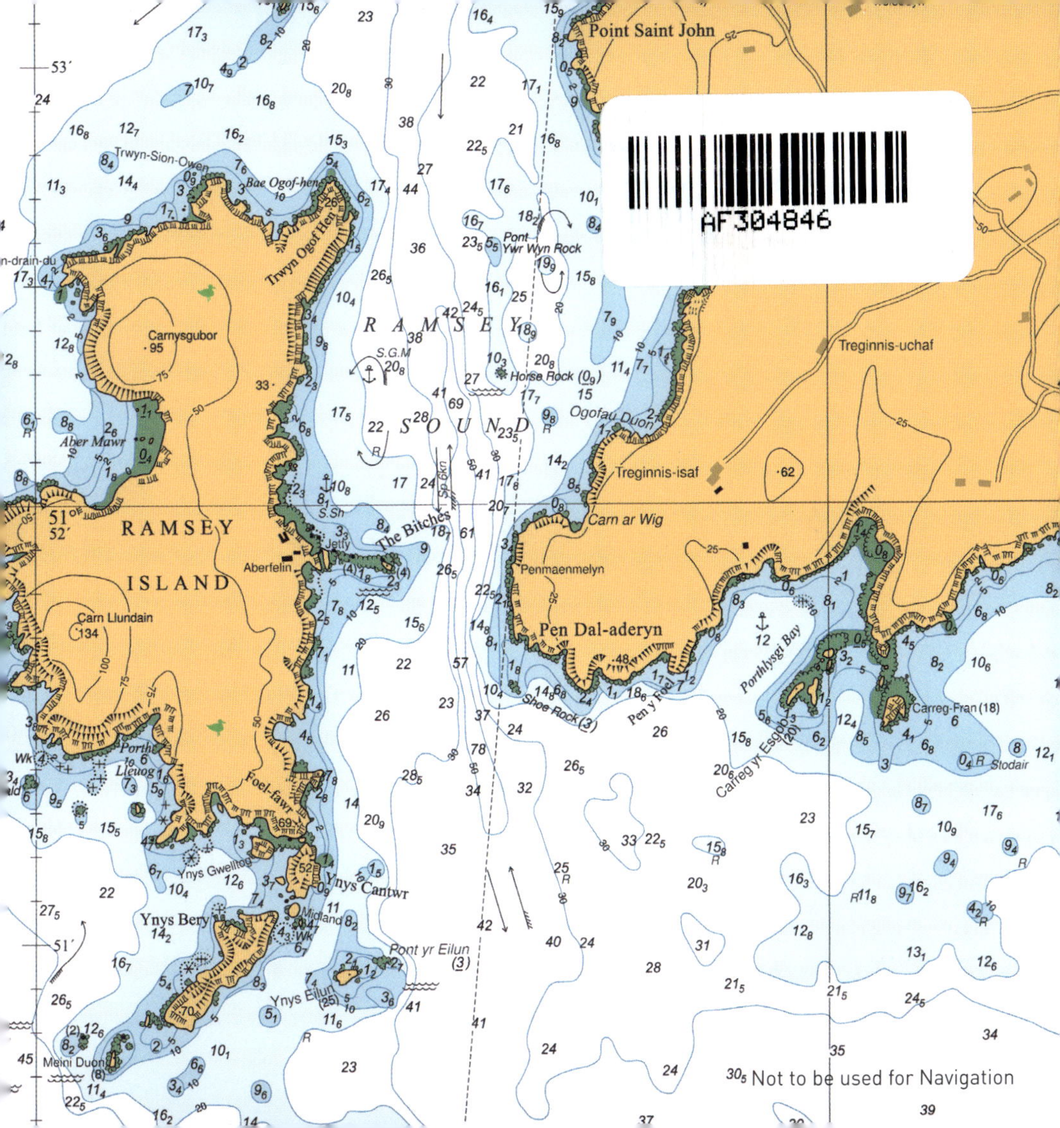
Point Saint John
Treginnis-uchaf
Treginnis-isaf
Ogofau Duon
Pont Ywr Wyn Rock
Horse Rock
Carn ar Wig
Penmaenmelyn
Pen Dal-aderyn
Shoe Rock (3)
Pen y Foel
Porthlysgi Bay
Carreg yr Esgob (20)
Carreg-Fran (18)
Stodair
Trwyn-Sion-Owen
Bae Ogof-hen
Trwyn Ogof Hen
R A M S E Y   S O U N D
S.G.M
Carnysgubor
Aber Mawr
RAMSEY
ISLAND
Carn Llundain
The Bitches
Jetty
Aberfelin
Porth
Lleuog
Foel-fawr
Ynys Gwelltog
Ynys Cantwr
Ynys Bery
Midland
Pont yr Eilun (3)
Ynys Eilun
Meini Duon (8)
Not to be used for Navigation
AF304846

Ramsey Island and beyond
Published in Great Britain in 2017
by Graffeg Limited

Written by Ffion Rees
copyright © 2017.
Designed and produced by Graffeg
Limited copyright © 2017.

This second edition 2023.

Graffeg Limited, 24 Stradey Park
Business Centre, Mwrwg Road,
Llangennech, Llanelli,
Carmarthenshire SA14 8YP Wales UK
Tel 01554 824000 www.graffeg.com

Ffion Rees is hereby identified as the
author of this work in accordance with
section 77 of the Copyright, Designs and
Patents Act 1988.

A CIP Catalogue record for this book is
available from the British Library.



Printed in China TT211122

ISBN 9781909823754

2 3 4 5 6 7 8 9

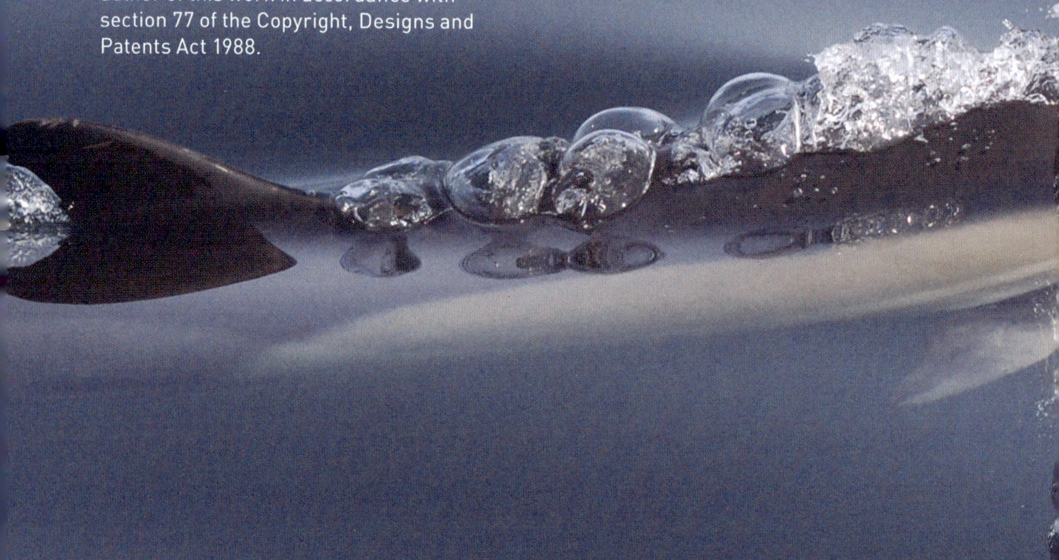

# Ramsey Island
## and beyond

a life on the water

Ffion Rees

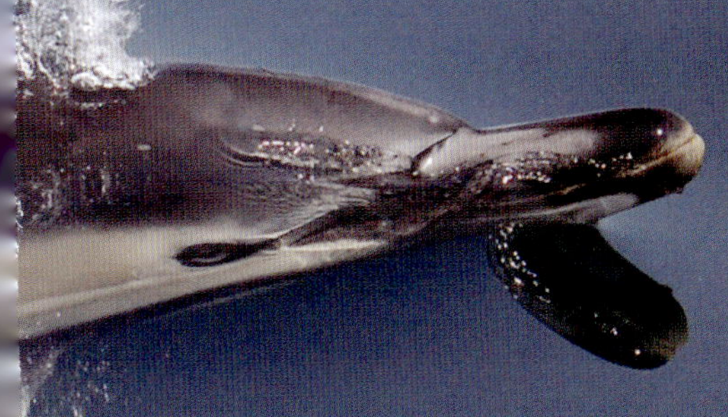

GRAFFEG

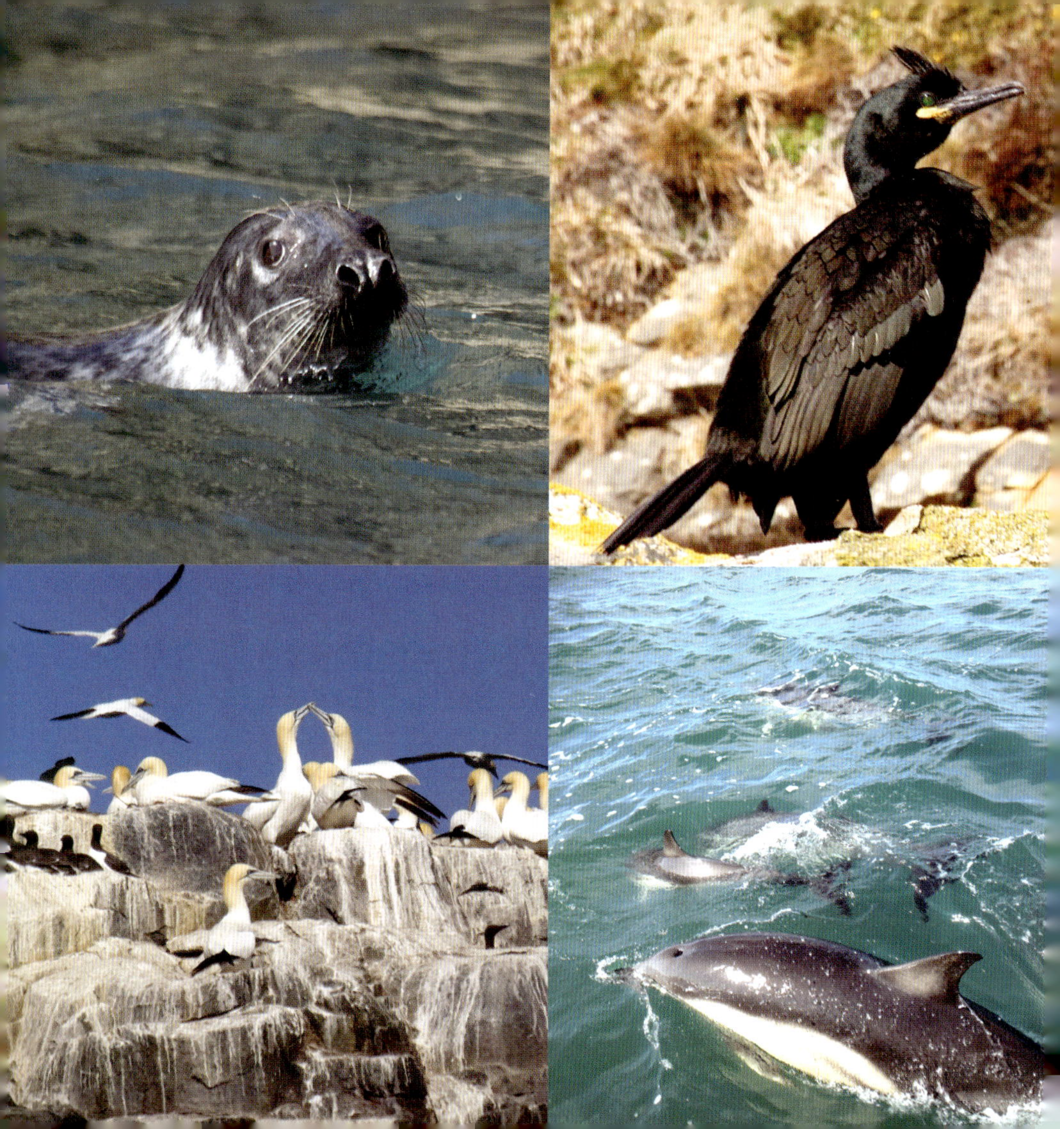

# CONTENTS



**Dedications**

I would like to dedicate this book to Jackie Morris, without whom it would never have been written. Not only did she have faith in me and introduce me to Graffeg, she also kick-started me into actually putting pen to paper. I would also like to thank my parents for introducing me to the sea and instilling in me a love of the natural world; to John Price for believing in my ability to hold my own in a male dominated world and for the opportunities he gave me; to my partner Dan for keeping me fed and sane whilst writing it, and to Deb who agreed to read the first draft when I was too nervous to send it anyone else. I would also like to thank all the team at Graffeg for their support and encouragement and for the wonderful job they have done on the design and production.

# RAMSEY ISLAND

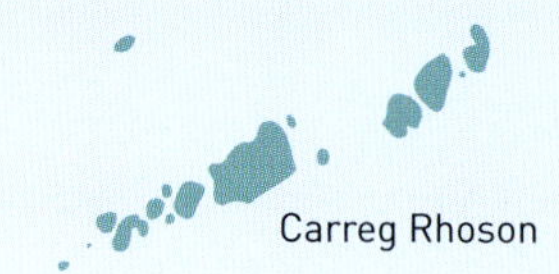


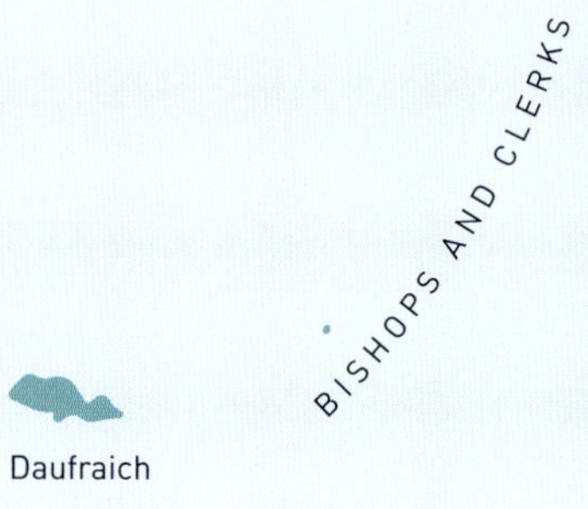



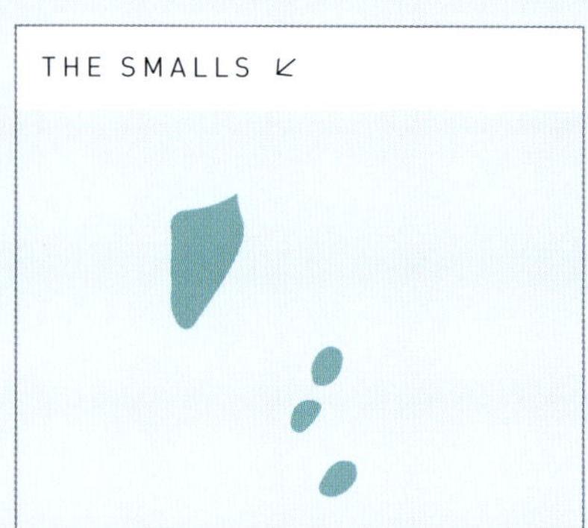



Key

Kilometres

0    0.5    1    1.5

0    0.5    1
Miles

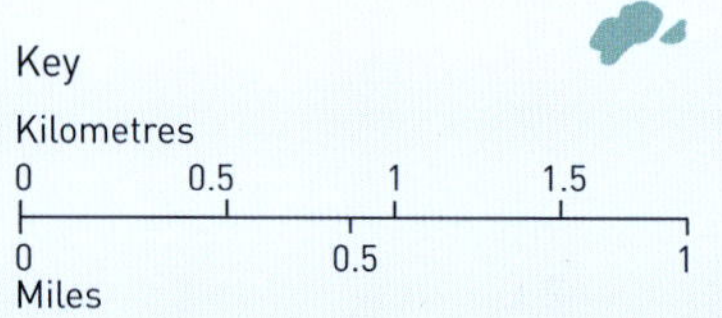

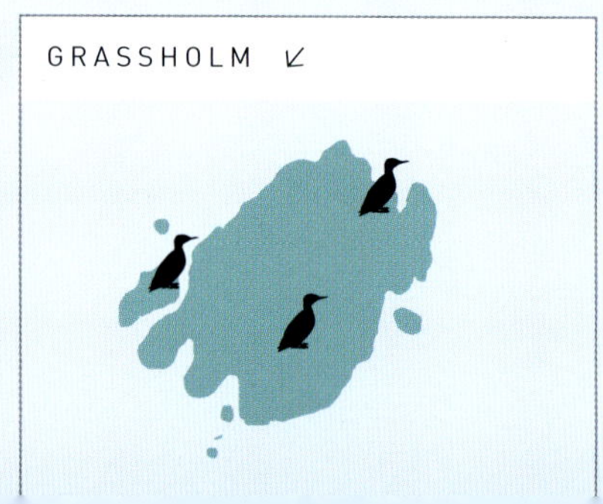

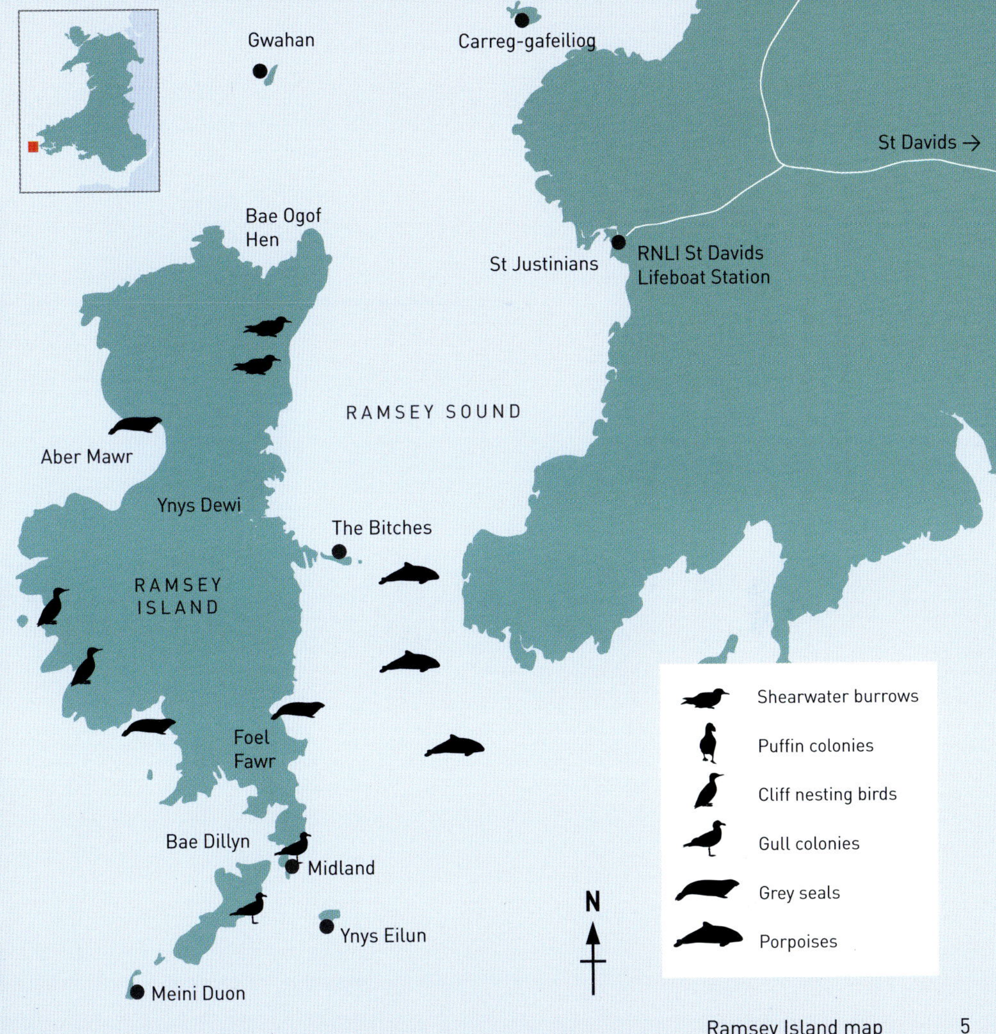


Ramsey Island map

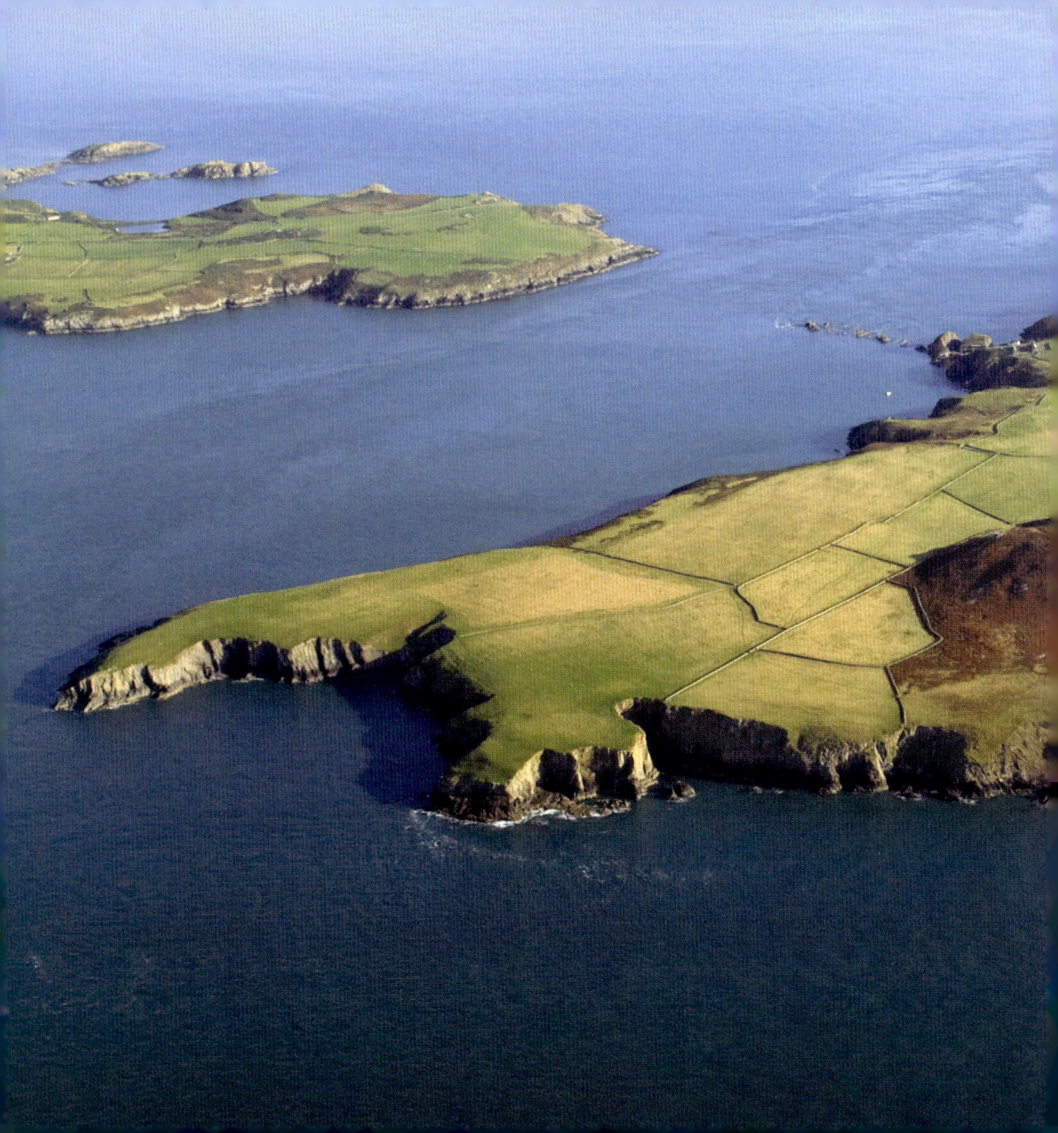

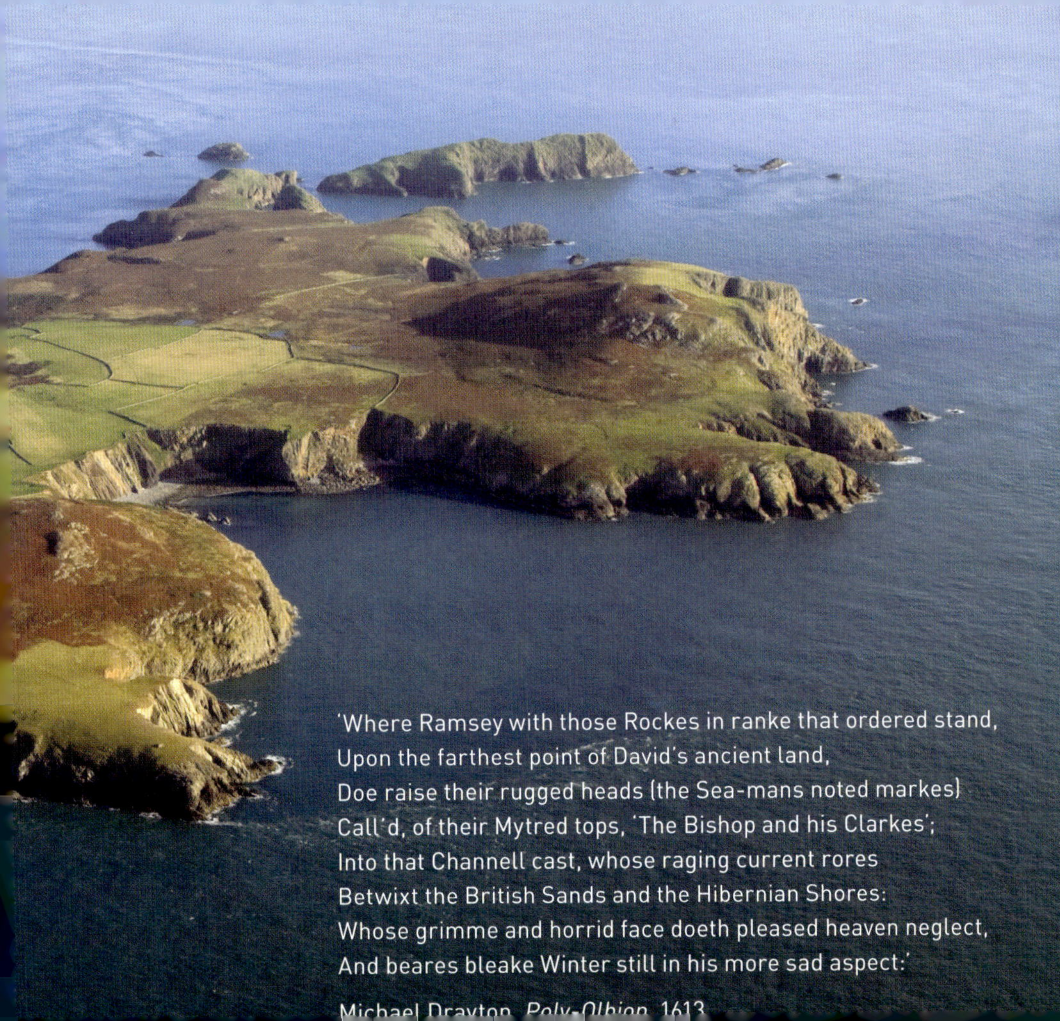

'Where Ramsey with those Rockes in ranke that ordered stand,
Upon the farthest point of David's ancient land,
Doe raise their rugged heads (the Sea-mans noted markes)
Call'd, of their Mytred tops, 'The Bishop and his Clarkes';
Into that Channell cast, whose raging current rores
Betwixt the British Sands and the Hibernian Shores:
Whose grimme and horrid face doeth pleased heaven neglect,
And beares bleake Winter still in his more sad aspect:'

Michael Drayton, Poly-Olbion, 1613

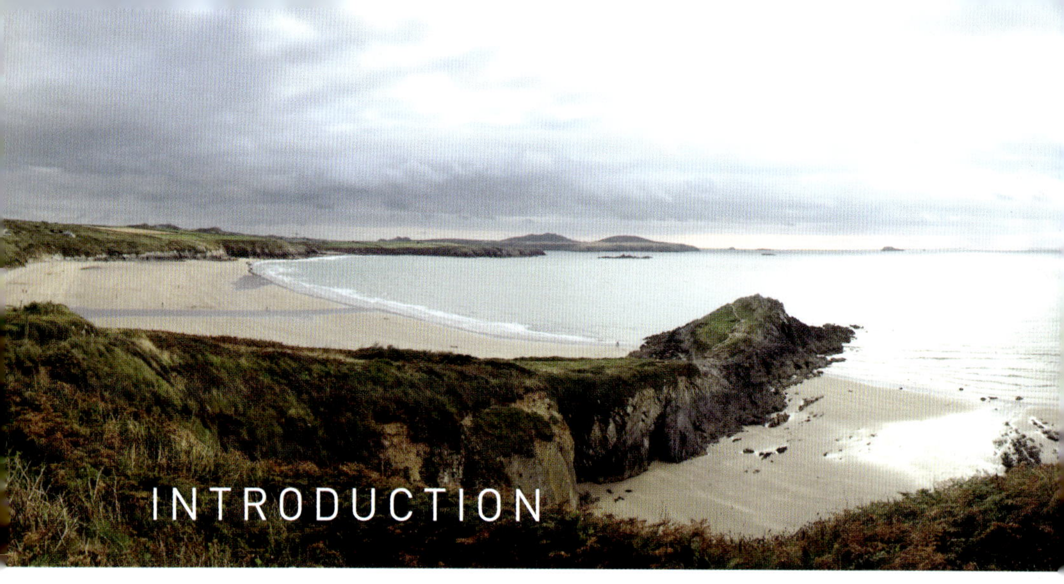

# INTRODUCTION

**Ffion Rees grew up beside the sea in Pembrokeshire, where the St Davids Peninsula slides out into the sea.**
Here the sea shows itself to be bigger than the land. It shapes the coast, drives the weather and the moods of the place, and no one knows this sea better than Ffion.

After completing a degree in German and Celtic studies in Aberdeen, she returned to Pembrokeshire. Later Ffion started Falcon Boats, taking people out to show the beauty of the coastal landscape and the wealth of wildlife that lives just off shore around Ramsey Island and Grassholm.

Low to the water, open to the sky, Ffion's guided trips enable us humans to be in the element of these wild creatures, so close to dolphin, porpoise, sometimes, rarely, even whales, unobtrusive observers.

Over the years Ffion has taught me so much about the shape of the sea, the creatures who live on, in and above it. I'd listened for years to Ffion talking with such passion about her life on the water, experiences, encounters, the histories of place. There is so much life out there. Ffion has so much knowledge, and to catch this, within the pages of a book, seemed a perfect idea.

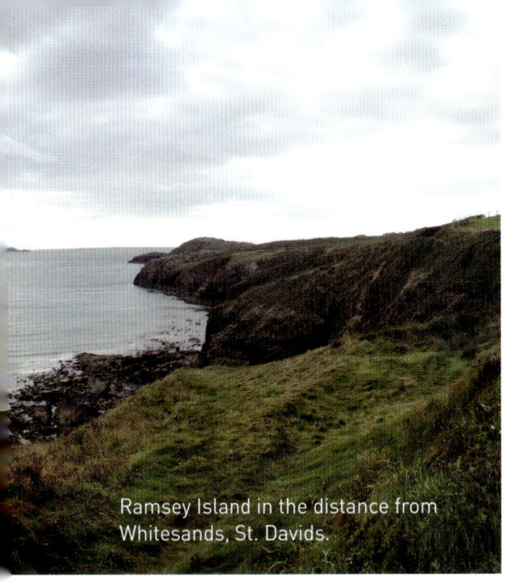

Ramsey Island in the distance from Whitesands, St. Davids.

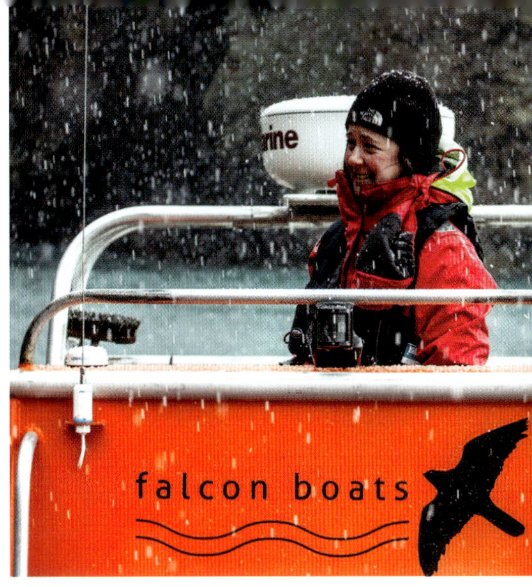


Writing isn't easy. The hardest part is beginning. So I asked her a question. "What keeps you on the water, what sends you back, time and again?" This book is the answer to my question.

**Jackie Morris**, illustrator and author

## The answer to a question

How do you describe how something has somehow become part of your soul? It is as if the sea is in my blood, exerting a pull that always draws me back. It gets like that if you spend long enough on it. I feel as if it somehow defines me.

For as long as I can remember I have spent time on or in the water; in boats, kayaks, even a surfboard on occasion, or maybe just swimming and snorkelling. As a child, given half a chance, I would happily spend all day, every day during the summer out on the boat with my father, fishing. Then, before I started working the waters of Pembrokeshire I always chose to live near the sea if I could. The first time I went abroad on a trip which landlocked me for months, I felt like something was missing. It was so subtle that I didn't really register it at the time, but when a friend came to pick me up in a camper van and asked me where I wanted to go, all I could say was, 'to the sea'. It didn't matter where; all the plans had gone out of my head. I think that was when I realised that not only did I love it, but that it was somehow part of me. Twenty years later it still feeds my soul.

I ended up working on the sea more by default than design, but maybe it was just meant to be. I remember saying, 'I can't spend the rest of my life driving a boat around Ramsey'. Well, it would appear that I can.

It is very difficult to contain in words why I stay; how the sea makes me feel. It has an ever-changing quality, more moods than I have myself. It commands respect, and I have always felt that the day you forget to respect it is the day you should hang up your waterproofs and step ashore. When I step back on the boat after a winter on the mainland, it doesn't just feel comfortable, it's like coming home. I relax, life is somehow simpler out there, it changes my perspective. No two days are the same; no two trips are alike between tides and weather, the seasons and creatures they give life to. I can drive out to Grassholm of a morning, on the edge of the Celtic Deep, and my worries seem to drop away. Not gone. They will be waiting for me when I step ashore, but somehow lessened, not so important or all-consuming, even if only for a short time. It is a constant challenge, and despite it being second nature the sea can still catch me out, surprise me, and I know it will always have that ability no matter how long I spend on it.

How can I swap that for a desk?

It is elemental. You can literally feel the seasons change under your feet when summer turns to autumn. Like the day you wake up and there is a change in the air, a chill or a scent that foretells winter. It is the same on the water. It will suddenly, somehow have more power one day in late summer, more energy behind the swells, a hint of danger, a warning that keeps you on your toes. You learn to read it, not only its changing moods but also how it plays with you. It reminds me of a poem by Lilian Moore:

### Until I saw the Sea

*Until I saw the sea*
*I did not know*
*that wind*
*could wrinkle water so.*

*I never knew*
*that sun*
*could splinter a whole sea of blue.*

*nor*
*did I know before,*
*a sea breathes in and out*
*upon a shore.*

The line 'I did not know that wind could wrinkle water so' is such a fabulous understatement that it has always stuck in my mind. The sea has a wonderful ability to lend your life perspective.

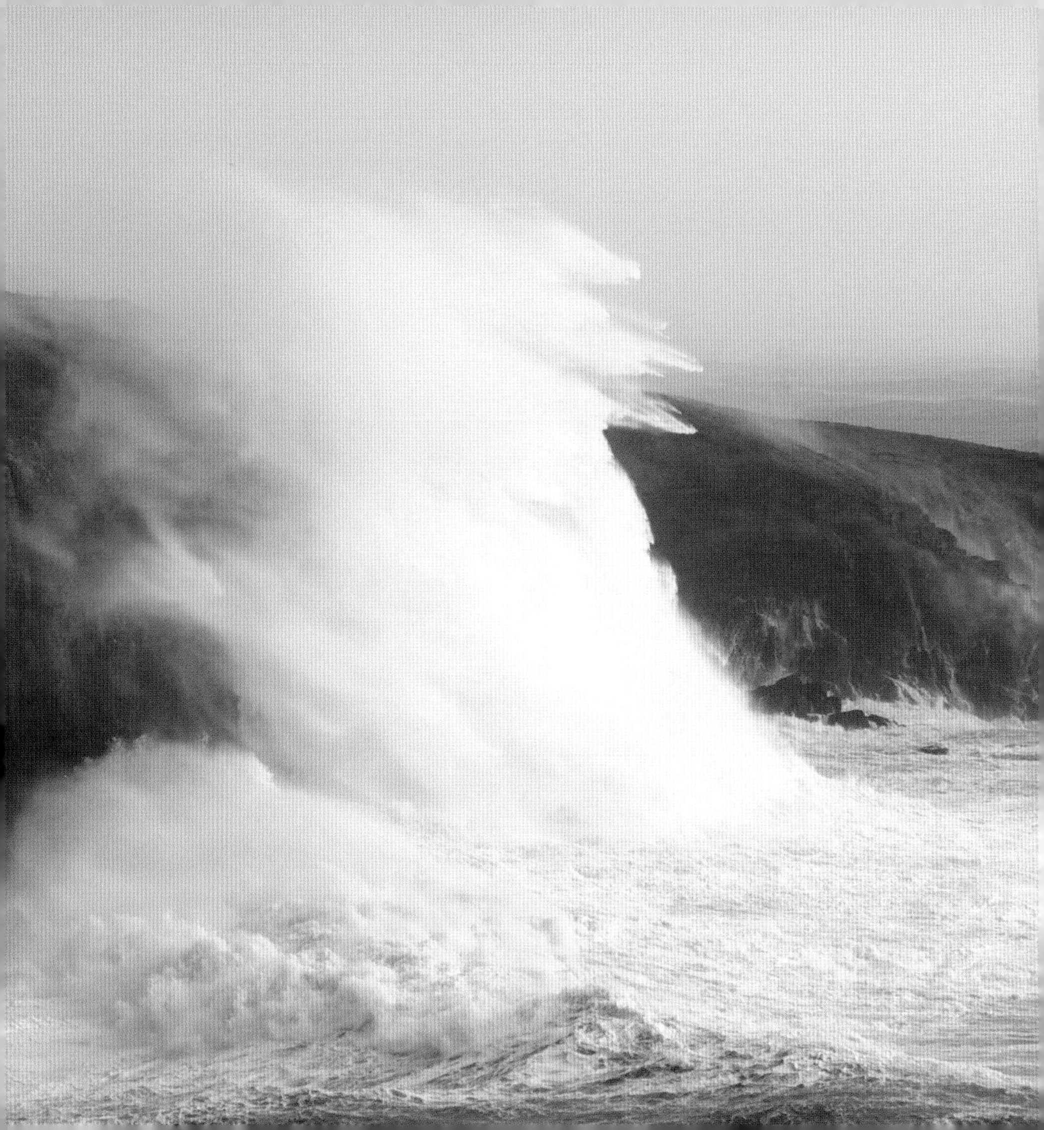

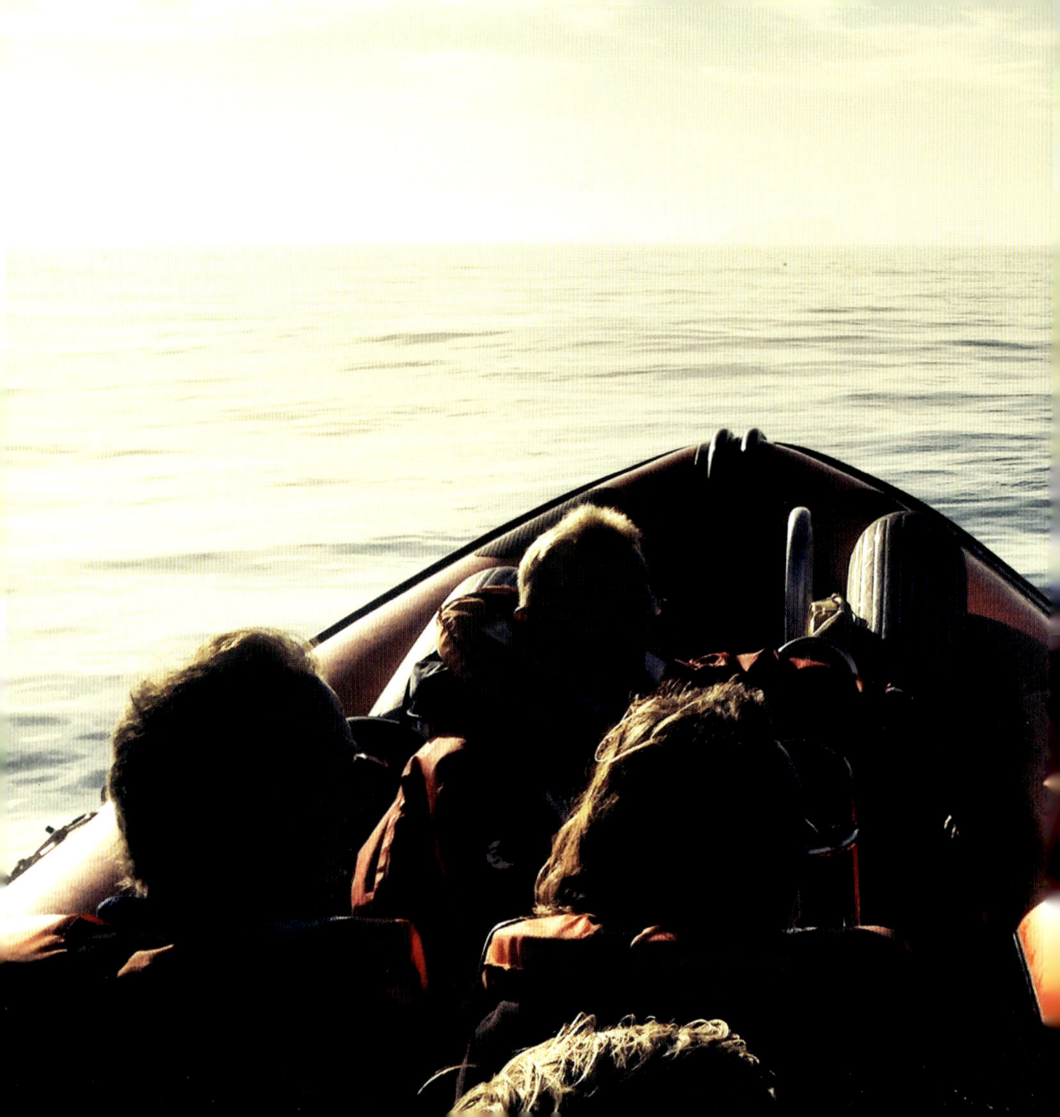

# LEAVING THE MAINLAND

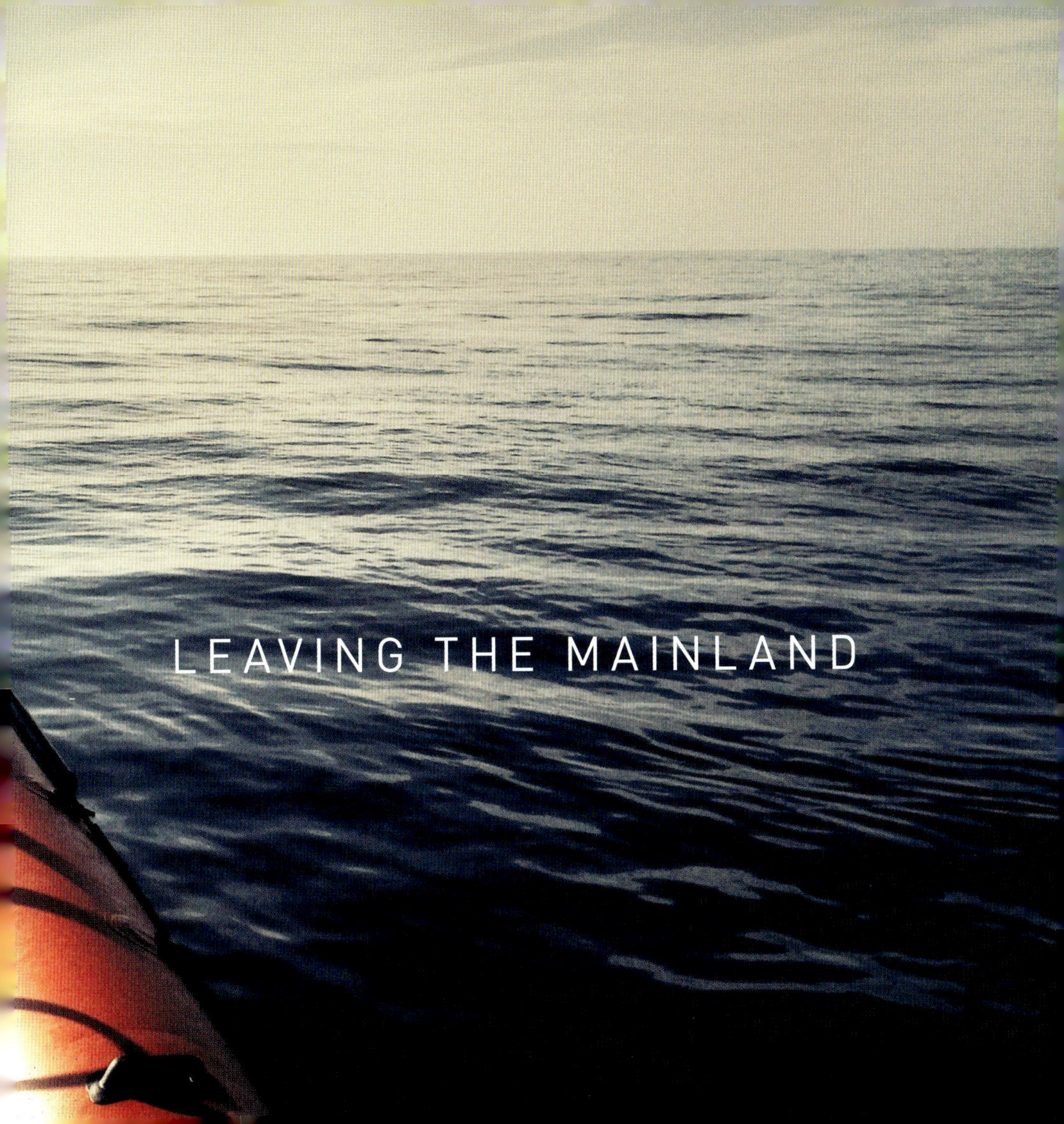

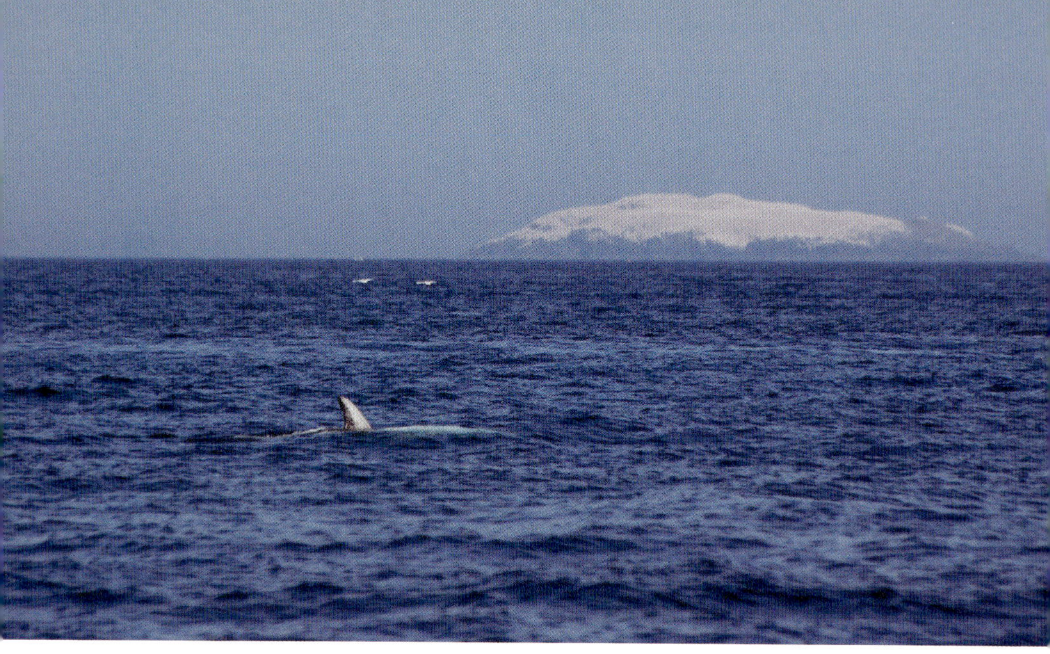

My morning typically starts with studying at least three different weather forecasts and taking a quick look at the barometer to determine what the day is likely to hold in store. The first trip of the day is generally an offshore sail to Grassholm, the Smalls and beyond and can take us up to twenty miles out to sea, so I need to be as informed as possible before deciding whether to go or not. Mind you, the weather can turn quickly in our little microclimate on the south-western tip of the peninsula, and the forecasts do not always get it right. If you're not careful, a change in conditions can transform the trip back to sheltered waters from what is essentially open Atlantic into an exhilarating or terrifying experience, depending on your perspective. Without sufficient experience, an intimate knowledge of the waters and sometimes an element of luck, it is easy to get caught out.

**Above:** Risso's Dolphin with Grassholm in the background.

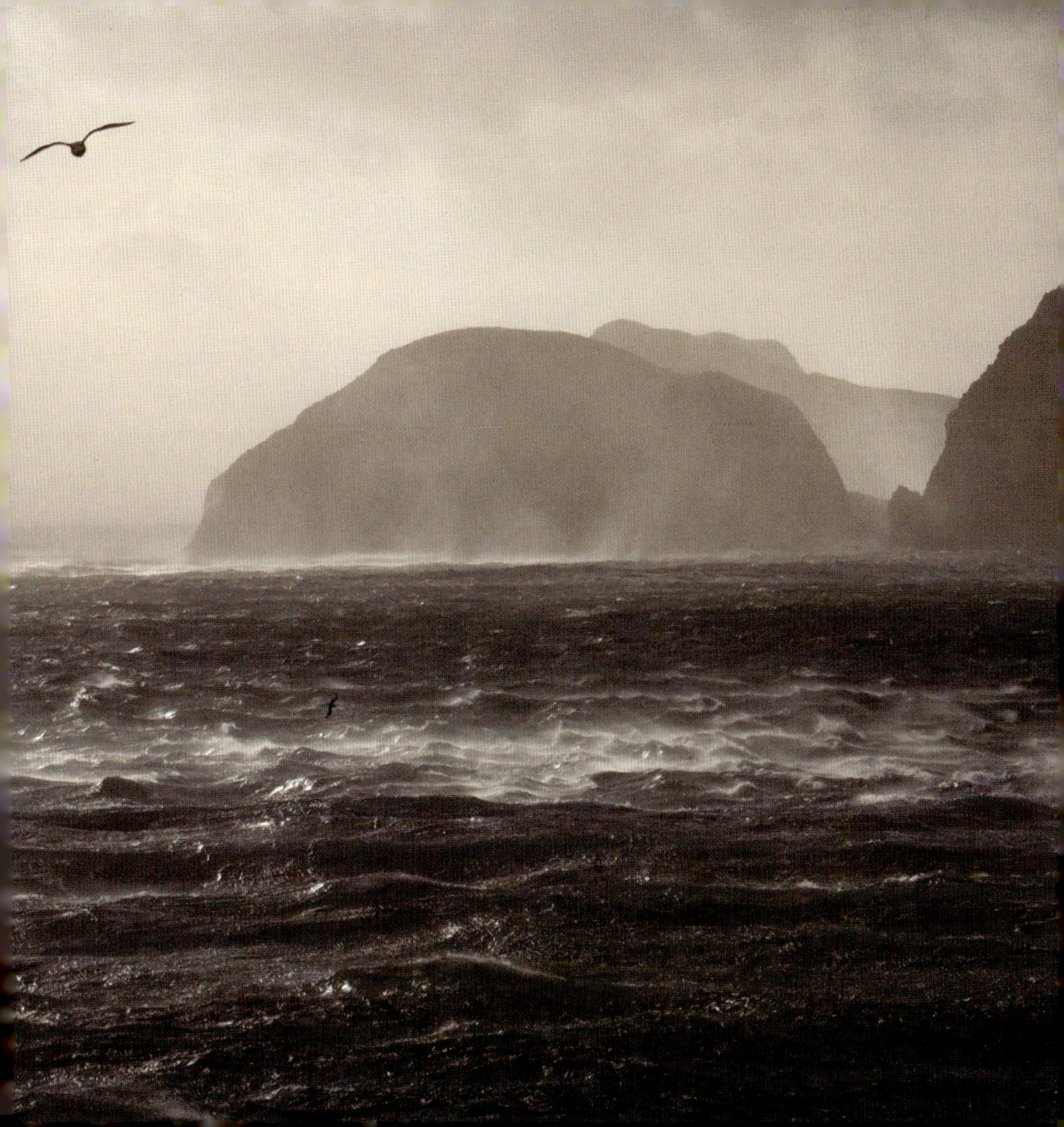

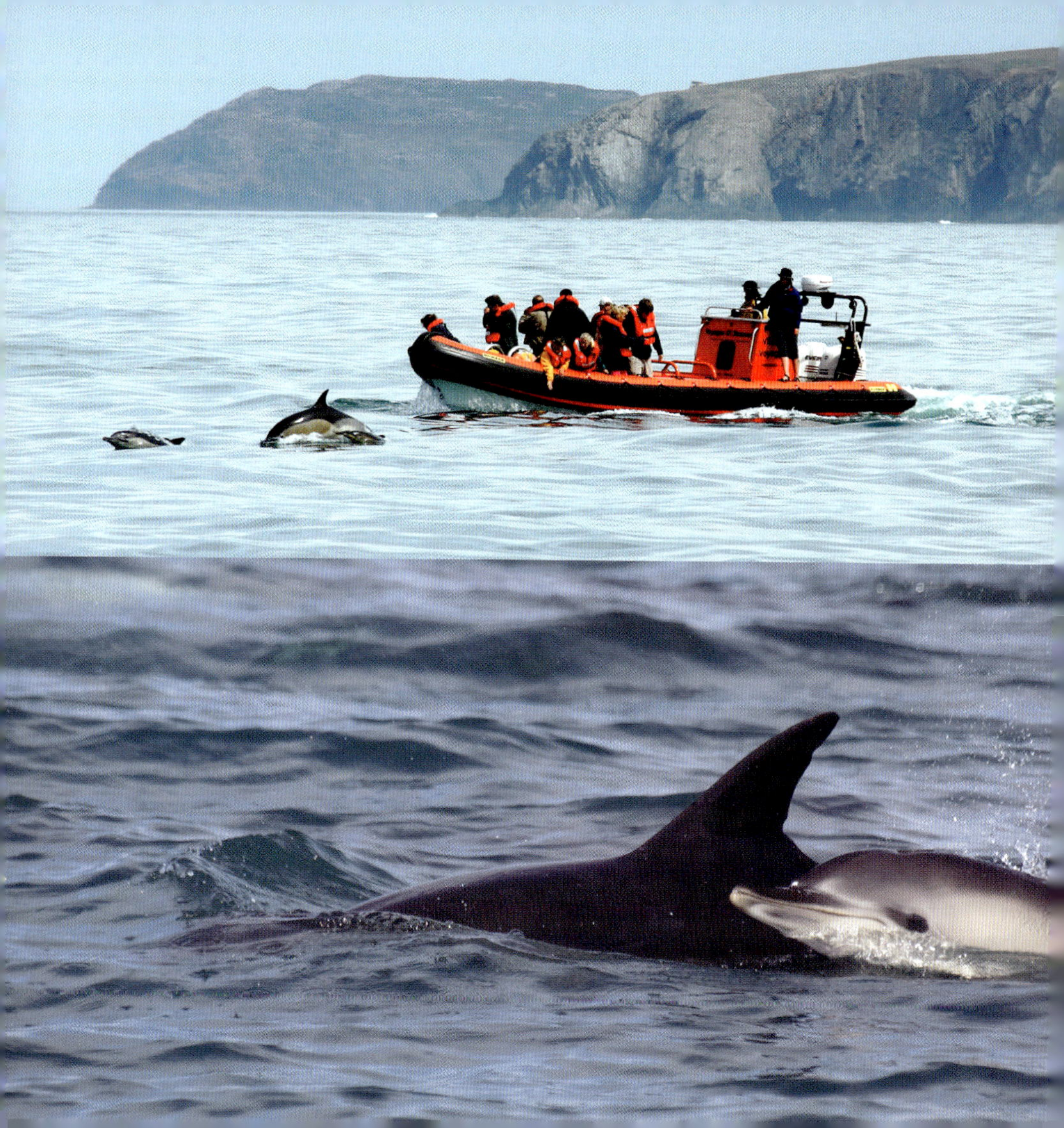

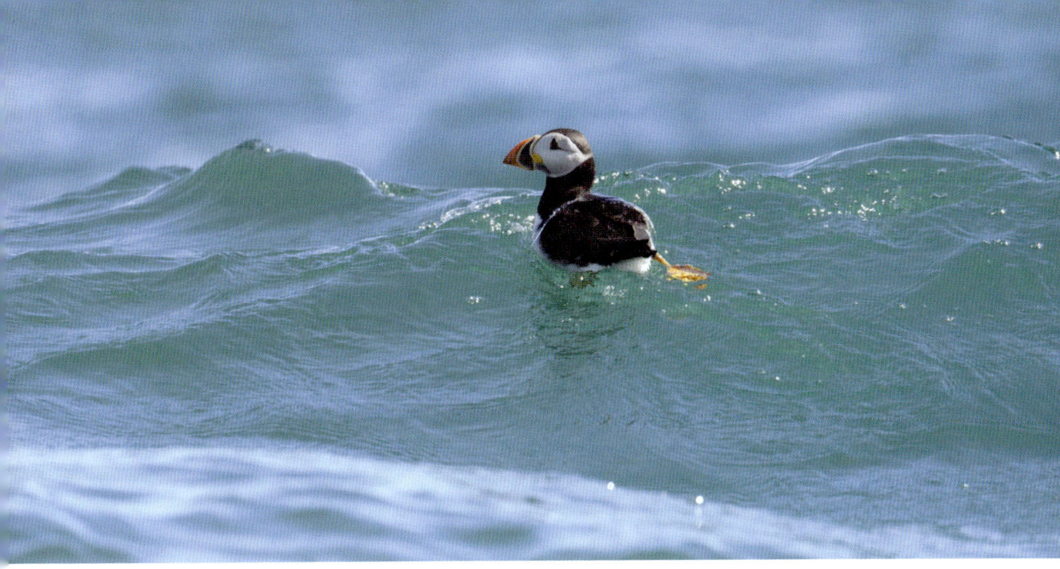

On a calm summer's day though, there is no better way to start your day than sitting offshore watching dolphins cavorting whilst consuming a lukewarm bacon sandwich and a mug of flask-flavoured tea! This is, of course, when all has gone according to plan. En route we will often stop to look at the many seabirds that are summer visitors to the islands, including auks such as the guillemot, razorbill and puffin. As we start to leave the shore behind we may get a glimpse of the land-wary shearwater, or even an elusive storm petrel. Sometimes called the sea swallow due to their size and flight, they are the smallest petrel found in our waters.

As we approach Grassholm the number of gannets wheeling above us increases and, depending on the wind direction, the smell will often announce the presence of the 100,000 gannets well before we arrive. In the fog you will almost certainly smell the island before you see it. If you look up, the sky above will be full of wheeling birds in a mesmerising display, leaving you wondering who is in charge of air traffic control, particularly when it comes to take off and landing!

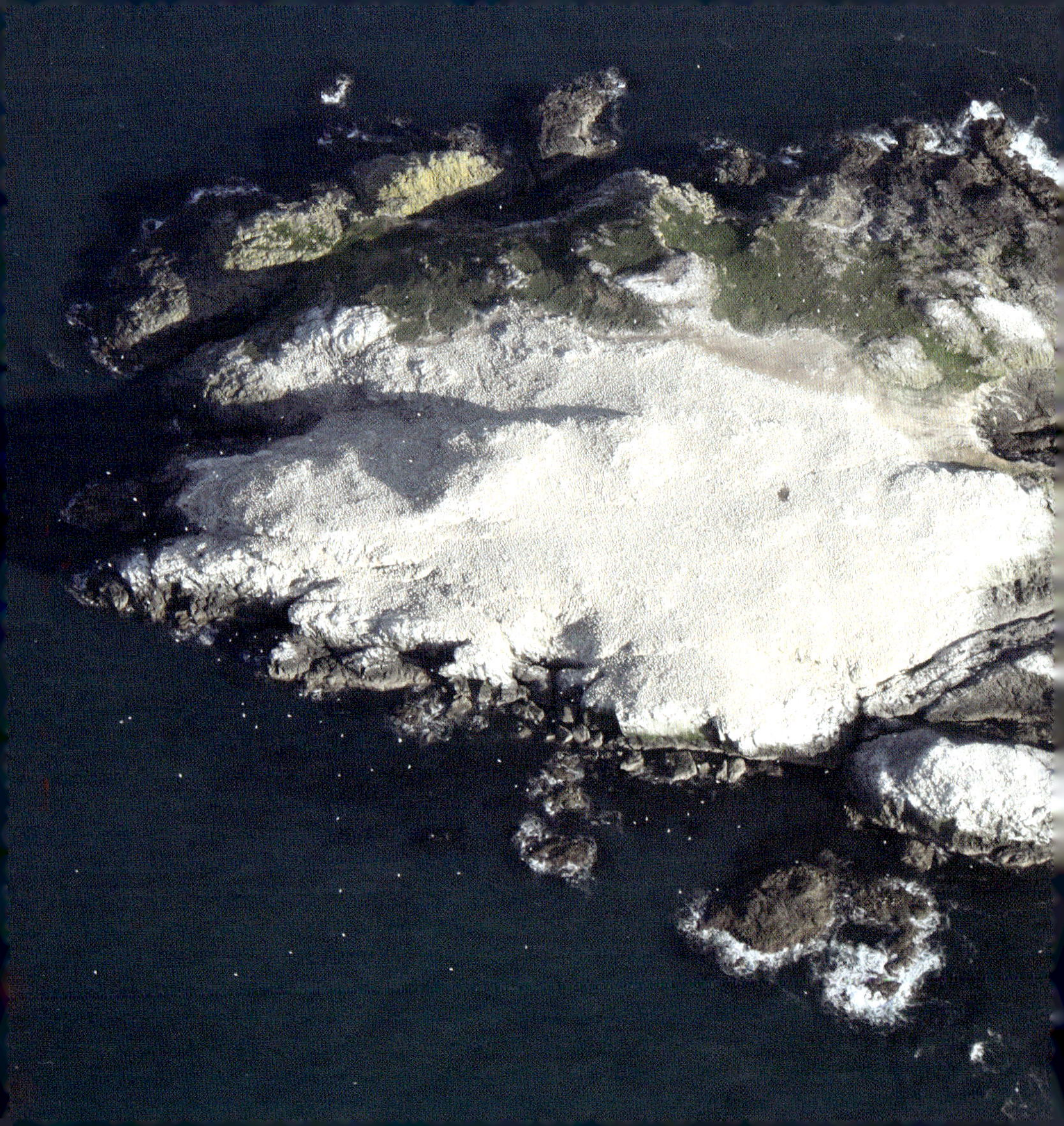

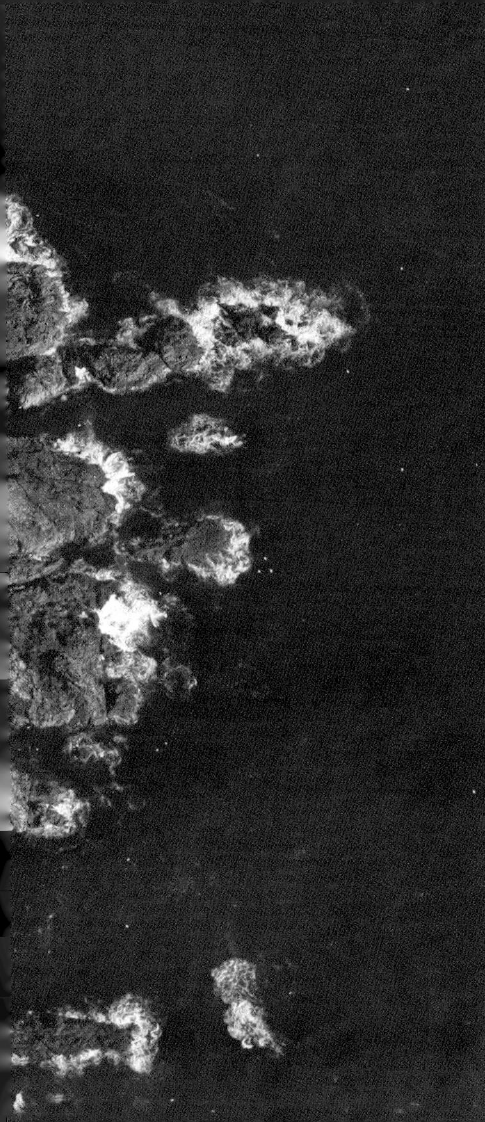

## Grassholm, 10 miles offshore

As with many of Pembrokeshire's islands, Grassholm is steeped in myth and has been associated with the name Gwales, a kind of magical underworld mentioned in the second Branch of the Mabinogi (a 14th century collection of Welsh myths and legends). The legend tells of a war between Wales and Ireland, following which the seven survivors of the army of Prydein (Welsh Britain) go to Gwales, a kind of magical otherworld where their sorrows were forgotten. They live in a royal palace for eighty years, feasting and drinking with the severed, but still living, head of Bendigeidfran (Bran the Blessed) until someone, as is the way of these things, opens the third door in the hall, the door facing Cornwall they had been forbidden to open. At this point the spell is broken, their sorrows return and they have to leave the island for reality.

This small island is twenty-two acres in size, lies ten miles offshore and is home to the third largest gannet colony in the world. Accounting for 10-12% of the world population of northern gannets it is, in my opinion, one of the most spectacular sights in Pembrokeshire. Seen in the morning sunshine from the mainland, on a clear day half of it appears white, and we often tease tourists that it is snowing out there! This is actually the birds themselves, as opposed to just guano, as they have the most incredibly brilliant

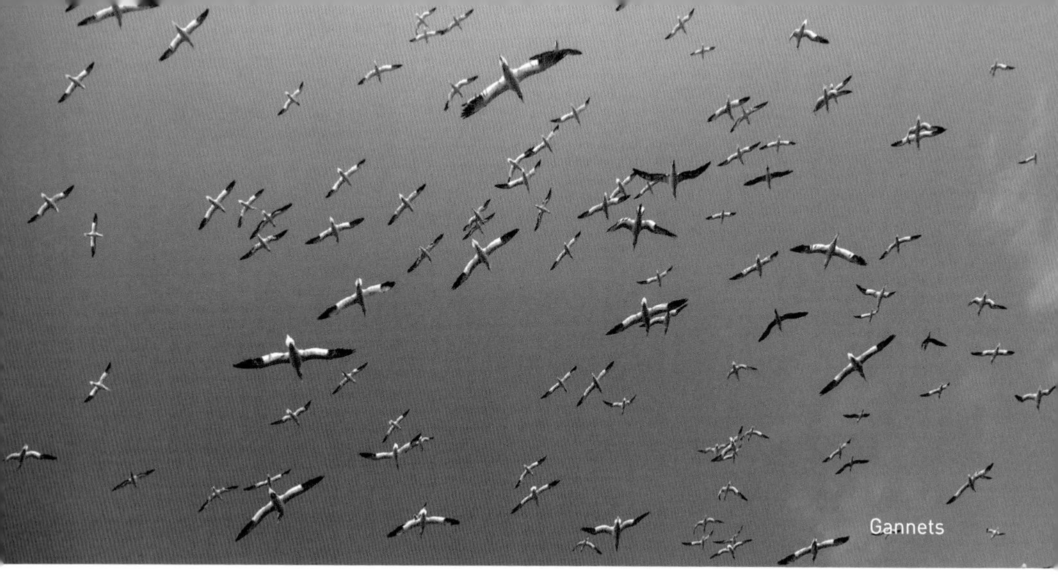

Gannets

white plumage. In certain conditions associated with hot weather, a mirage effect called *Fata Morgana* after Morgan le Fey can sometimes be seen where Grassholm can assume all sorts of odd shapes, including a table-top island.

Gannet nests are uniformly spaced across the island, just a neck and beak's distance away from their nearest neighbour in every direction. This is because, whilst space is at a premium, gannets are also quite an aggressive bird. When establishing their claim to a nest, males will often have to fight for their territory. Fights between male gannets can last as long as an hour, and after one such fight witnessed on Grassholm, the victor was recorded sleeping for three days.

In 1802 there were no records of any gannets on Grassholm, and it is thought that, prior to their arrival, there were as many as 250,000 puffins breeding on the island. There were so many in fact that it is likely they became a victim of their own success and, being burrow nesters, burrowed themselves out of existence as their nests in the thin top soil all collapsed. It is also believed that the sheep who used to graze the island may have contributed to the collapse of the puffin burrows.

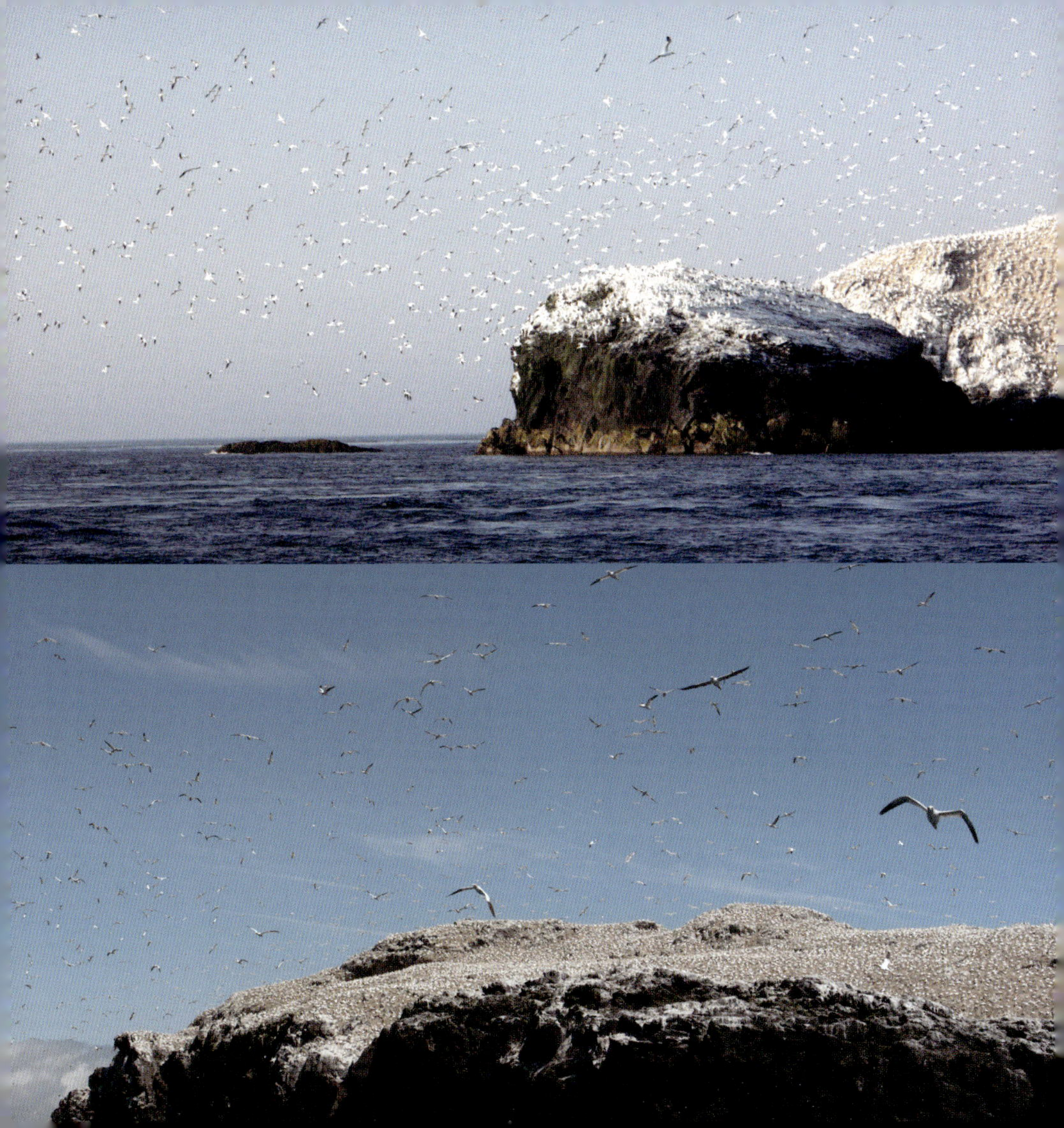

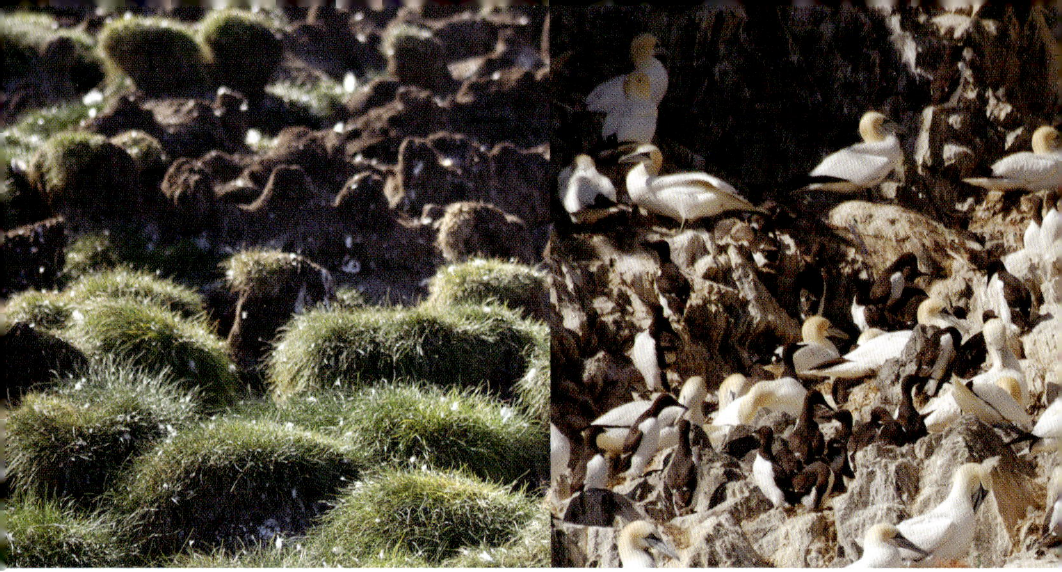

The remnants of these burrows can still be seen today in small areas not inhabited by the gannets.

In 1860, twenty pairs of gannets were recorded on Grassholm; by 1905 this had risen to 300, and when the RSPB bought the island in 1948 there were 8000 pairs on the island. It is thought that the dramatic increase in numbers may have been due to Lundy birds leaving their colony as a result of disturbance with the building of the new lighthouse and the introduction of a fog horn.

The gannets colonised Grassholm from west to east, as the western side of the island boasts the highest cliffs and faces the prevailing winds, making for an easier take-off. Due to weight and wing proportions gannets need quite a bit of lift to get airborne. The colony has been steadily increasing in size since the island was bought by the RSPB in 1948, with the nests spreading over to the less desirable areas of the central and eastern parts of the island. However, it is now thought to be not far off capacity and growth has slowed in the last couple of decades.

Unlike other west-Wales seabirds, gannets will tend to gravitate in large

**Above left:** Collapsed puffin burrows.
**Above right:** Gannets and guillemots.

numbers to one breeding site, rather than nesting in small colonies throughout the Pembrokeshire islands. In addition to the nest sites there are a number of 'club rocks' on Grassholm peripheral to the main breeding sites. These are where juvenile gannets will hang out and learn about life in the colony and where the best feeding grounds are, a bit like the local youth club. Recent research has suggested that these may also include juveniles from other UK populations, as these large 'club rocks' are notably absent in other British gannet colonies.

Whilst definitely in the majority, gannets are not the only birds to breed on the island. In the years I have been sailing out to Grassholm I have noticed the colonies of breeding guillemots increasing, as they appear to have discovered that if you live in close proximity to large, aggressive neighbours you are much less likely to be attacked by predators. As a result, they are often to be seen scattered in amongst the gannets, to whom they pose no threat.

Other species of bird recorded breeding on Grassholm include storm petrels, shag, oystercatcher, kittiwake, razorbill, ravens, rock pipits, and even a pair of peregrine, as well as the inevitable herring, lesser black-backed and greater black-backed gulls. Since 2005, the RSPB have recorded 78 species of bird on or around Grassholm.

## Gannet Research on Grassholm

Since 2006, Dr. Steve Voitier and his team from Exeter University have been carrying out annual data-gathering work on Grassholm, attaching tracking devices and cameras to the birds to collect information on the foraging and migration strategies of northern gannets. This work actually involves camping out on Grassholm during the summer months with the 100,000 gannets; probably the same again in fly numbers and large infestations of earwigs!

The cameras, which are attached to the tail feathers of the birds, were designed to find out to what extent gannets follow trawlers and feed on 'by catch'. It was already suspected that this was the case due to the large variety of fish species that

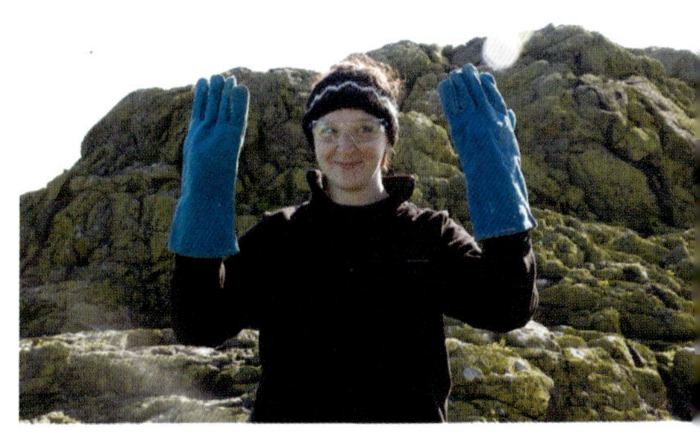

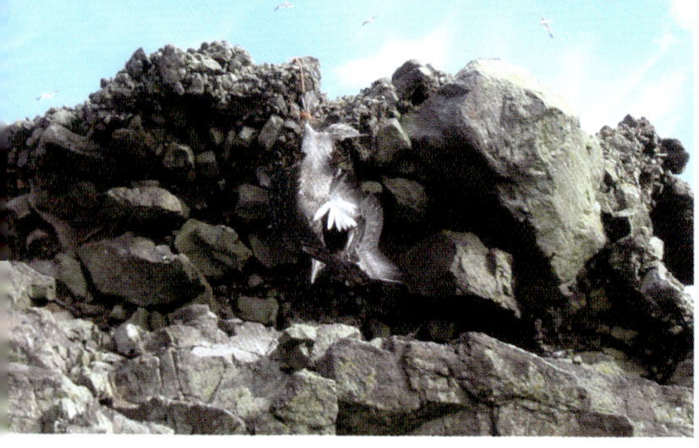

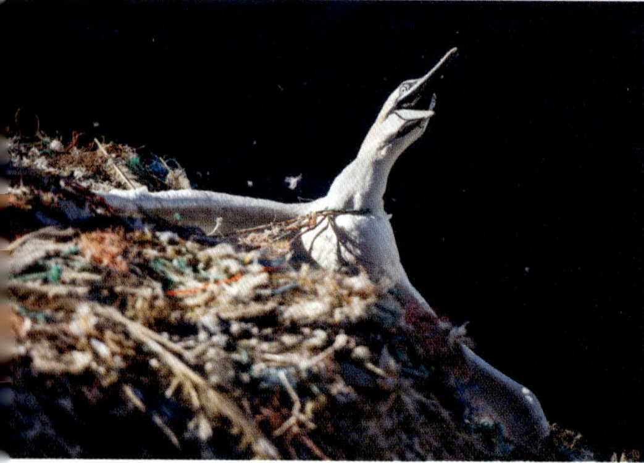

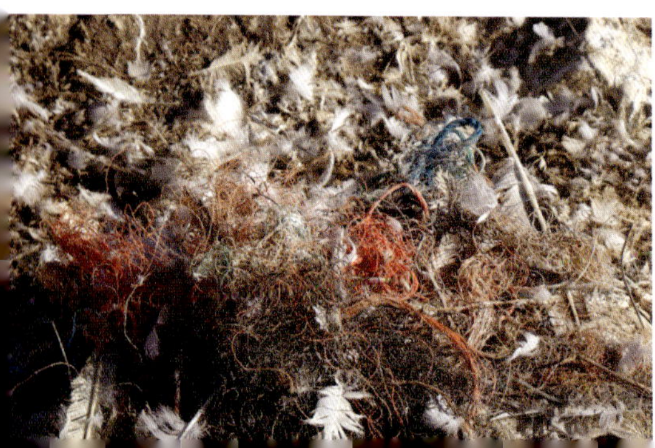

have been found regurgitated around nest sites, many of which would not normally be part of the birds' diet.

These suspicions were confirmed by results produced by the cameras, although interestingly the research suggests it is predominantly male birds who followed the trawlers, whilst females went and caught their own dinner: 80% of males have been associated with fishing boats as opposed to only 20% of females. Not surprisingly, birds only home in on fishing boats when they are processing their catch, not when they are steaming. The 300 GPS loggers which have been attached to birds and later retrieved, show core foraging areas to the south and west of the island, with individual birds using the same foraging routes year after year. Certain areas, such as those with a lot of tidal front activity, are very popular. The Celtic Deep has a lot of frontal activity, making it a good foraging ground. Foraging trips made by individual gannets have been recorded that range from 77km–1782km in total length, and birds can travel from 33km to 472km away from the island on each trip. For further information on the gannet see page 68.

## Conservation work on Grassholm

Gannets build their nests out of anything they find floating on the surface of the water. Historically this would have largely consisted of seaweed but, sadly, in more recent years there has been a dramatic increase in discarded plastic in the form of rope and netting being picked up and used by the birds. This can have devastating effects on the nest's inhabitants. Every year, weather permitting, at the end of the breeding season, the RSPB, along with a team of volunteers, will spend a day on Grassholm, when the majority of the chicks have fledged, cutting free any birds that have become entangled in their nests. Twice I have been lucky enough to join them on these rescue missions, which involve being fully kitted out in safety goggles, gloves and with a sharp knife. Gannet wrestling requires a team of two and is not for the faint hearted, as they are not noted for being grateful towards their rescuers. Gannets should always be approached with caution, as they have exceptionally sharp beaks, will attack first, ask questions later, and have a tendency to go straight for the eyes! It is great to be involved in helping with work like this, but it is a heartbreaking sight seeing gannets tethered to their nests by our discards, and inevitably there are

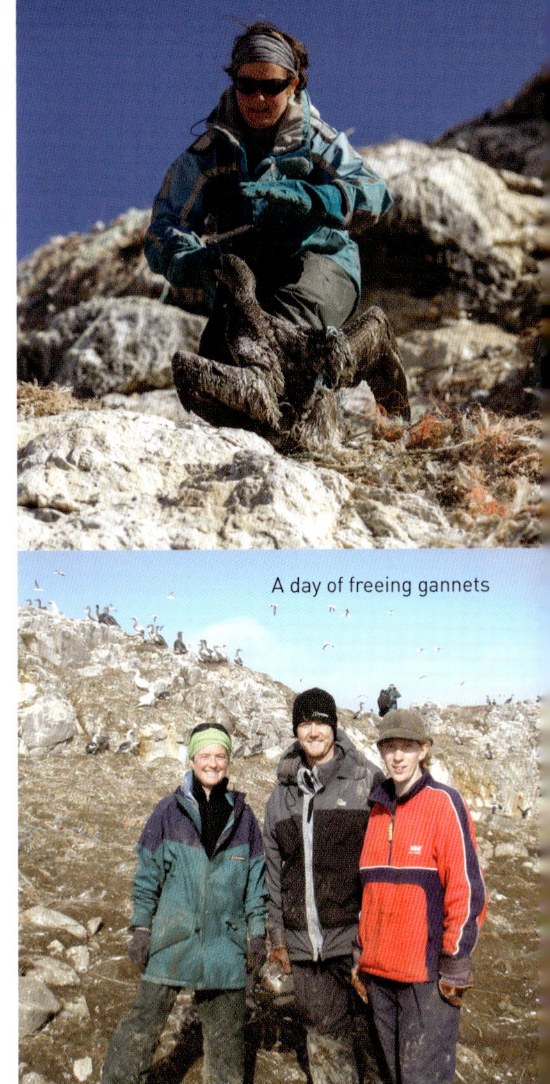

A day of freeing gannets

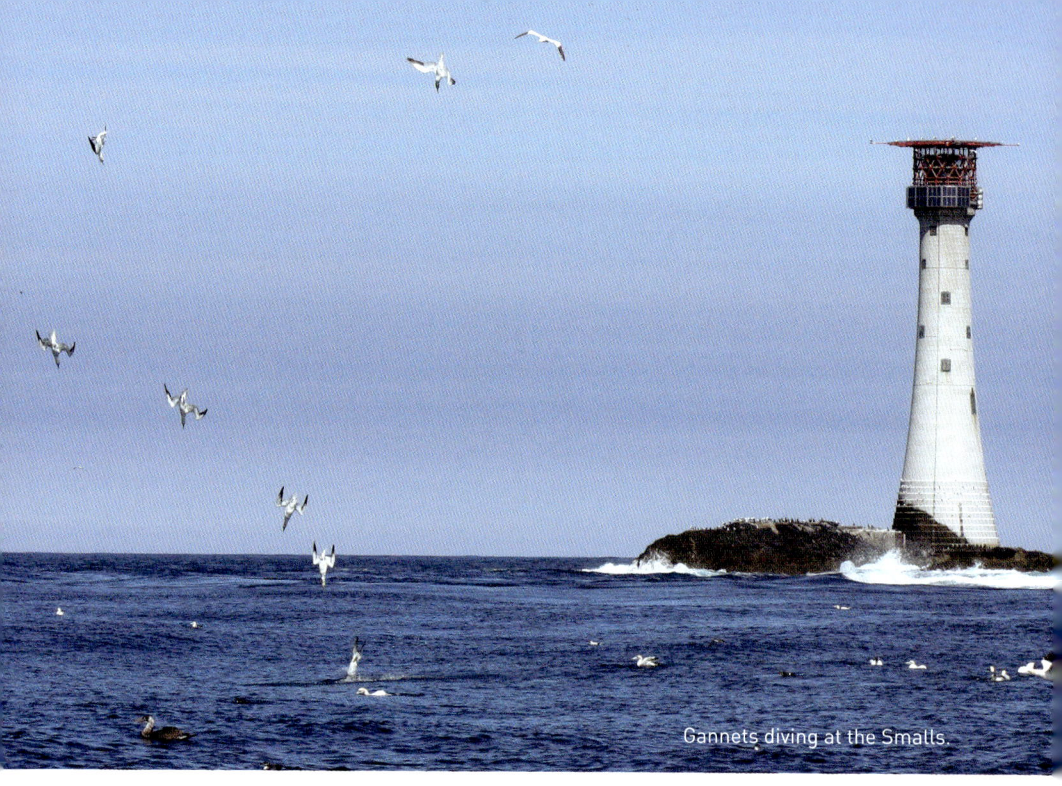
Gannets diving at the Smalls.

those for whom our arrival is too late.
In 2015, we cut free fifty birds that had
become trapped this way. The majority
were chicks, but even the occasional adult
can become entangled and these often
starve to death. Occasionally a bird will
lose a leg due to the blood supply having
been cut off, but these are set free as they
still have a chance of survival.

I found one unfortunate individual
tethered by its neck one year, and having
cut it free I discovered it had lost both feet
and sadly had to be dispatched.

We often get asked why we don't just
do a big clean up to remove the plastic,
but unfortunately it's not that simple.

The plastic has built up over years of nest building, layer upon layer, and a study carried out by the RSPB with Plymouth University estimated there could be up to eighteen tonnes of plastic contained within the gannet nests on Grassholm. Whilst much of this is marine waste, there is a surprising amount of domestic plastic on the island as well. Removing all this from a small, isolated island is not only impractical but would also completely destroy the existing nest sites.

## From Grassholm to The Smalls

After leaving Grassholm we head off towards the waters of the Celtic Deep, past turbulent currents created by the treacherous reefs known as the Barrels and Hats. Lying to the west of Grassholm, these culminate with the Smalls rock and its lighthouse. We will often see large numbers of seabirds out here rafting on the water, where they gather together sitting on the surface or diving in after fish. A lonely tower standing 42m high, the tallest of the Welsh lighthouses stands on a low lying, wave-washed reef of rocks a mere 4m above the water, which become fully submerged during storms. When I first visited the Smalls lighthouse many years ago, it was painted with distinctive red and white stripes to distinguish it from other lighthouses, but the costs of repainting

became prohibitive and, given its isolated situation and treacherous surrounding waters, it is not often that conditions are suitable for landing people on the rock for maintenance. In 1997 it was sand blasted back to the original stone.

## The Smalls, 20 miles offshore

The Smalls has a fascinating history. The original lighthouse was designed by a musical instrument maker, Henry Whiteside. Completed in 1776 and operational in 1777, it was an octagonal wooden structure built on 8" x 42" oak posts, set in deep holes drilled into the rock and secured with molten lead. The idea was that the fury of the ocean would pass between the pillars beneath the tower, rather than battering against a more substantial structure. This worked up to a point. The original structure was 66" tall, 17" in diameter, and has some interesting stories associated with it. The first was that of the proverbial message in a bottle, when, on 13th January 1777, Whiteside decided to join the lighthouse crew to see for himself how his design was faring. The weather deteriorated and, lashed by gales, the light went out. Marooned with dwindling rations and no sign of being relieved the crew resorted to sending a number of messages in corked bottles encased in barrels, outlining their distress and requesting help. Three days later, one of the barrels came ashore in Solva Harbour and Whiteside and the crew were finally rescued. However, this is not the only tragic story to unfold there.

In the early 1800s, Thomas Howell of King Heriott and Thomas Griffith of Solva were lighthouse keepers for the Smalls Light. On the occasion in question they had supposedly been seen fighting when leaving the pub the night before they were due to go on duty, a fact that was to play heavy on the mind of Thomas Griffith in the days to come. Within a few days of arriving at the Smalls, Howells was taken ill and died, leaving his unfortunate colleague with the dilemma of how to summon help and what to do with the corpse in the meantime. He was unable to commit it to the deep for fear of being accused of murder. Inclement weather meant it was months before the relief boat would arrive and it wasn't long before the body began to decompose. So Griffith resorted to fashioning a makeshift coffin out of a cupboard and lashing it to the rails outside the tower. One night in a storm, however, so the story goes, one of the doors came off and one of the dead man's arms swung out of the coffin, appearing to beckon ships towards the rocks and wave to his colleague in the lighthouse. As this was before the days of radio communications and Griffith had to keep the light in the tower burning he had no way to communicate his distress to the mainland. In that bleak, storm-blown isolation, with nothing but a corpse for company and the fear that foul play might be suspected, he slowly started to lose his mind. When the relief boat finally arrived, they found a rotting corpse strapped to the outside of the lighthouse and a disturbed Griffith inside. One of the results to come out of this tragedy was that Trinity House, who subsequently owned all the British lighthouses, insisted that from that point on all offshore light houses were to be manned by three keepers rather than two. (*The Solva Saga*, Eric Freeman, 1958)

Later, it became apparent that the wooden structure was not strong enough to cope with the hostile conditions that batter this reef on a regular basis, and in 1861 it was replaced by the current structure, based on the design of Smeaton's Eddystone tower. It was the second one built on Eddystone, and a fine example of recent innovations in lighthouse building at the time. It is made of interlocking blocks of cut stone, constructed on shore then deconstructed, shipped out and rebuilt in situ, the blocks fitting so perfectly that no mortar is used in the construction. As anyone who has been to the Smalls even on a calm day can imagine, the construction of anything on this isolated wave-washed rock, the last piece of land between us and America, required superhuman effort, let

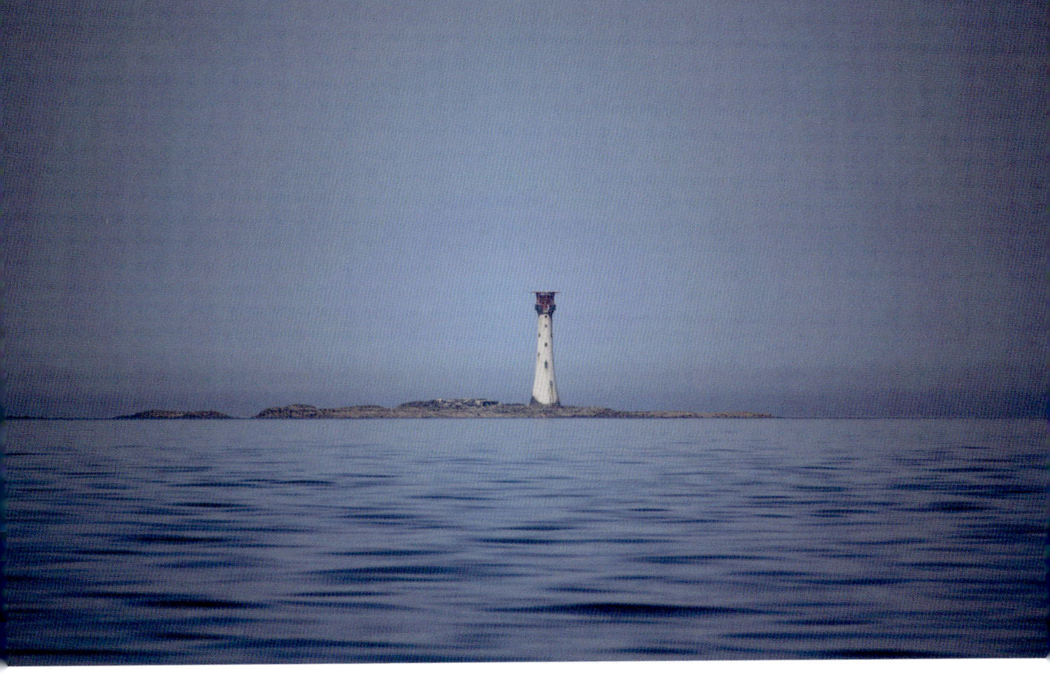

alone the imposing tower that still stands
sentinel today, warning passing ships
of the dangers lurking just beneath the
waves.

Today, the light can still be seen for
25NM (nautical miles), with a signal of
three flashes every fifteen seconds. A
more recent addition is the helipad, built
above the tower in 1978, and used today
by maintenance crews to access the
lighthouse. The light became automated
in 1987, and it was the first offshore
British lighthouse to have a flushing
toilet. Trinity House maintain all the
offshore lighthouses, using a ship with a
small helicopter to drop off maintenance
crews and supplies, a testament to the
difficulties posed by trying to land people
by boat.

## Discovering Viking relics

In 1991, whilst diving on the Smalls reef, a sports diver found a blueish object in a gully in 11m of water, under a much later wreck thought to be of the steamship Rhiwabon, wrecked in 1884. It was declared to the Receiver of Wrecks and further investigation identified the find as a Viking sword guard.

Its elaborate decoration is in a late Viking style called Urnes, whilst the ornamentation is reminiscent of metalwork produced in Ireland and was cast in brass, with inlays in silver wire on black niello. This has dated it to the first quarter of the twelfth century and it is thought likely to signify the capsize and loss of a Viking vessel, rather than a single casual loss. Viking ships were not only an integral part of Viking culture, but also became a symbol of the terror they wrought on the British coastline. Based on other Viking finds, this vessel could have been anywhere between 13m and 28m long. As a result of this find the site has been designated under the Protection of Wrecks Act 1973 to safeguard it from further disturbance.
(*Discovered in Time*, *Treasures From Early Wales*, Dr. Mark Redknapp, 2011, Item 56)

From the Smalls we track to the northwest in a wide sweep back towards the mainland in search of cetaceans. For a full account of sightings of the common

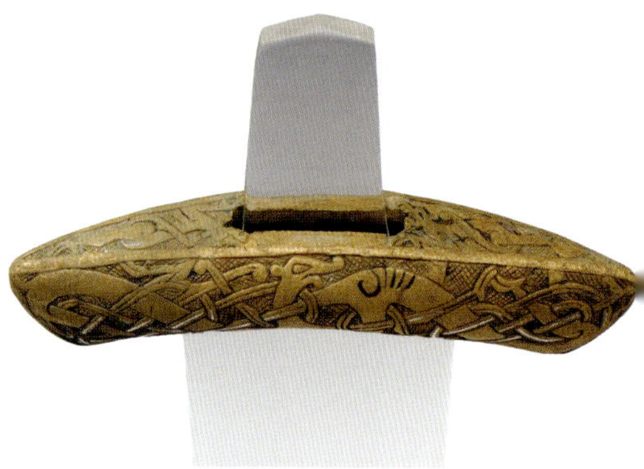

**Above:** Guard of a Viking sword, dated to about AD 1100. Image © Amgueddfa Cymru – National Museum Wales

**Right**: Minke Whale

dolphin and Risso's dolphin around the north Pembrokeshire islands, see page 162.

Occasionally, as we journey back to the mainland, we will see a seal popping up literally out of the blue and, although it shouldn't, it often seems a little incongruous in open sea because we are so used to seeing them just off the coast.

On our return from Grassholm it is time for a quick refuelling of both boat and crew at St Justinian's before we turn our attention to Ramsey.

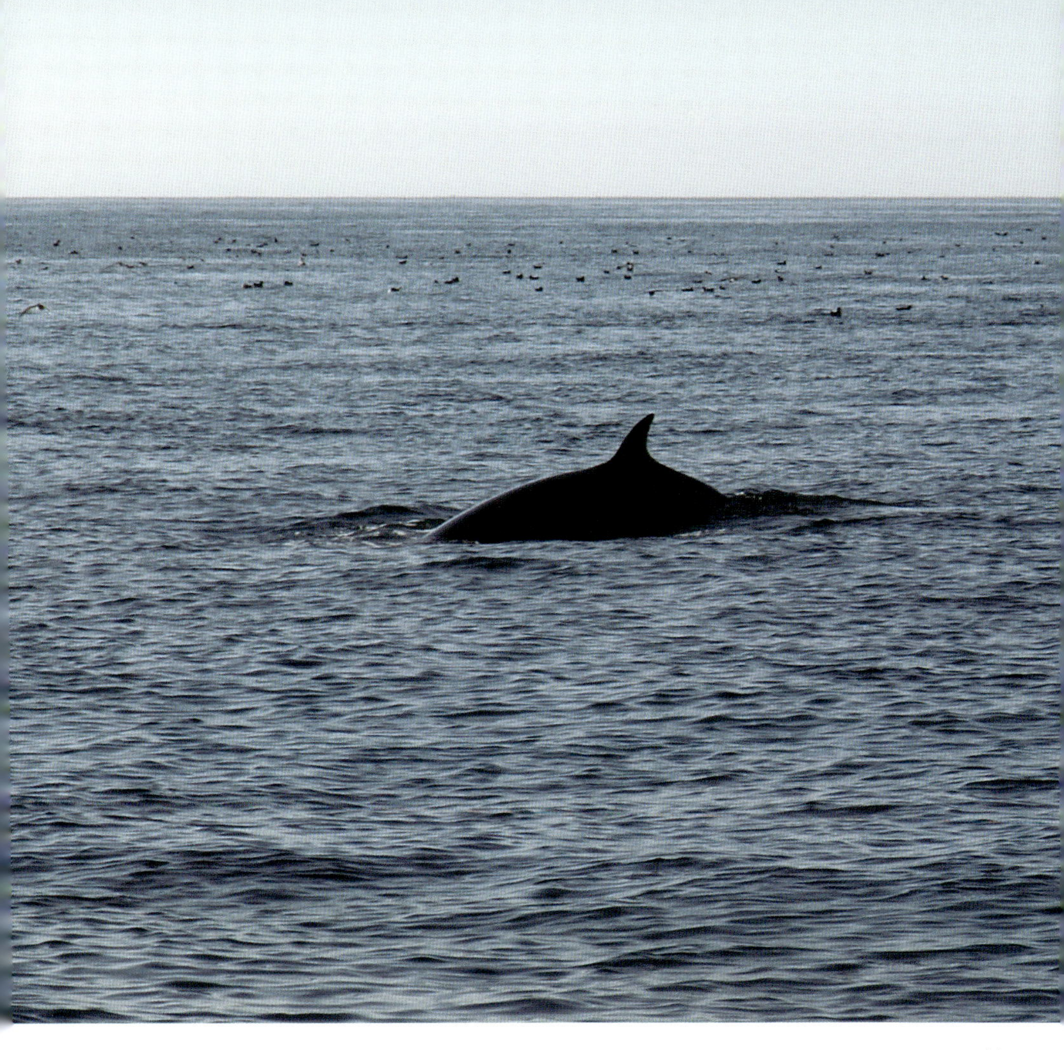

# A TRIP AROUND RAMSEY

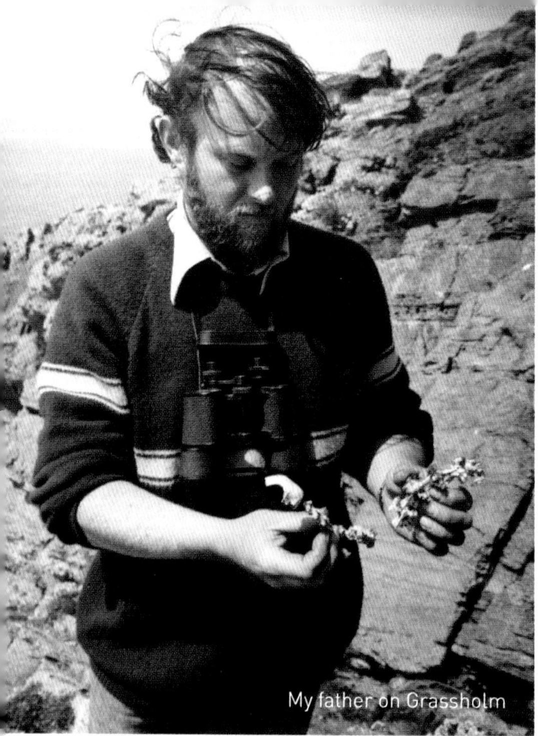


Ramsey and its offshore islands are steeped in myth and legend, with tantalising glimpses of part-remembered stories only adding to the allure of these islands. From the burial place of 20,000 saints to the source of magical otherworlds, Ramsey is a place of enchantment on many different levels.

My first memories of Ramsey are from early childhood, when the island belonged to the Allpress family, whose daughter Judy and her husband, Robin Pratt, were family friends. K.P. Allpress bought the island in 1959, and after his death in 1968 Robin and Judy introduced the red deer, descendants of whom still inhabit the island today. It was run commercially as a venison farm for a number of years and, although deer were new to the island, farming in various forms has been a large part of Ramsey's history over the centuries.

When I was eight years old, myself and my best friend Jemma, the Pratt's oldest daughter, persuaded one of the farm workers to accompany us as we wanted to bivvy out on the island in our sleeping bags in the heather – my first taste of wild camping and one that has stayed with me. I can still remember the excitement of two small girls off on an 'island adventure'.

As a family we would often make the trip across the Sound to visit our friends on the island, but the Sound, with its ferocious currents, can be a wild and unpredictable place. On one occasion, after spending the day on the island with my mother and brother, the weather took a turn for the worse. Robin, being keen to get his guests safely back to the mainland, brought the boat into the harbour to pick us up. We hadn't gone far when disaster struck and one of the engines broke down. With conditions worsening and darkness not far away, Robin decided not to risk the crossing on just one engine. We headed back to the island, much to the delight of myself and my brother, for whom this was just another adventure (my mother was somewhat less enamoured of the situation) and so another night was spent on Ramsey.

I loved the island, it was a big playground where they even had ponies to ride and I was very jealous that every time the weather was bad Jemma wouldn't be able to get across the Sound and had to miss school.

My early love of the island and the sea was further encouraged by my father who, in those days, was a fisherman. He would take me to sea with him every day during the summer holidays. At the age of eight or nine I would get to work the controls of his small dory while he hauled the pots, bringing up lobster and crab.

When I came back to Ramsey's waters it was as a student at university in Scotland many years later. My father, who was then working for one of the local boat companies as a skipper running wildlife trips around the island, asked if I fancied crewing for him again during the summer holidays, an opportunity I couldn't resist – like me he found it hard to stay away from the sea for any length of time. So once again I took to the seas with my father,

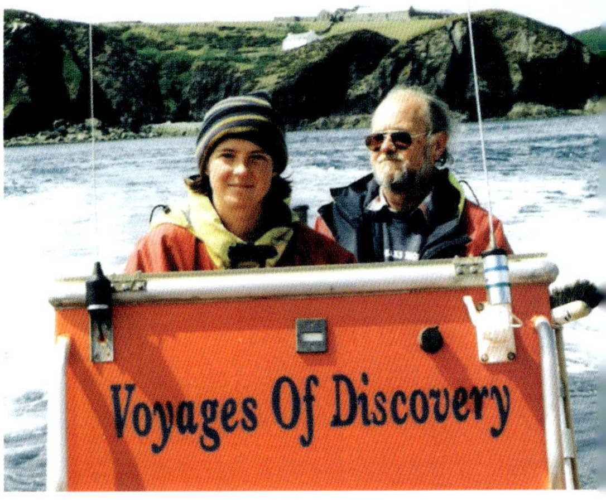


**Above:** Learning the ropes with my father

this time to do a very different job, one in which I was to learn a huge amount about the island's history and wildlife and the many moods of its waters.

Spending all day, everyday (weather permitting) on the boat, this time a rigid hull inflatable (rhib) rather than my fathers' small fishing dory which was a very different creature, has given me an intimate knowledge of and huge respect for the sea. Yet twenty years later it still has the ability to surprise.

The waters around the Pembrokeshire islands, with their strong tides and exposed location on the westernmost tip of Wales, made a fantastic training

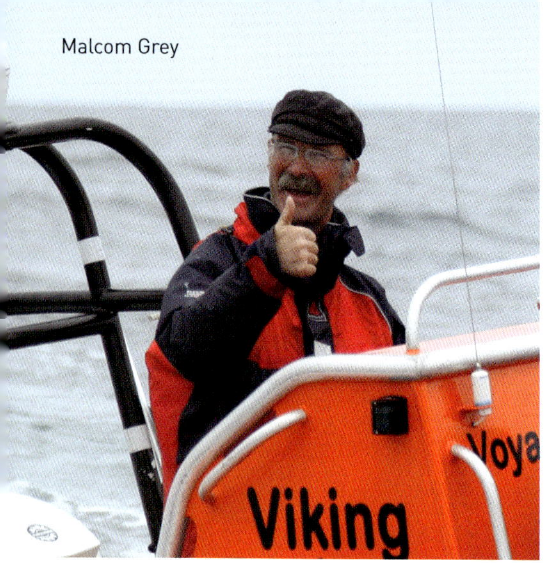


Graham Dove, the only person I have ever met who had actually been shipwrecked on a desert island. Watching him manoeuvre many a boat out of a tricky situation it always struck me that, as well as inordinate skill, he had the luck of the devil. Maybe that was something that ran in the family, as his father survived ditching his light aircraft off the west coast of Ramsey. He was picked up off one of the rocks by the St Davids Lifeboat, which 'just so happened' to be round the corner shortly after the 'accident'!

Ramsey and its waters started off as my playground, ended up being my office, and have lost none of their magic to this day.

ground, being some of the most challenging waters in the UK. With nothing standing between us and America to the south-west, the waves that pound our shoreline may have travelled thousands of miles across the Atlantic Ocean.

I was lucky to learn my trade from some of the most experienced skippers in the area. They had worked in waters all over the world and on many different boats and were very much 'old school', but most importantly, they knew these waters like the back of their hands. Not only my father, but Malcolm Gray (OBE), the then coxswain of the St Davids Lifeboat, and

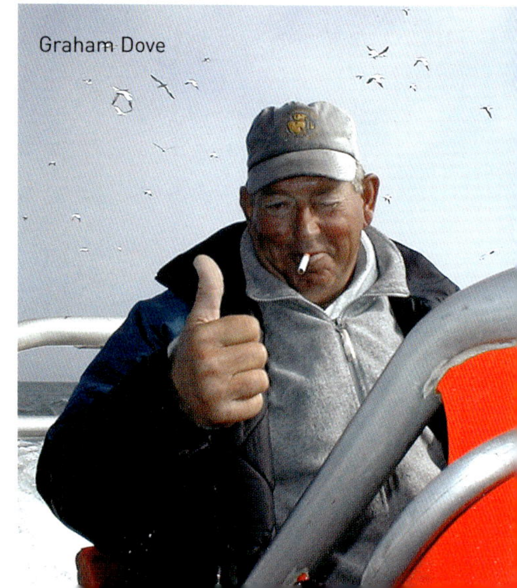

Graham Dove

## Origins of 'Ramsey'

The island has not always been known as Ramsey, and the earliest reference to it is by Ptolemy, the Greek geographer, who calls it Limnou Eremos (meaning desolate or solitary) on the earliest map of Britain.

Ramsey, which is possibly of Norse origin, along with the neighbouring islands of Skomer, Skokholm and Grassholm, is thought to be from a combination of the Norse personal name 'Hrafn', also Norse for Raven, and 'Ey', meaning island, so either Hrafn's Island or Raven's Island. It could, however, also come from the Old English 'rams' or 'ramsa', meaning wild garlic, and there is a cove on the island called Aber Garlic, which might support this theory.

One of the early, if not very well known, names for the island is Ynys Tyfanog after Saint Tyfanog, an early Celtic Saint to whom a medieval chapel, in the vicinity of the present day farmhouse on the island, was dedicated.

Ramsey is also more commonly known as Ynys Dewi or David's Island after St David, and legend would have us believe that Ramsey is the burial place of 20,000 saints!

## A history of Ramsey Island

Ramsey is currently owned and run by the RSPB as a bird reserve. They bought it in 1992 because of its importance as a breeding site for a number of nationally rare species of bird, the most notable of these being the chough. Its importance in conservation terms does not stop there though, as not only is it an SPA – Special Protection Area (an EU directive on the conservation of wild birds) but the surrounding waters and inter-tidal zone are covered by the Pembrokeshire Marine SAC (Special Area of Conservation) and it is also an SSSI (Site of Special Scientific Interest). In addition to the birds, some of its features include internationally rare plants, as well as marine mammals, fossils and even a nationally rare spider!

There are signs of human habitation on Ramsey dating back over 4000 years, and evidence that the land has been farmed for centuries. Ancient field patterns, which are still visible in the areas around the two hills of Carn Llundain and Carn Ysgubor, are suggestive of the Bronze Age period.

From its early Christian history, with its links to the 6th century St David, right up until relatively recently, Ramsey has been owned or at least associated with the Church. It formed part of the medieval bishopric of St Davids, known as Dewisland, which comprised the area of the pre-Norman Cantref Pebidiog, one of the original Seven Cantrefs of Dyfed. There is an early account from 1293 in an inventory of goods of the Bishop of St Davids, who was Bishop Martyn at that time, which records mixed farming taking place on Ramsey, including beef cattle, sheep and goats, as well as wheat, oats and barley. A later account in the 1326 *Black Book of St David*, which also documented the holdings and rents of the Bishop of St Davids, states that "2 carucates of land on the island, containing 100 acres...and there can be kept 10 horses, 100 head of 'great cattle' and 300 sheep...and 100 loads of rushes and heath" were taken per annum. It is also from this source that we first learn that rabbits were being farmed on the island, and the annual rent included 500 rabbits for cooking worth 33s 4d. (*Sounds Between*, Roscoe Howells, HG Walters, 1976. p.51)

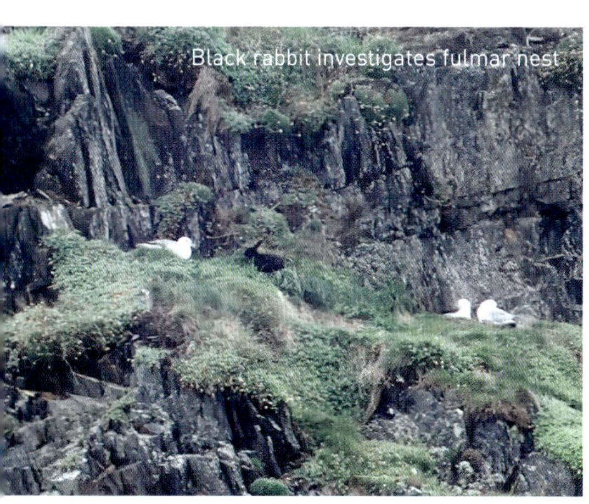


Rabbits are not actually a native species of the British Isles. Having been introduced by the Normans as a luxury food crop for the aristocracy, they would have to have been brought to the island initially in man-made warrens, before it became apparent that rabbits could survive very well without help. The original rabbits were black, and it is thought that their fur was especially prized by royalty and the clergy for ceremonial cloaks. Interestingly, you can still see black rabbits on the island today, although latterly other additions have meant you also see a variety of other colours, from white through to ginger. It is likely that the black rabbits here have survived due to the lack of ground predators, as they do tend to stick out like a sore thumb. There are a number of aerial predators such as buzzards, ravens and greater black-backed gulls that are partial to the occasional bunny, but little else to keep the numbers down. Myxomatosis, which was deliberately introduced to the island, does lead to large crashes in the population every few years. The farming of rabbits continued on Ramsey into living memory, and Malcolm Gray OBE tells of an entry in his grandfather's diary. Ifor Arnold and his brother Adrian were tenant farmers on the island, talking of the rabbit catchers with their long nets, who apparently weren't very popular: *"Rabbit catchers*

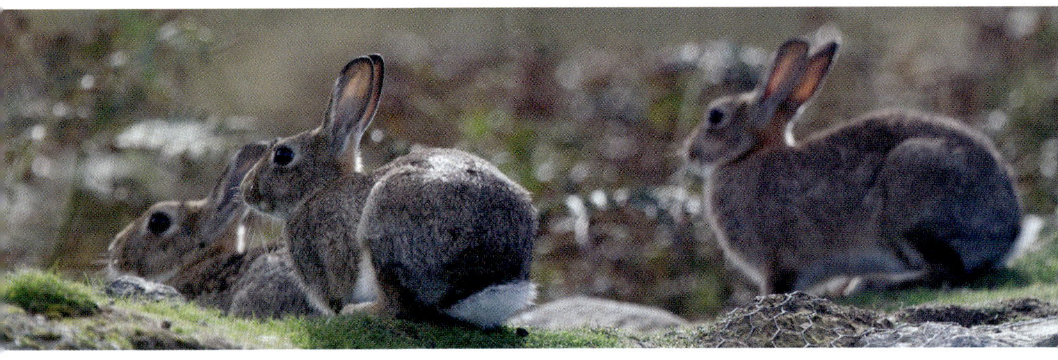

gone ashore now with all the rabbits, glad to see the back of them". One of the last entries in his diary was "came ashore in Porthstinian, Adrian and I, with 500 guillemot eggs". Seabird eggs were considered a delicacy in those days and would have been sold. The exploitation of seabird eggs was common practice on many of the islands and coastal communities around the coast of the UK until relatively recently. As a child, I can remember my own father coming back from Ramsey with gull's eggs.

The island was sold by the Church into private ownership in 1904, bought by Wynford Philipps, Lord St Davids, and farming continued, with the Arnold brothers taking over as tenant farmers. For the next few decades, under a number of different owners and tenants, it continued to run as a reasonably successful mixed farm, growing barley, potatoes, turnips, peas and rearing sheep, pigs and some horses until, with increased mechanization and the necessity of handling everything twice just to get it on and off the island, it ceased to be commercially viable. The red deer were perhaps one of the more unusual farming ventures on Ramsey. One of the biggest expenses in deer farming is fencing, given deer's ability to jump, so as they were reasonably contained on the island this was one cost that could be kept to a minimum. Nonetheless, quite a lot of deer fencing was erected and it was not unheard of for the occasional deer to end up over the cliff. They were not only farmed on the island but also slaughtered and the meat processed, as transportation of live animals was such a major operation.

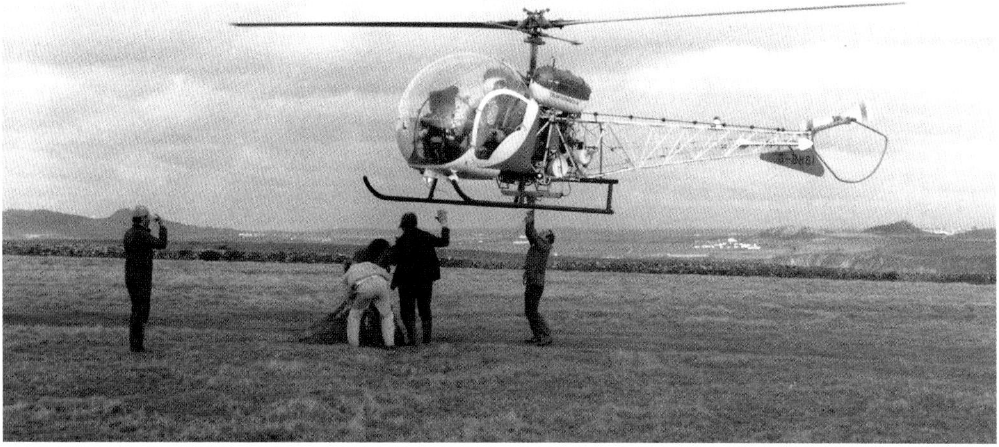

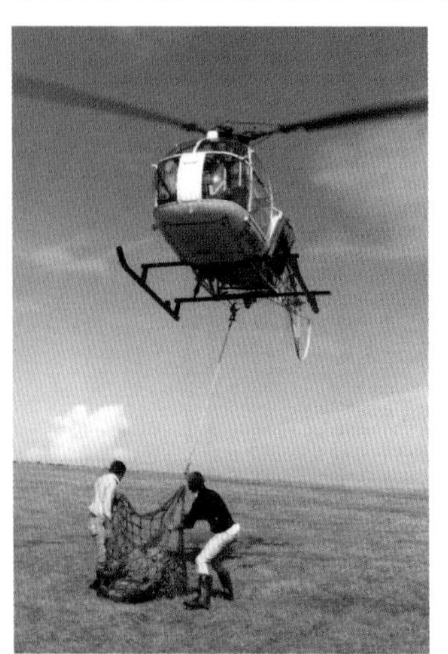
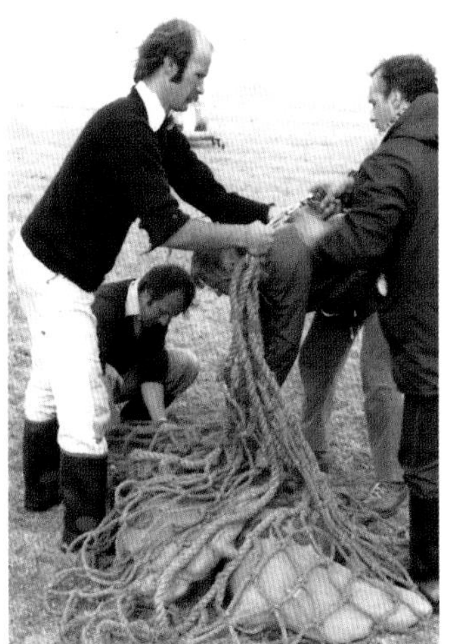
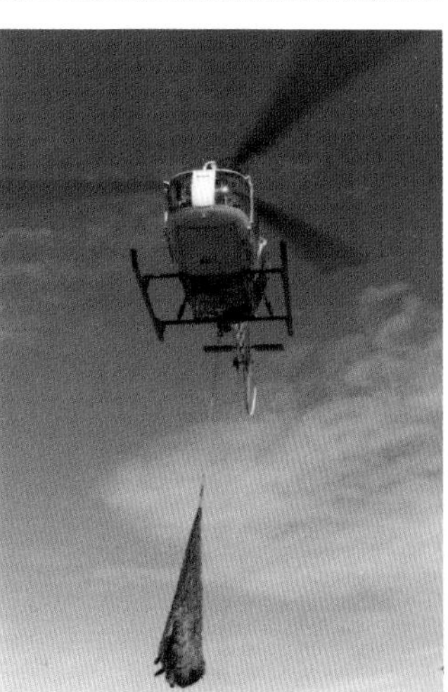

When the deer farming came to an end and the animals were rounded up to be airlifted off, a few escaped, thus accounting for the small 'wild' herd of red deer left on the island today. These are managed by the wardens and are occasionally selectively culled to control numbers and maintain a healthy population. They can occasionally be seen from the water, where they make a majestic sight. They are wary of visitors, but if staying on the island it's not unheard of to find a deer peering at you through the farmhouse windows.

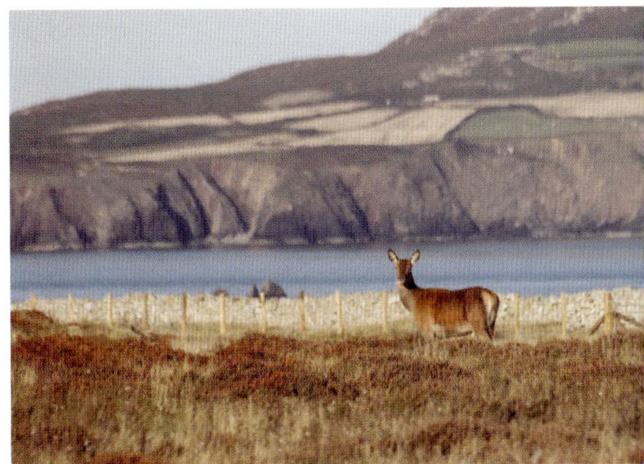

Methods of transporting animals across Ramsey Sound have been many and varied over the years; cattle and horses were tied together and swum across tied to boats, pigs were tied to barrels and towed across, as they risk cutting their throats with their trotters if they try to swim, whilst sheep, not being natural-born swimmers due to their thick woolly coats, had to be loaded into boats to be transported. In fact, if you have ever been down the steps at St Justinians you will notice that the steps themselves are too deep to walk down comfortably. This is because they were designed for animals to use as well as people. Even today it is not unusual to see a herd of sheep at the bottom of the steps at St Justinians.

During the island's venison farming days, transporting the deer was to pose more of a problem. Being an animal that

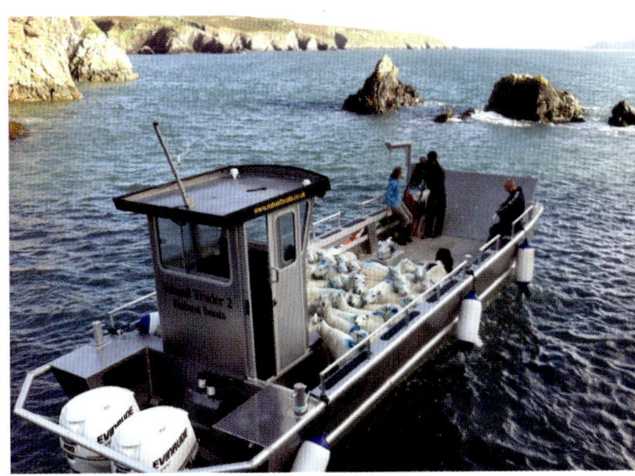

is easily stressed, an alternative method of transportation needed to be found, and the Wessex helicopter from the Navy ship HMS Bulwark was used. The main stag on Ramsey for many years was named Bulwark, after the ship. The deer had to be sedated and were then airlifted from St Justinians to Ramsey one at a time in nets slung underneath the helicopter. This was probably one of the most unusual, labour intensive and expensive methods of animal transportation to the island. It involved darting the deer, the help of a vet and, as deer can respond to certain types of sedation by getting an adrenalin rush, it was not always an exact science. On one occasion, a stag, after what should have been more than ample sedation, proceeded to jump a six foot fence.

In addition to farming, the Church played an important role in Ramsey's history, and there are a number of place names around the island that bear testament to its ecclesiastical links.

## Religious sites

There are two medieval chapel sites on the island, and the seventeenth-century historian George Owen recorded that each chapel had a 'fine spring of running water by it'. Whilst there is little evidence of either of these chapels today, the chapel dedicated to St Tyfanog, mentioned earlier, is associated with records c.1811-1963 of stone coffins and headstones having been unearthed in the area around the farmhouse. The 'coffins' are in fact what archaeologists call 'long-cist' graves,

and could date anywhere from the fifth to the eleventh centuries. The only surviving engraved headstone is that of the 'Saturnbiu' stone, named after the inscription on it. In addition it has an incised cross and sundial and is possibly as old as the eighth or ninth century. It has been suggested that this could have been the burial site of Saturnbiu Hail (the generous), who was the first recorded Bishop of St Davids and whose death was recorded in the medieval chronicle *Annales Cambriae* in 831. He was later sanctified.

The second of the two chapel sites is that of Ogof Capel, on the eastern side of the island. Today it is a beautiful half-moon shaped cove which, as its name suggests, was originally a cave above which was once the site of the other medieval chapel, dedicated to St David. Today there is no evidence of either cave or chapel, as the wisdom of building above a cave proved questionable and erosion led to both collapsing into the sea a couple of centuries ago. What has been left as a result is a very sheltered cove, one with a narrow entrance not open to the prevailing winds and an abundant supply of fresh spring water at the back. This has led to a microclimate developing, whereby fourteen species of plant grow in this cove which would not normally be associated with a maritime environment. It is also home to one of the best examples of the Ramsey juniper,

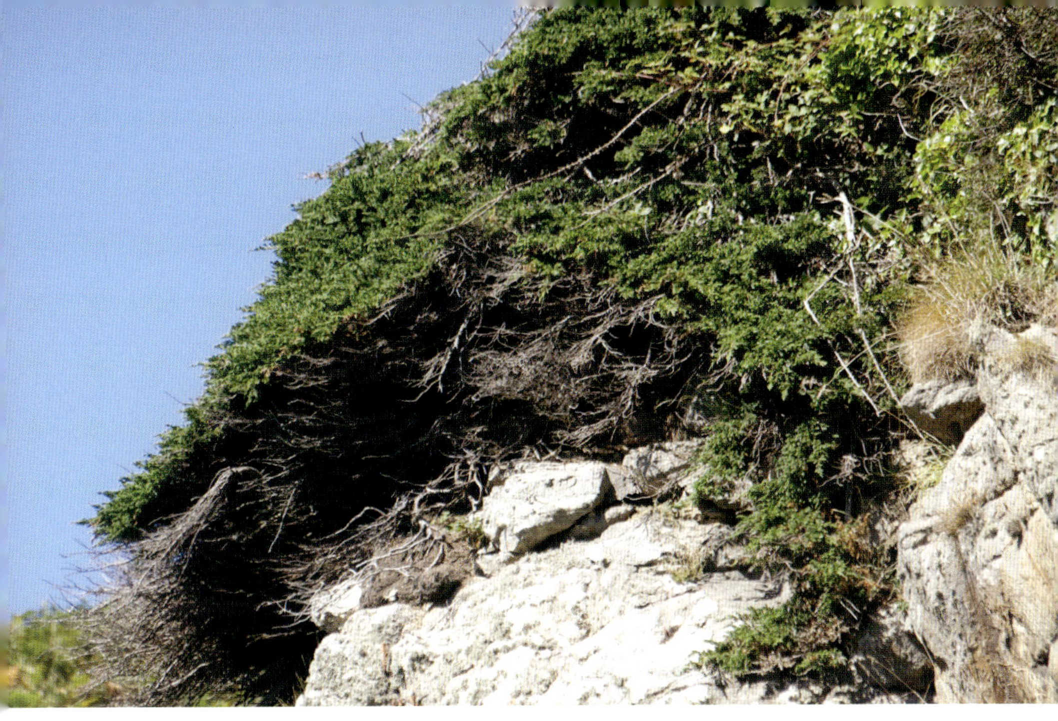

one of four examples of a subspecies of prostrate juniper bush on the island. It is so rare, having been isolated for so long, that only seven exist in the world, and all of these are to be found in Pembrokeshire. They are a relict population which possibly dates back to the end of the last Ice Age, some 11-12,000 years ago. Evidence found in peat bogs suggests that juniper was abundant in Pembrokeshire, and it is possible that the bushes surviving today could be up to 1,000 years old. Although both sexes occur on Ramsey, there is no evidence to suggest any regeneration is occurring. They are considered so important that cuttings taken from Ramsey junipers are now growing in the botanic gardens at Cambridge.

## The legend of St Justinian

There are many legends associated with Ramsey, one of the more far-fetched being attributed to St Justinian. The story tells that back in the sixth century, when St David set up his monastery on the site of the present day cathedral, St Justinian, also a monk, was his confessor. It is reputed that over time Justinian disapproved of the lax ways of David's monastery, so he departed with a number of followers to set up a monastery in glorious isolation on Ramsey, where he could ensure a much stricter regime. According to the legend, Ramsey at that time was joined to the mainland by a causeway, so to complete his isolation Justinian took his axe and hacked it away. He went about cutting the island off, but the closer he got to it the blunter his axe became, leaving great chunks of rocks behind and forming the reef now known as the Bitches. On reaching the island he buried his axe in the last rocky islet off the harbour, which to this day is still called 'The Axe'. His monastic settlement was not to last long however, as his monks soon mutinied under his austere regime and cut off his head. Apparently undeterred by this turn of events, Justinian picked up his head, tucked it under his arm and walked back across the waters of the Sound, placing his head on land when he reached the shore at St Justinians and causing a well to spring up out of the ground. The well can still be seen today above the stone steps, and the small chapel there is dedicated to Justinian, who was later sanctified. The murderers were reputedly struck with leprosy and isolated on Gwahan Gleifion – Leper's Rock, a small rock to the north of Ramsey, still called the Gwahan to this day. This somewhat unbelievable tale is typical of the hagiographies of the early Celtic Christian saints. No hagiography worth its salt didn't have at least a few miraculous events attributed to its saint, the more unbelievable the better.

## The Waterings, south of the harbour

As you move south from Ogof Capel down the east side of the island, you come to the bay known as the The Waterings, a sheltered bay just north of the harbour. It gets its name from the waterfall coming over the cliff at the back of the beach which has never been known to dry up. Down through the centuries this water source has been well documented, as it was well known and extensively used by trading skippers delivering goods around our coastline before the advent of a reliable road and rail network. They would anchor up in the bay, which is charted as a safe anchorage, and from here they would not only be able to wait for a favourable tide and shelter from the

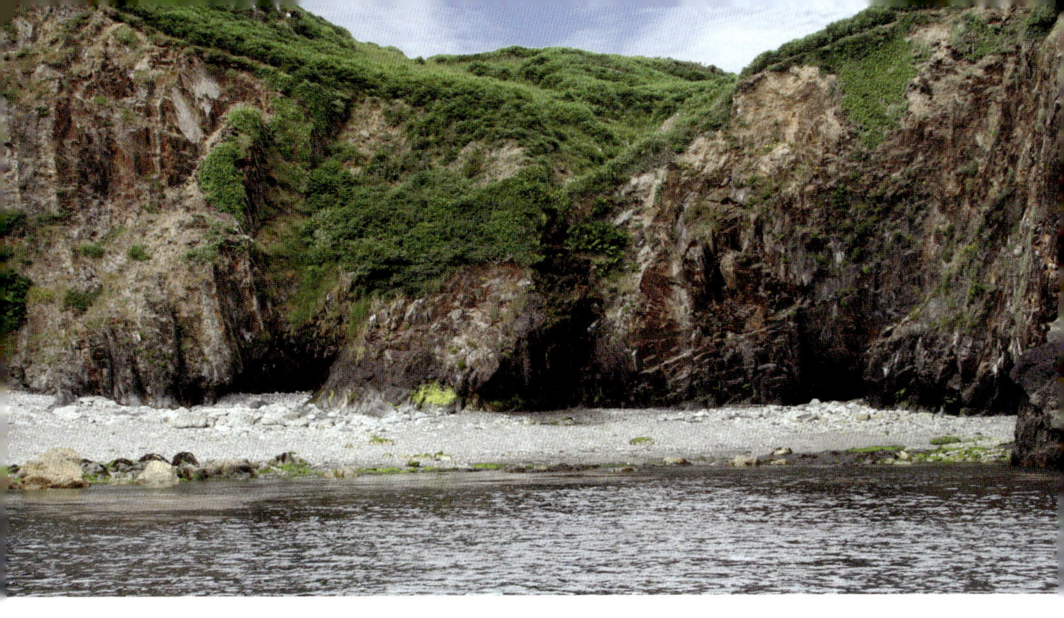

prevailing bad weather, but they would also be able to row ashore and fill their water barrels from this spring. At a time where ports were often rife with diseases such as cholera and typhoid, a guaranteed uncontaminated and easily accessible source of water was worth its weight in gold, particularly if embarking on a trip to the Americas where contaminated water meant you were likely to lose your crew, and with it your ship. It had the additional advantage from a captain's point of view of not having any hostelries ashore, so there was no chance of losing your crew overnight and possibly not getting them back in the morning.

It was even used, on one occasion we know of, by a German submarine during the Second World War, surfacing in the Sound where their silhouette was unlikely to be seen by the coastal lookouts. Some crew were sent ashore and made use of the spring to top up their batteries. The first record of this water source is written in the Doomsday Book, containing records of the 'Great Survey' commissioned by William the Conqueror in the eleventh century.

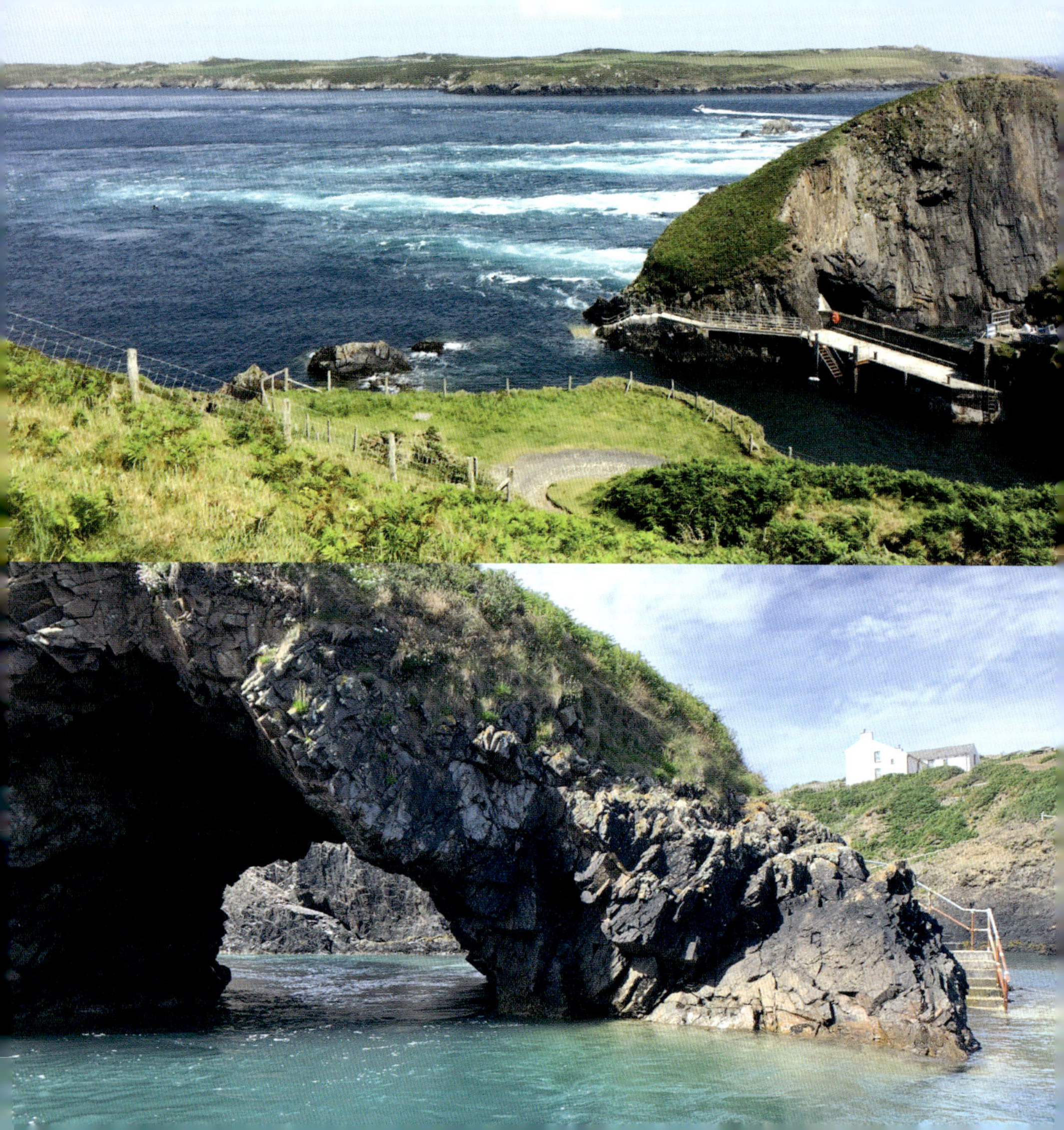

## Ramsey harbour wall

The island harbour is the only landing place on the island. It is situated on its sheltered eastern side, directly below the farmhouse, and today is enclosed by a harbour wall. The wall itself was built relatively recently, in the 1930s by Captain Whitehead, the then owner of the island. The main reason for building it was to stop the ferocious tidal flow that runs through the Sound from running straight across the harbour. Prior to the building of the wall, Ramsey was quite a tricky and often dangerous place to land a boat at anything but slack water, which only gives a very short window in which to work. In the past, animals would often have to be landed on the beach at Aber Felin, just to the south of the present-day harbour. Stores would more often be offloaded from above the cave on the south side of Ogof Capel. Being out of the tide and relatively sheltered, the boat would sit in the cave entrance whilst the stores were hoisted up with a block and tackle and a horse on the cliff above. On one memorable occasion during the Arnold brothers' time on the island they apparently misjudged the weight, and as Donald Arnold recalls, the horse came down on top of them with everything, including the horse, ending up in the sea. Horses would have been swum over for the harvest, where they would have had to use the last of the ebb tide so that if they misjudged it, the beginning of the flood would carry them back in the right direction.

When they built the wall they actually had to dynamite an existing cave in The Axe, the last islet at the western end of the Bitches. This was enlarged in order to divert the tide away from the back of the harbour wall and allow it to flow through the tunnel, thereby relieving the tidal pressure from the wall. On large tides, a torrent of white water pours through The Axe, highlighting the necessity of the tunnel, and it proved a very successful project, with the wall having since stood the test of time. The successful completion of the wall was to totally revolutionise island life by providing a relatively sheltered harbour and therefore significantly easier access. The much later addition of extending the steps to include a low water embarkation point now allows access to the island at almost any stage of tide, although it is still unusable in large swells, strong north-easterly winds and large spring tides at low water.

## Twll Y Dillyn, an exhilarating channel

The narrow gap at the southern end of Ramsey between Ynys Cantwr and the Midland is usually our egress to the western side of Ramsey. With sheer cliffs to either side and fast-flowing

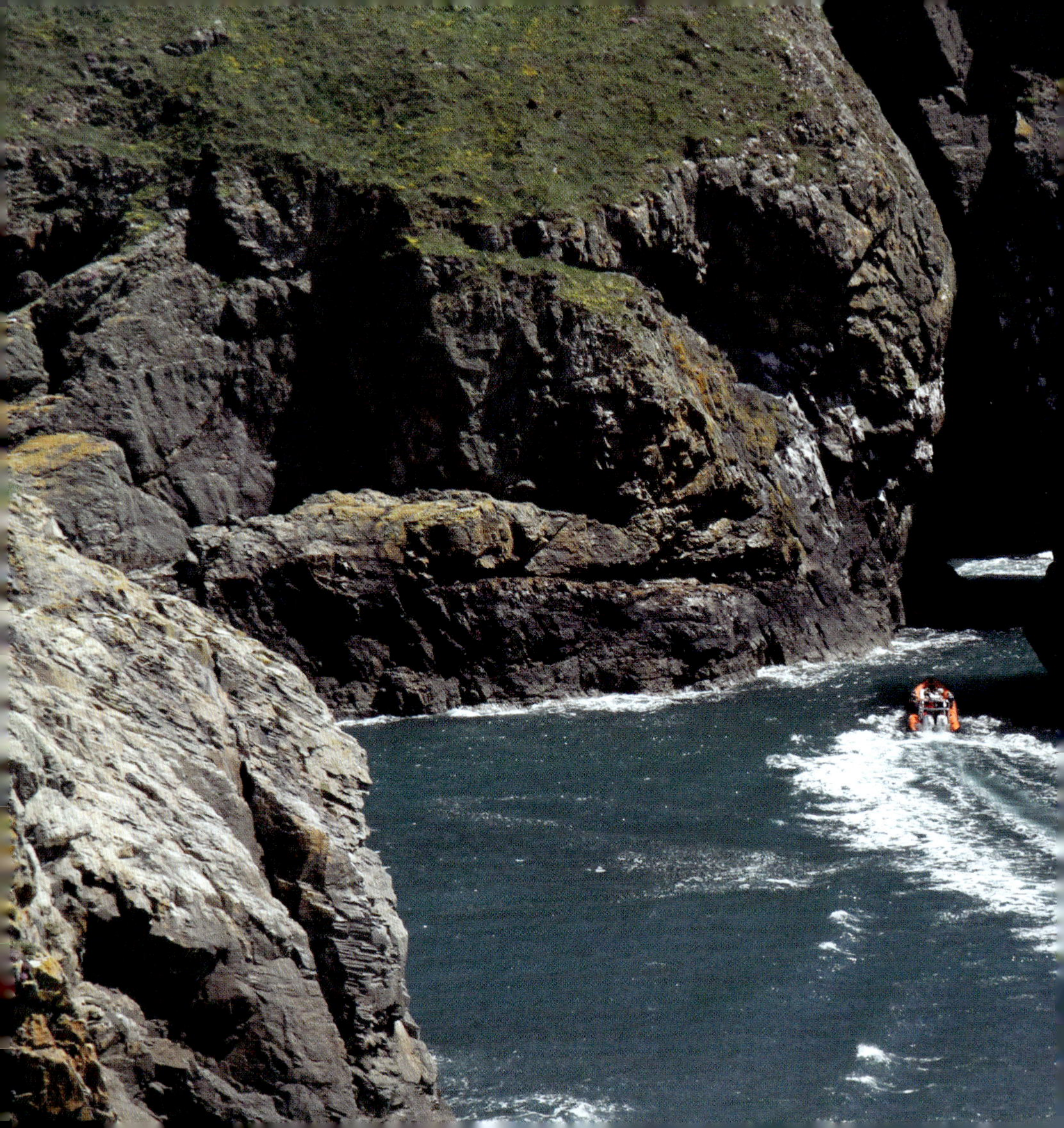

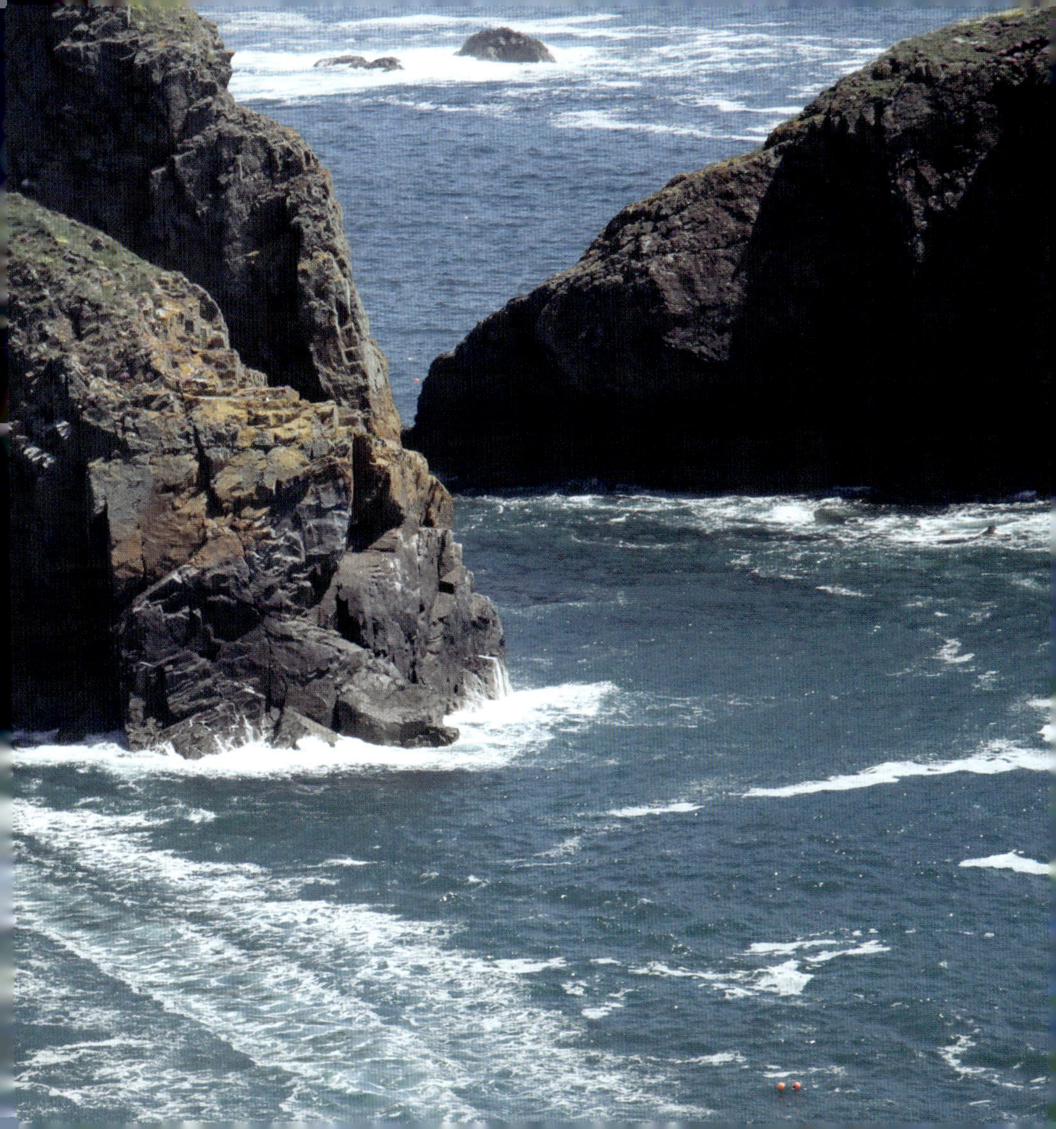

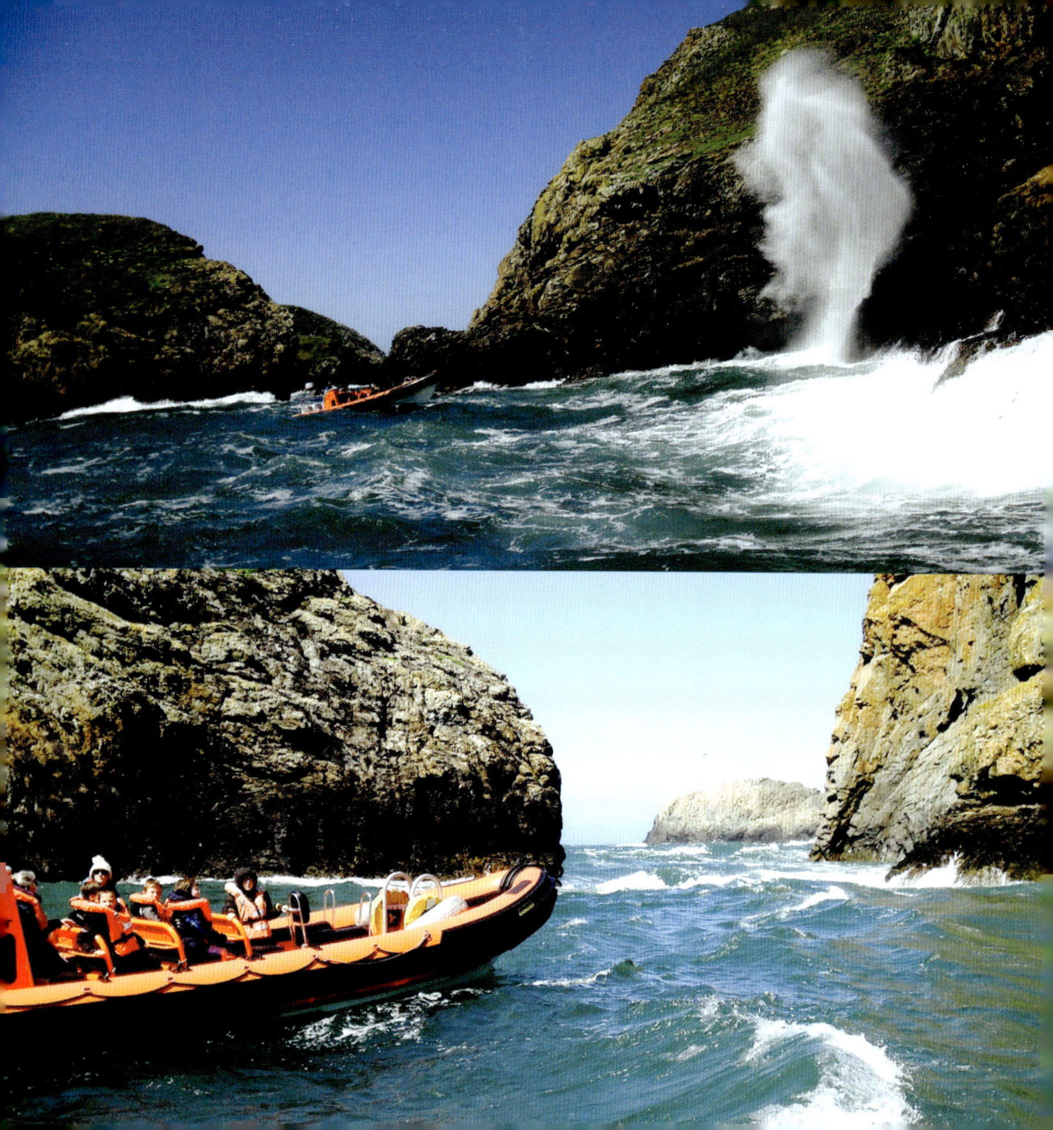

water through a narrow channel littered with rocks, it is often an exhilarating prospect. It does not take much to make it impassable, and it can turn into a veritable cauldron of white water in bad weather. It is an area of the island where the tidal movements are even more unusual than in the Sound, as the tide flows east on the beginning of the ebb for 3 hours, then west for 9 hours. With a strong westerly wind blowing against the flood tide this gap can turn into a pretty hostile environment, as overfalls build up, compounded by the swells, increasing in size and power as they are funnelled through the narrow gap. It is another spot on the island where it's easy to get caught out, as the waves are inevitably almost always bigger than they look once you have committed to go through, by which point there is no turning back.

Having ventured through the notorious Twll Y Dillyn, on the south side of the channel stands the dramatic volcanic cave Ogof Cantwr, Chanters Cave. Carved into one of the islets off the southern tip of Ramsey, this also has a story associated with it. The story again dates back to when there was a monastic settlement on the island and could tie in to the story of St Justinian, though he is not mentioned. The cave in question has also in more recent years been called Cathedral Cave, due to its dramatic high ceiling and amazing acoustics.

The large rock in the entrance to the cave can stand several metres high at low water but covers at high water on larger tides, and is often submerged by large Atlantic swells. The story tells that any monks caught misbehaving would be rowed out and left on this rock, where they were expected to chant their penance for two turns of the tide and appreciate the amazing acoustics of the cave. Given the propensity of this side of the island to be subjected to big Atlantic swells, the likelihood of being swept off was quite high. Presumably the theory was if you were still there when you were picked up twelve hours later you had been forgiven by God, and if not you had met your just desserts. You would definitely have wanted to time any misdemeanours to coincide with small tides and calm weather! More recently it has been used on the odd occasion to drop off misbehaving boat crew! Other ecclesiastical names include Trwyn Mynachdy, Welsh for monastery point, which is the headland on the north end of Dillyn Bay.

## Ogof Thomas Williams

As you head further into the southern bay of Ramsey, known as Dillyn Bay, the north side has a narrow inlet surrounded by sheer cliffs, named Ogof Thomas Williams. This dramatic cove was

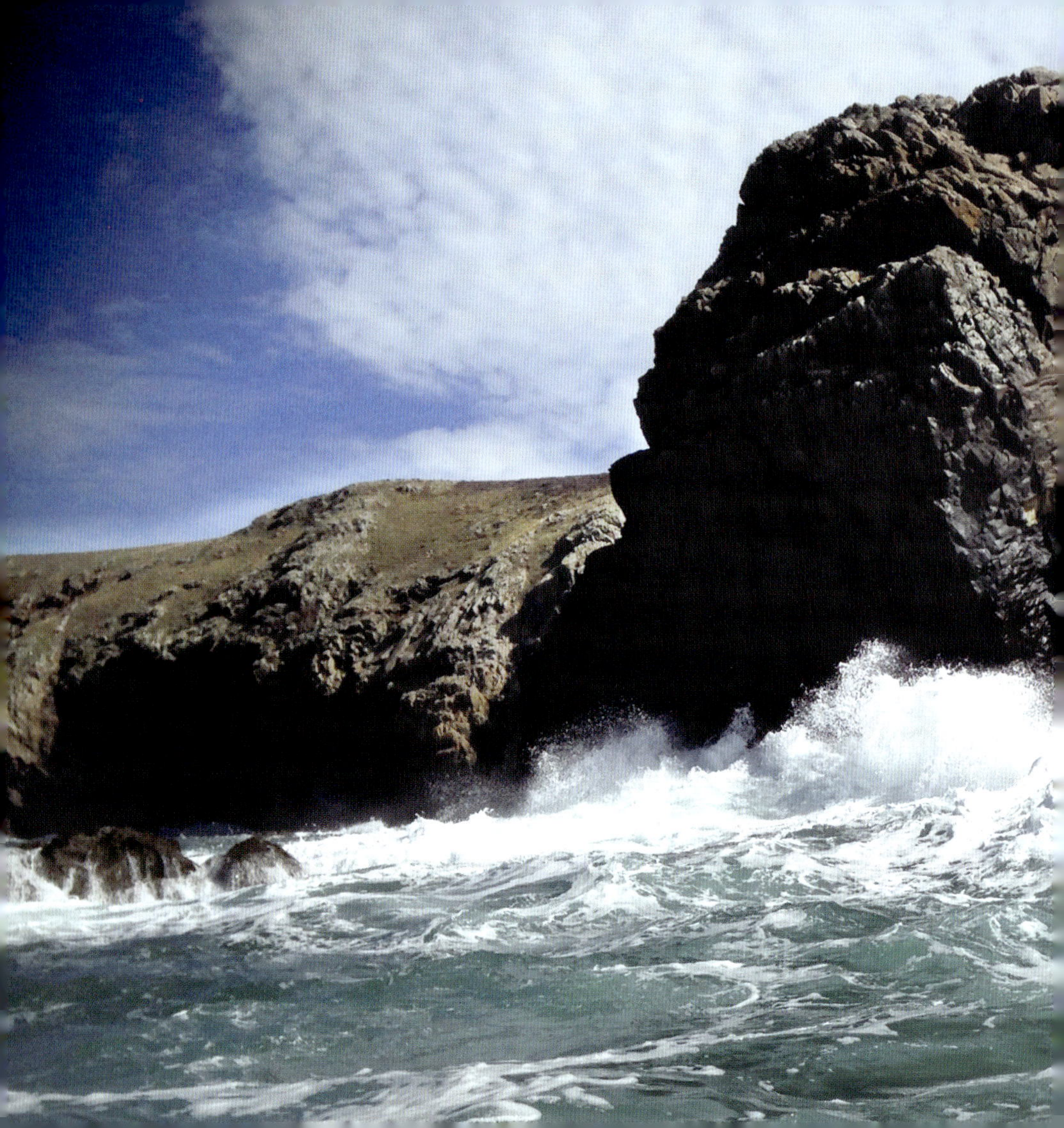

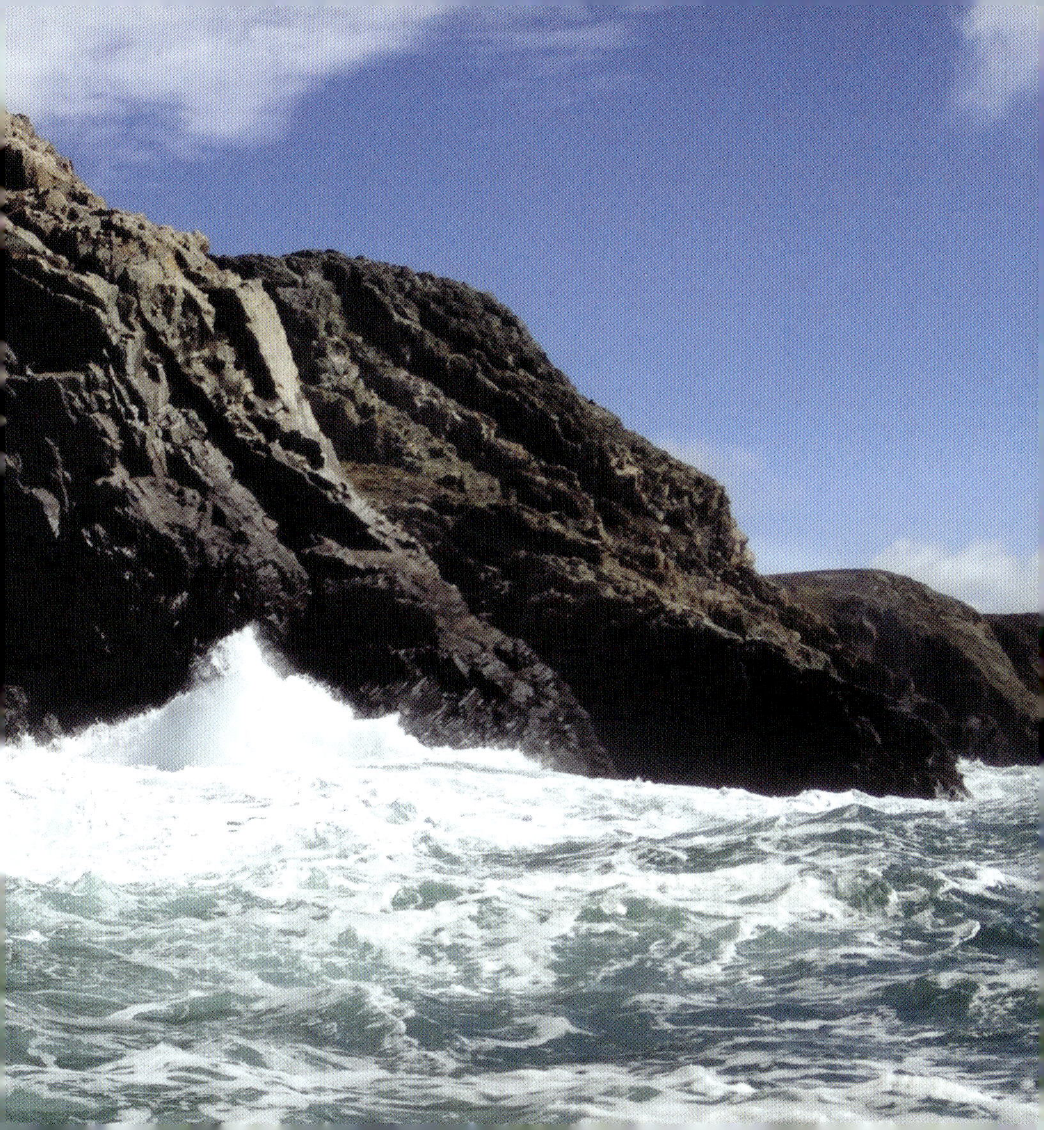

named after a certain Thomas Williams of Treleithyn, who was a retired sailor credited with alerting the local militia to the last invasion by the French on British soil. On 22nd February 1797, he spotted a fleet of four French warships and, not fooled by the fact that they were flying British colours, raised the alarm. After landing at Carregwastad, near Fishguard, things initially looked good for the French troops from La Legion Noire, but a combination of ill-discipline in their ranks, clashes with hostile locals and Lord Cawdor's forces ultimately led to their unconditional surrender. This was not before local heroine Jemima had single-handedly rounded up twelve of the French soldiers armed only with her pitch fork, and locked them inside St Mary's Church. The story, which has likely been much elaborated over the years, tells that the French may have mistaken the women, dressed in their National costume of red shawls and tall black hats, for British grenadiers when they saw them from the cliffs.

## Shipwrecks

As you traverse the dramatic and exposed coast of the south-west side of the island, littered with wave-washed reefs and outlying rocks, it is easy to see why it has been the scene of many a shipwreck.

Looking out from Ogof Cantwr, you can see another narrow, rock-strewn channel to the south of the Dillyn, running past Ynys Beri, the last of the islands that make up the southern part of Ramsey. It is possible to navigate this channel in a small boat with local knowledge, but its name is testament to the dangers here, as it is named after the SS Graffoe, a 314ft steamship which was wrecked here on 25th January 1903.

The second wreck, also off the south-western end of the island, happened on 28th September 1908, this time in the bay known as Porth Lleuog, which aptly translates as 'Lousy Harbour' due to its exposed location and the storm beach at the back of the bay. On this occasion it was a 285ft steamer called the Szent Istvan which hit the rocks in the early hours of the morning in dense fog, or 'pea soup' as the locals refer to it. The crew managed to reach the shore in their own boats, where they wandered around the island till they found the dwelling house. Both of these wrecks happened during the tenancy of the Arnold brothers, and Ifor gives an account in his diary of how during the night the Szent Istvan was wrecked he 'heard a lot of noise and being on his own locked the door and went upstairs not knowing who it was.' The following day when chopping logs, he found the shipwrecked crew in the barns and comments, 'I was chopping up sticks in the house when three men came to the door at 7am. They had a

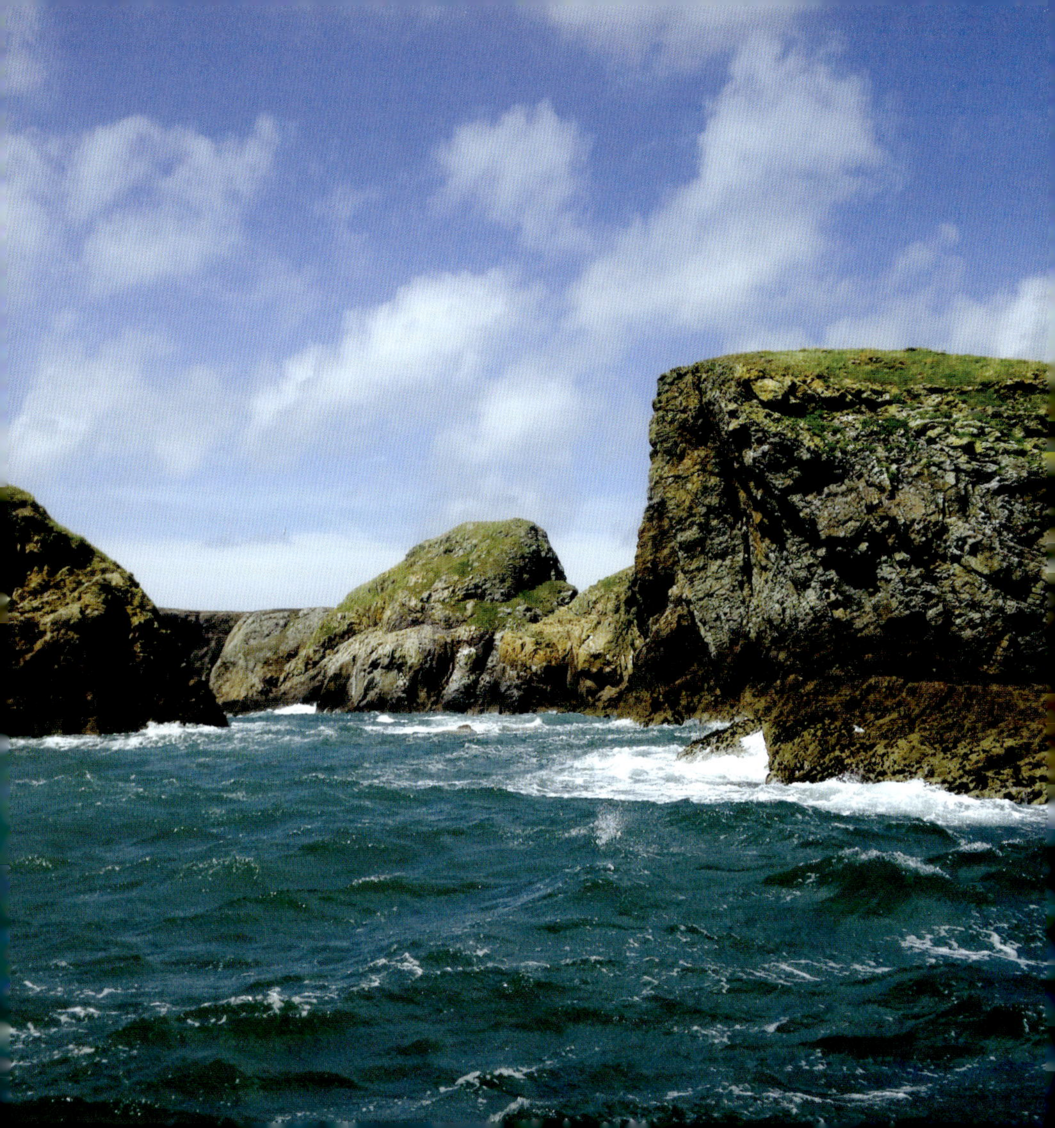

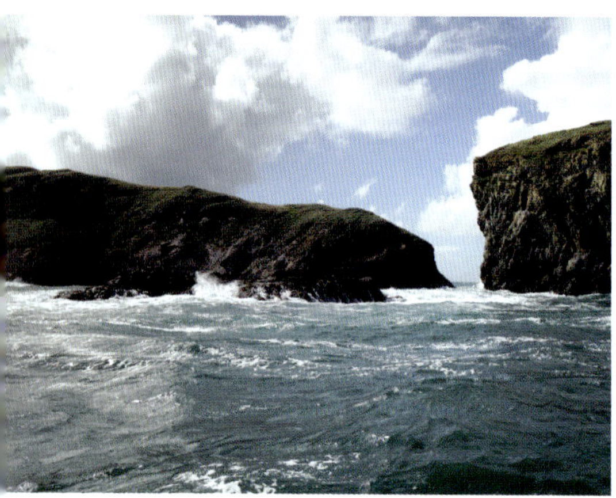

boiler of the Szent Istvan lies a mere 6m below the surface.

'Grandfather and his generation were very much into recycling!', Ifor's grandson Malcolm explains to me. On both occasions, Ifor went down to see the wrecks for himself and whether anything could be salvaged. One of the items he did salvage from the SS Graffoe was the ship's bell, which is still in the family, and interestingly the name on the bell is the Graphic. Malcolm explains that this would have been the boat's original name as, if you go on to any boat and look at the ship's bell, it will carry the original name of the boat. Although the boat may have changed names a number of times, the name on the bell is never changed. In his diary entry about the Graffoe, Ifan mentions that rats were pouring ashore from the stricken vessel, unsurprisingly proving the truth in the saying about 'rats leaving sinking ships'.

The rats, which may well have come onto the island with farming supplies as well, were to become a considerable problem for ground and burrow nesting birds, particularly with no ground predators to keep their numbers down. This was a problem which the RSPB were to inherit, and after buying the island they embarked on an extensive rat eradication project.

Lisa, one of the wardens, has said the successful eradication of the rats is one

hatchet and a long knife in their hands, which I couldn't help keeping an eye on. They were jabbering something which I couldn't understand, so I brought them an Atlas and they pointed out Fiume in Austria and from there to Lisbon and then to Ramsey. I came to the conclusion they were shipwrecked on the island. These three men landed on Aber Mawr and lost their boat. I went out with them to look for the rest of the crew and found them at 10am. They had landed (on the NE corner of the island) and moored their three boats there. The men had lost everything. I gave them tea and two loaves of bread, 1lb butter which included all I had. They ate it ravenously, though sad to say some of the youngest boys had none.' Today, the

of their biggest conservation success stories in the last twenty years. It took a single winter of concerted effort by the RSPB wardens, that of 1999-2000, to successfully eradicate rats from Ramsey, with the help of experts from a New Zealand company, Wildlife Management International. This was achieved by laying poisoned bait in raised pipes, so that only the rats were targeted and other species would not be affected.

Shearwater numbers have increased by 590% in the 22 years since the eradiation of the rats. Wheatears, also easy prey for rats, have increased in number and it has seen Britain's smallest seabird, the elusive storm petrel, breeding on Ramsey for the first (recorded) time, when five pairs were discovered in 2008.

Puffins, also susceptible to rats, haven't bred on the island since the late 1800s and they are next on the list of species which the RSPB are hoping to encourage back.

## West cliffs

As you reach the western side of Ramsey by sea you are dwarfed by the dramatic sea cliffs. Rising to some 120m in height, they are the second highest sea cliffs in Wales. Before the building of the South Bishop Lighthouse they would have been used as a navigation aid for mariners approaching the area, as they can be seen from many miles out to sea. Indeed, on a very clear day, it is possible to see across to the Wicklow Mountains of Ireland from the top of these cliffs.

The cliffs are at their most beautiful in the early evening sunshine, when the setting sun illuminates the colours of the lichens which grow on the rock so they almost appear to glow.

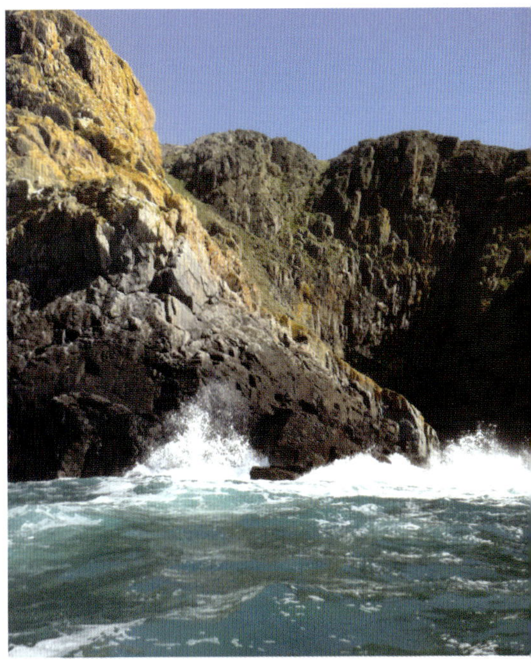

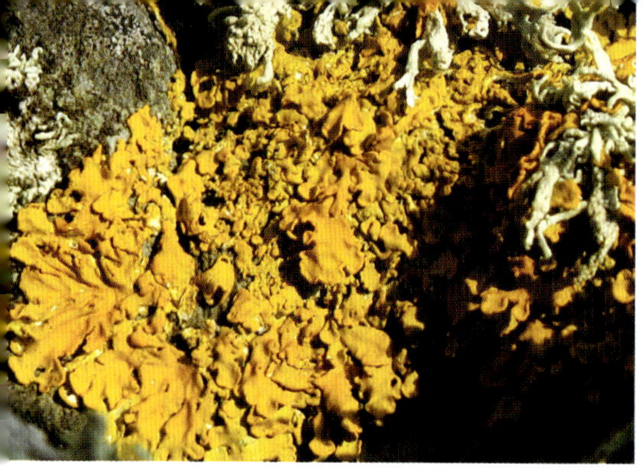

## Lichens

Lichens are not a plant but rather a symbiotic relationship between a fungus and an algae or cyanobacteria. They are extremely slow growing organisms which exist in some of the harshest and most barren environments in the world. The oldest recorded lichen is 8,600 years old. Ramsey's lichens, which include the nationally rare *Ramolina polymorpha* and golden hair lichen (*Teloschistes flavicus*), are testament to the lichens' ability to survive in hostile environments, clinging to the spray-lashed cliffs where little else can. They grow in bands on the cliff relative to their salt tolerance, so the higher up they grow the less they like the salt. The lowest band of lichen is called black tar lichen (*Verrucari maura*), and it has adapted to grow in the upper intertidal zone and into the splash zone, where it is regularly submerged by waves.

Above this, in the splash zone, grow the yellow and orange lichens and higher up again the green lichens. As a result, they are a good indicator of how exposed the coast is. In more sheltered areas, where the waves do not reach as high, these layers can be quite close together and near the water's surface, whereas on the west cliffs of Ramsey they grow in wide bands spread out over the full 120m.

From May through to early July these cliffs are teeming with life as this is when the auks come in to breed, with as many as 4000 guillemots and 1500 razorbills occupying precarious ledges high up on the cliff face where space is at a premium.

## Coastal flowers

In addition to the lichens, which are present all year round, during the spring Ramsey comes alive with a riot of colours, as coastal flowers such as thrift, squill, and sea campions come into bloom. Although not as hardy as the lichens, these also have the ability to grow in the salt-laden winds that regularly batter our shores. Perhaps more unusually, Ramsey, like neighbouring Skomer, also has carpets of bluebells more usually associated with woodlands; and some years it plays host to spectacular displays of foxgloves, a species that benefits from the disturbance caused by the large rabbit population.

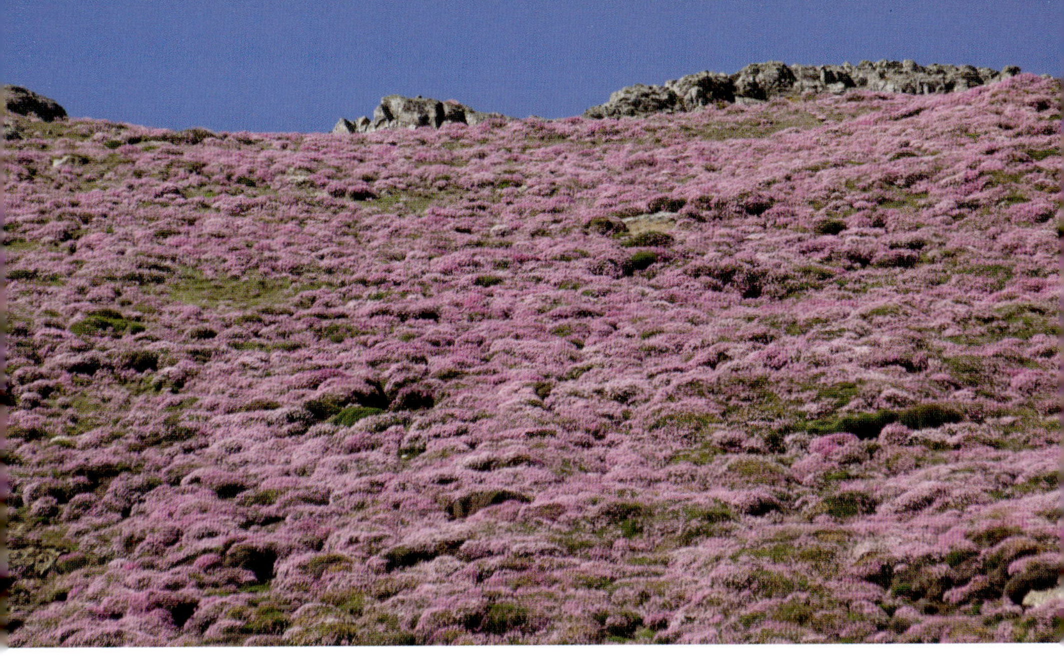

## Heather

Towards late summer, long after the spring flowers have gone, the island turns to gorgeous hues of pink and purple as the heather starts to flower.

There are always special moments out on the water, no matter how long I have spent working on it or how hard the day has been, that remind me that, as offices go, this is not a bad one. For example, on a late summer morning, returning from a sojourn offshore to the land of gannets and the search for sea creatures, when the sun is out and the wind is in the east (a rare occasion), we will reach a point a couple of miles south of Ramsey where a wall of warm air hits me that speaks of hot sunny days on shore. A welcome change to the cold maritime air that has been assaulting my senses for the last twenty miles, but also air that is laden with the sweet honey smell of the heather. A heady scent so strong you can almost taste it, so alluring it entices bumblebees

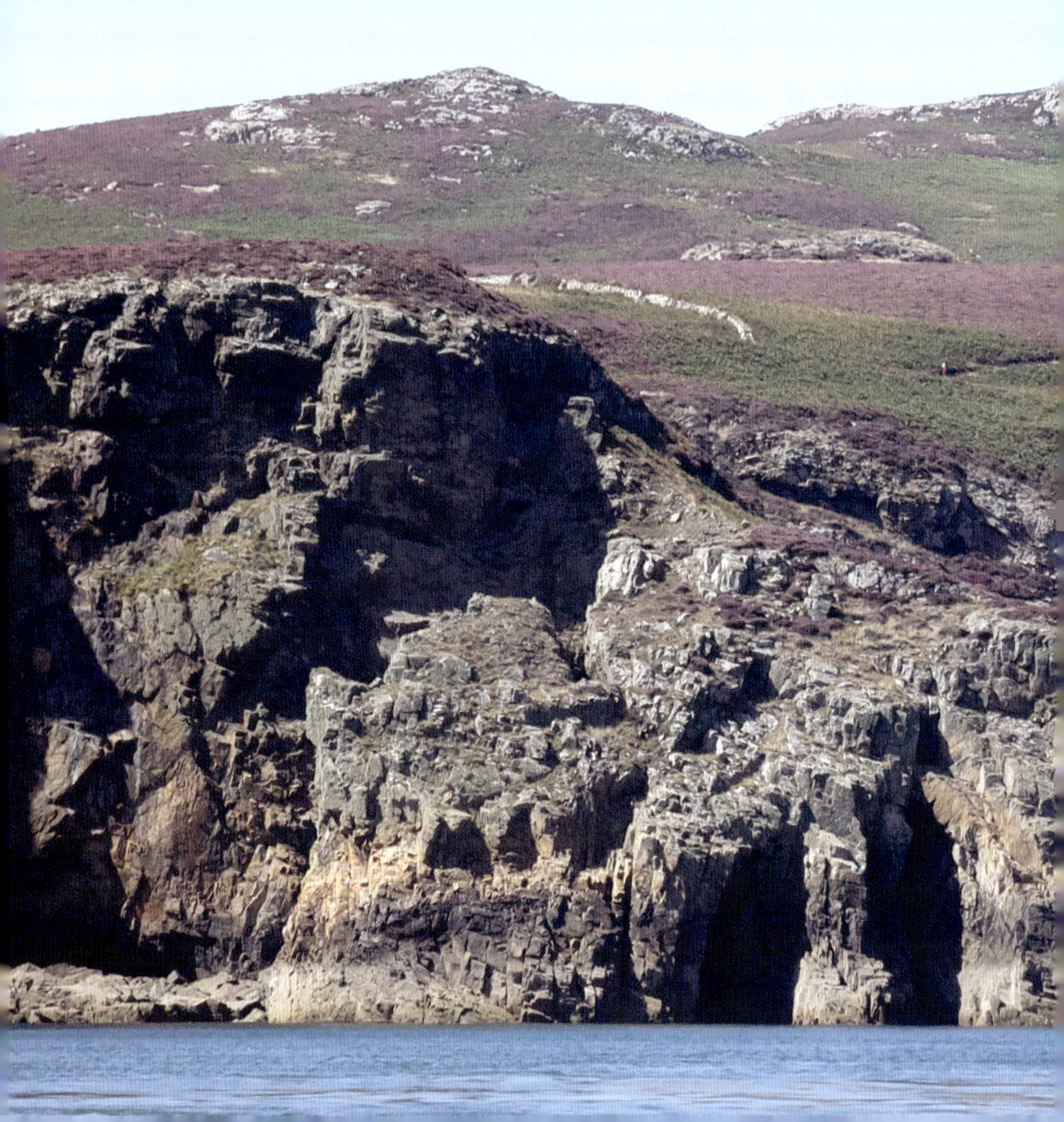

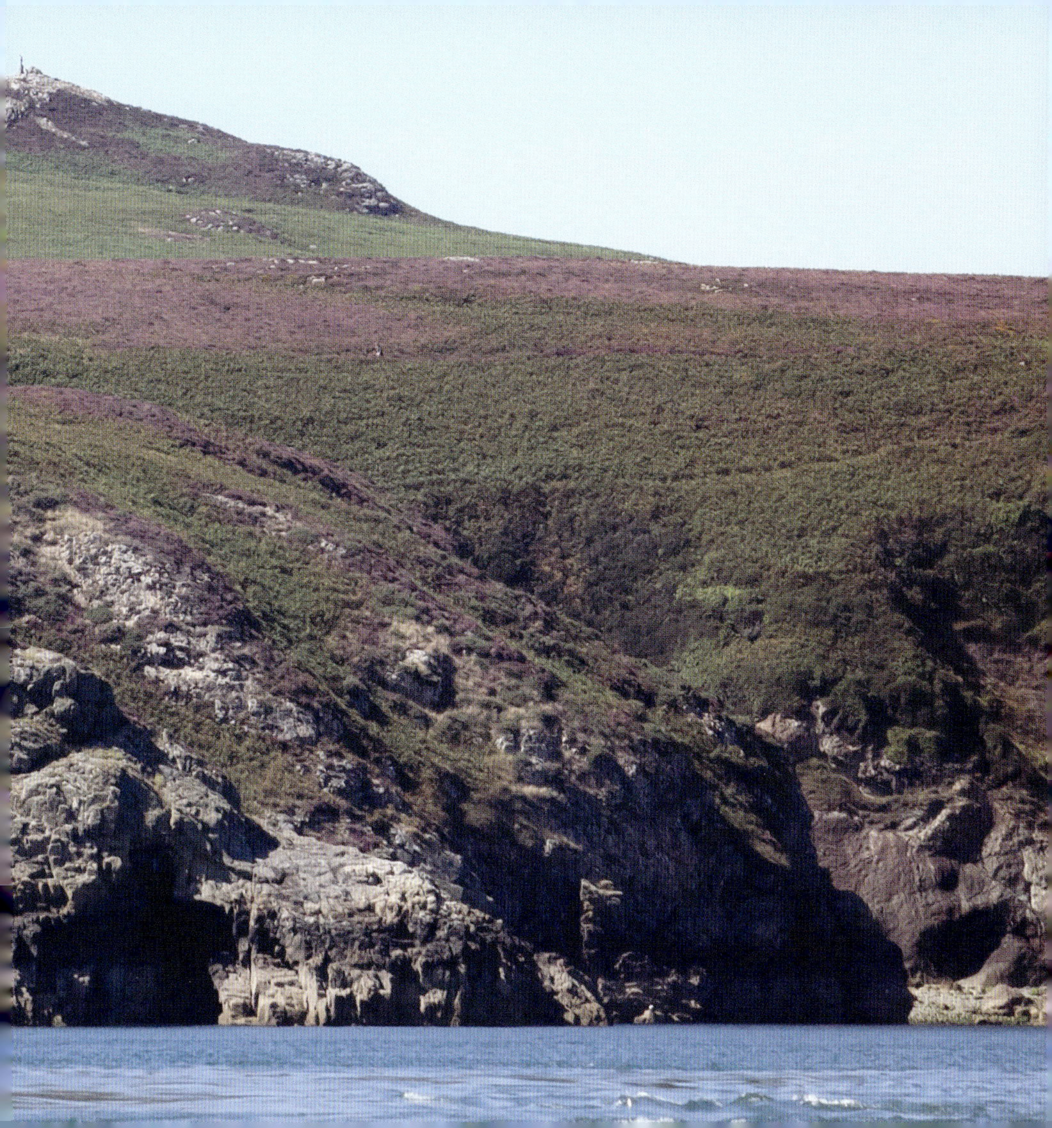

from the mainland to venture across the Sound and feed on the abundance of heather, occasionally even hitching a ride on the boat.

## Geology

The geology of Ramsey is both varied and complex, including examples of sedimentary and volcanic rock as well as intrusive igneous rock from the Paleazoic Era, to the extent that even geologists have not always agreed on certain elements of it. The island has a geological fault running north to south from Aber Mawr to Port Lleuog, dividing it into two distinctly different rock types. These range in age from Arenig Llanvirn (mid Cambrian Period) through to the Ordovician Period. The majority are igneous rocks from the Ordovician Period,

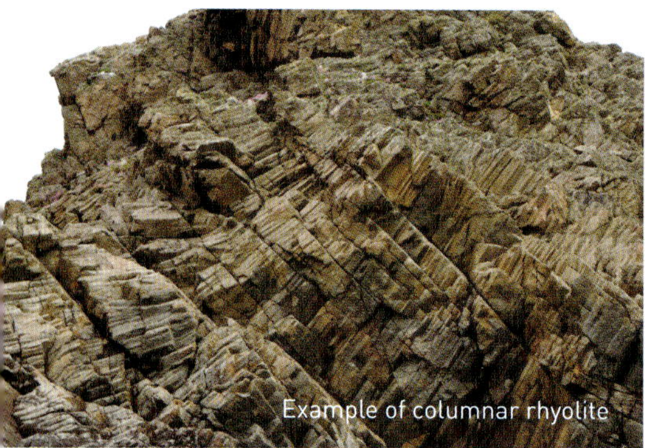
Example of columnar rhyolite

443-485 million years ago, largely making up the southern and western area of the island. On the north and eastern side of the island, sandstones and mudstones from the older mid-Cambrian period are to be found. During the Ordovician Period, when much of the island's rocks were created, there was widespread volcanic activity in the area of their origin and many of the offshore islands and higher mainland peaks are made predominantly of igneous rocks.

Even to the untrained eye, it is easy to see as you move around the island that the rock type changes dramatically. The igneous rocks on Ramsey tend to be characterised by the more rugged coastline and dramatic scenery, with high cliffs including both Carn Llundain, the highest hill at 130m high, and Carn Ysgubor to the north, which is an igneous intrusion. Most of the volcanic rocks are made up of rhyolite and various tuffs, including turbiditic and ash-flow tuffs, all of which are now believed to have been formed by violent subaqueous or underwater eruptions. There is also a fine example of rhyolitic conglomerate of the Ogof Colymenod Conglomerate Member to be found overlying the sandstones, where rounded pebbles of rhyolite are set in a finer mix of rhyolite and rhyolitic sandstone.

The extensive exposures of rhyolitic volcanic rocks provide some of the

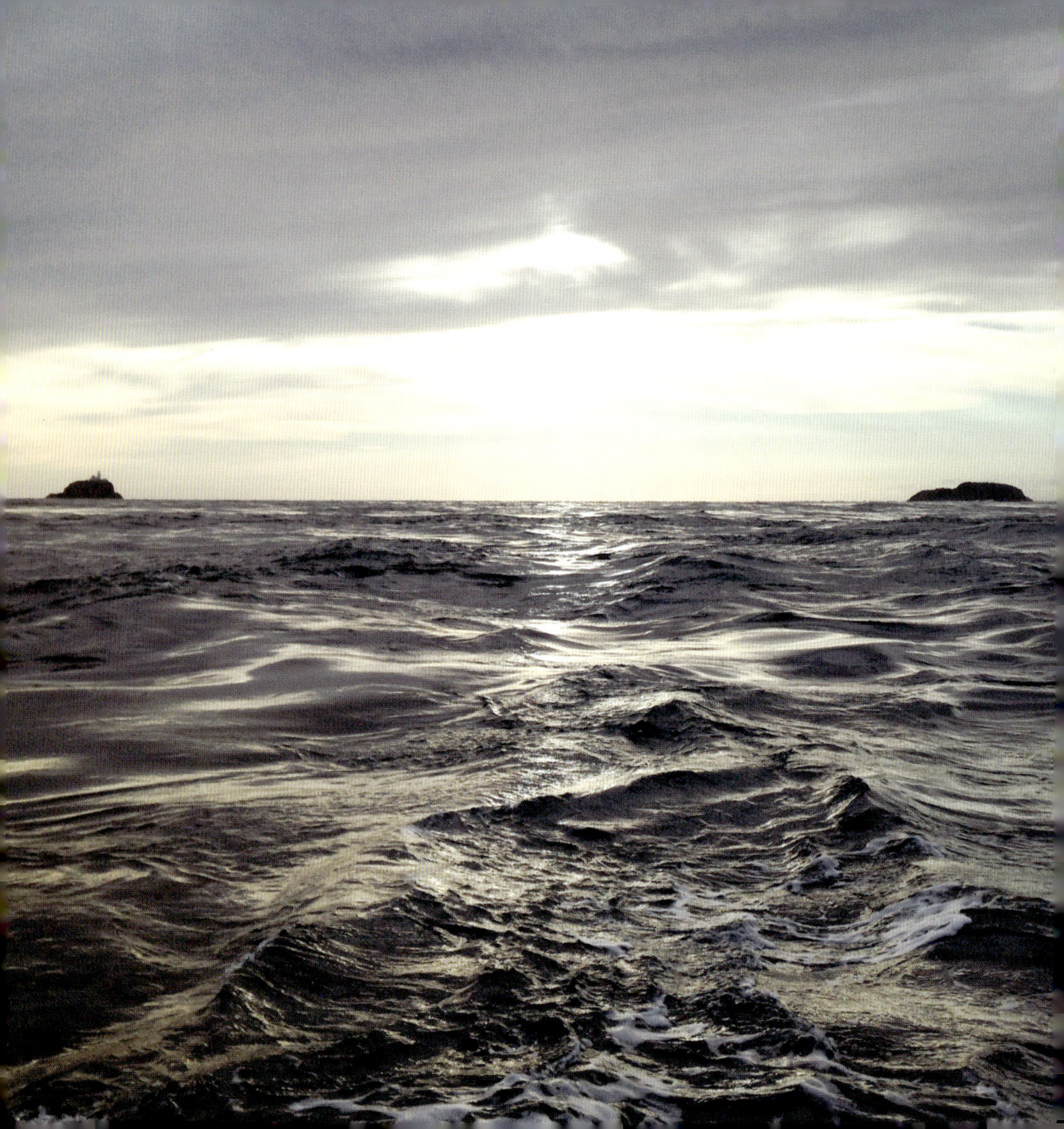

most important sites in the UK for interpretation of submarine, silicic volcanic processes, and the first record of submarine welding of a silicic ash-flow tuff in the world. Fine examples of columnar rhyolite can be seen in various areas around the south of Ramsey, where rapid cooling of magma has formed distinctive column structures.

The background sediments to this volcanic activity consisted largely of black muds and sand, which probably accumulated in a low-energy outer shelf-like marine environment. They are rich in marine fossils, including trilobites, graptolites and brachiopods, making them of national importance to paleontological research.

## Shearwater trip at sunset

The last trip of the day is a shearwater trip, and just before sunset we will head offshore to the Bishops and Clerks to see the breeding puffins. On our return, we sit and watch one of nature's most amazing spectacles, as tens of thousands of shearwaters head back to their burrows on the islands at the end of a day's fishing. It is a beautiful time of day to be out on the water, just drifting with the engines off. Watching this silent daily migration as the sun sets is nothing short of magical. If you sit here for long enough of an evening you will see over half the world's population of

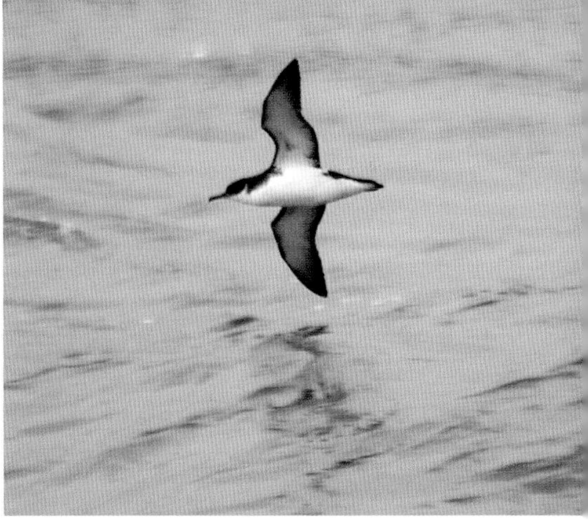

Manx shearwaters fly past.

Watching shearwater flight is like watching poetry in motion. Like all the petrels, they use what is called the ground effect, utilising the updrafts from the waves to gain lift. They have a stiff, straight-winged flight on long, narrow wings, getting so close to the surface of the water that their wing tips appear to brush the surface as they bank and glide, hence the name shearwater, and Manx because they were first recorded on the Calf of Man, a small island at the south western extremity of the Isle of Man. They will never fly over the boat, always choosing to fly around us, as we are quite a large obstacle and disturb the updrafts. This has to be one of the best ways to end a day out on the water.

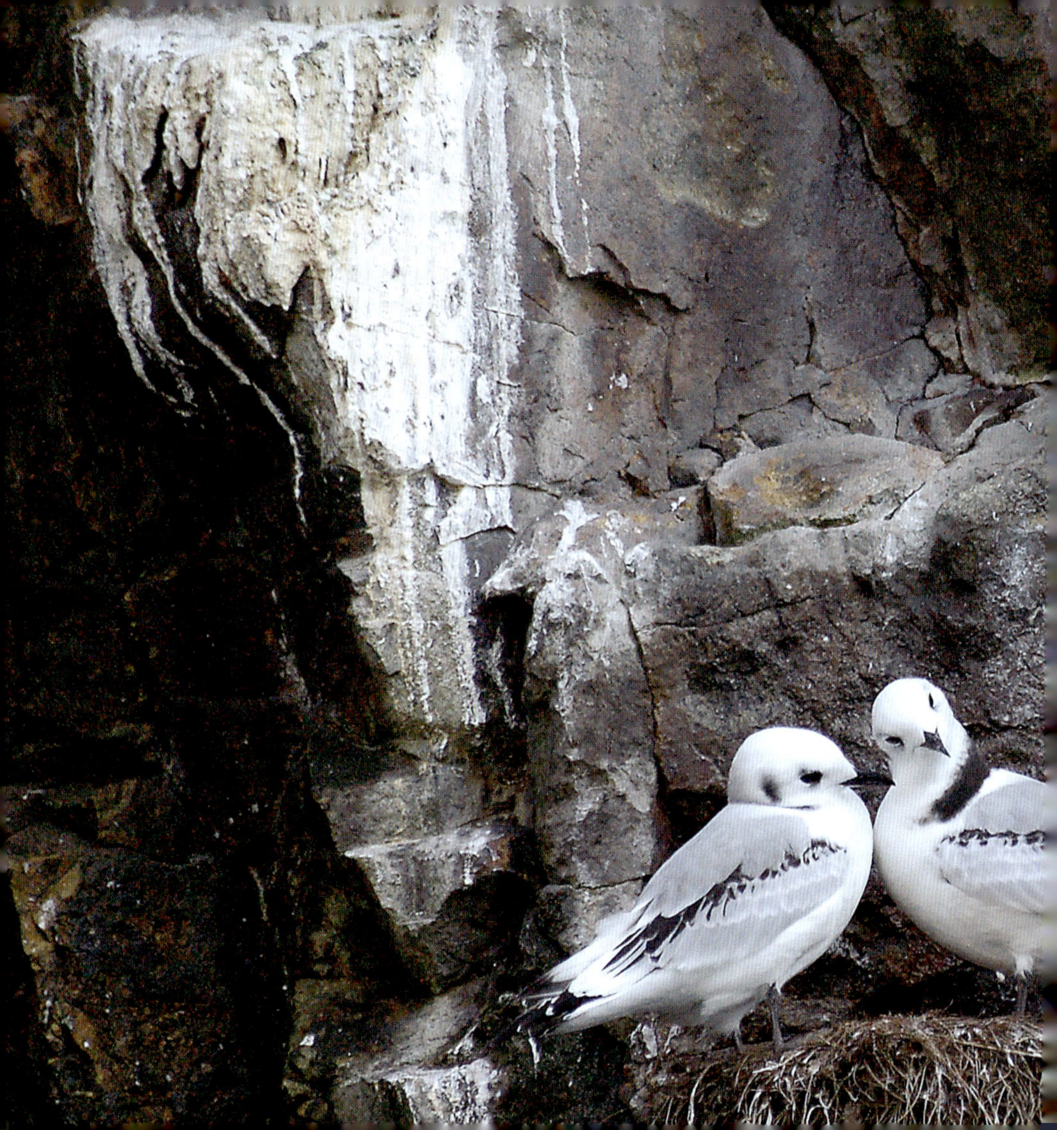

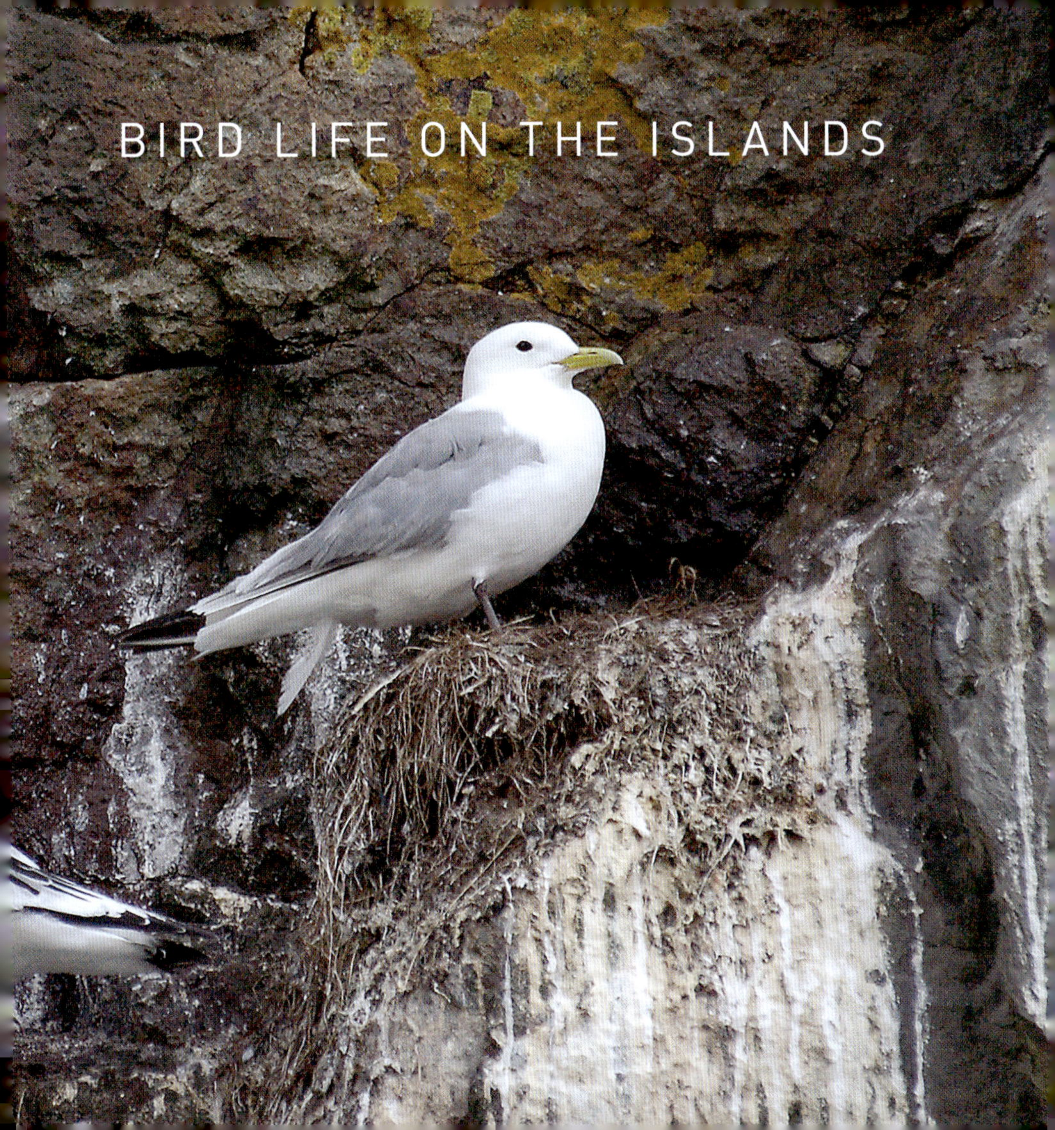
BIRD LIFE ON THE ISLANDS

Whilst the Pembrokeshire islands are renowned for their seabird populations, they are also home to many species of land-based birds, some of which are nationally rare. In addition, due to Pembrokeshire's exposed location on the very western tip of Wales, we often see interesting migrants passing by on their journeys north and south to and from breeding grounds. The following are descriptions of some of the species you will encounter; it is by no means an exhaustive list.

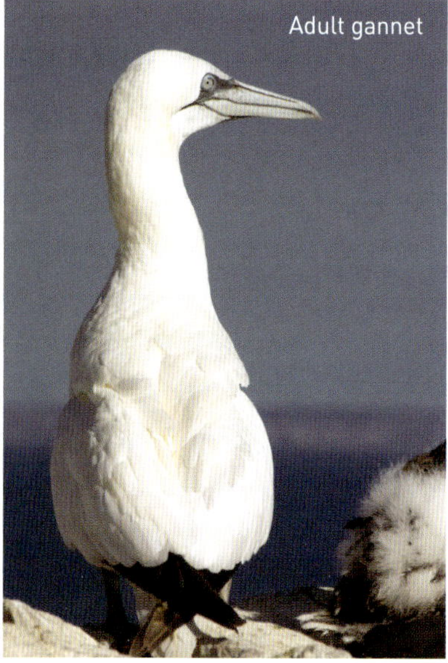
Adult gannet

## Northern Gannet
### *Morus Bassanus*

Gannets are not only the largest but also one of the most impressive looking of Britain's seabirds, with a two metre wingspan, a long neck and pointed beak and tail. They are perhaps best known for their highly specialized hunting technique, which has led them to develop a number of remarkable adaptations. Gannets are what are called plunge divers; their shape is remarkably streamlined to enable penetration of both air and water, and they have binocular vision which enables them to spot their prey from heights of up to 30m. They will initiate their dive, dropping from the sky and hitting the water at speeds of up to an astonishing 60mph; the deepest dive recorded from a Grassholm gannet was 22.2m. To spot your prey over this distance, allowing for the refraction of the water, and still be on target 20m under is a phenomenal feat. The impact associated with hitting the water at those sort of speeds is immense, and to minimise this a split second before they enter the water Gannets fold their wings back against their bodies to increase their streamlining, their pointed bills breaking the surface tension as they pierce the water like a feathered dart. It is an incredible sight to see close up, and I have been lucky enough to see one enter the water a couple of feet from the side of the boat, so close you could hear the impact and see the white plume of bubbles disappearing off into the depths at incredible speed. They rely largely on their momentum to carry them through the water, but can also use their feet and wings to propel themselves deeper to reach their prey. Further adaptations include internal nostrils that can be closed when in the water to stop water ingress, reinforced skulls, air sacs in their body which inflate to cushion the impact with the water, and a secondary eyelid which comes across to protect their eyes. All in all they are a highly adapted hunter. Recent research has discovered they can also change the shape of the lens of their eyes from oval to round on impact with the water so they can see as well underwater as in the air.

They often gather in large numbers to hunt shoaling fish, and watching hundreds of circling birds turn into arrows to pierce the ocean's surface before disappearing is a breathtaking sight that I never tire of. An average dive will last 5-7 seconds, with a maximum duration of 37.5 seconds (recorded on a Grassholm gannet). If they are successful they will usually swallow their fish before they reach the surface, they then rest on top of the water for a while to digest, or if unsuccessful they will immediately take to the skies again and continue hunting.

One of the funniest gannet sightings I have seen was when two gannets and one

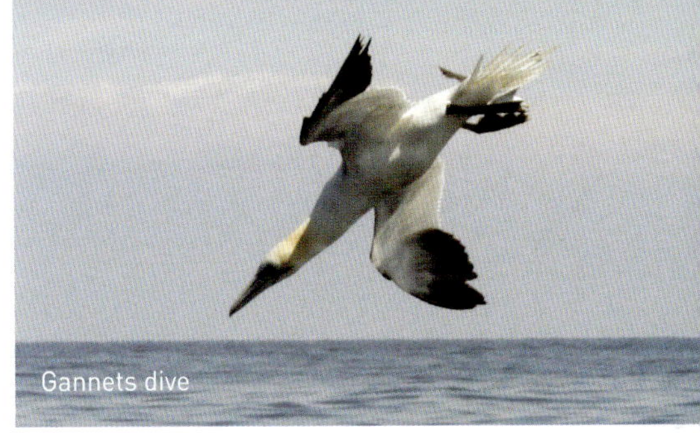
Gannets dive

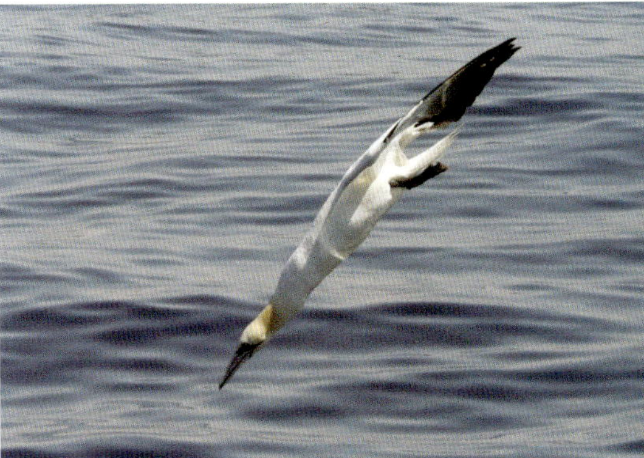

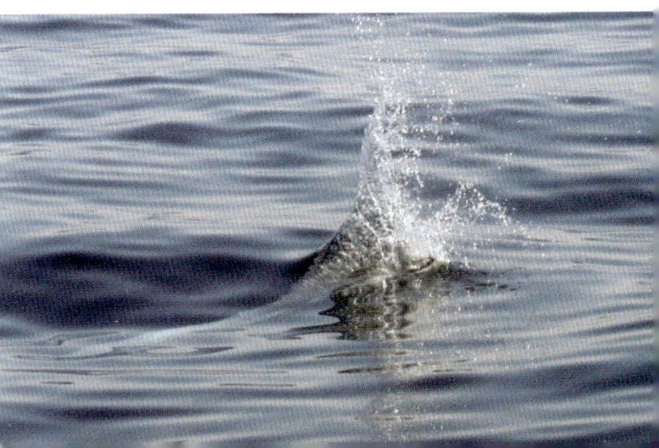

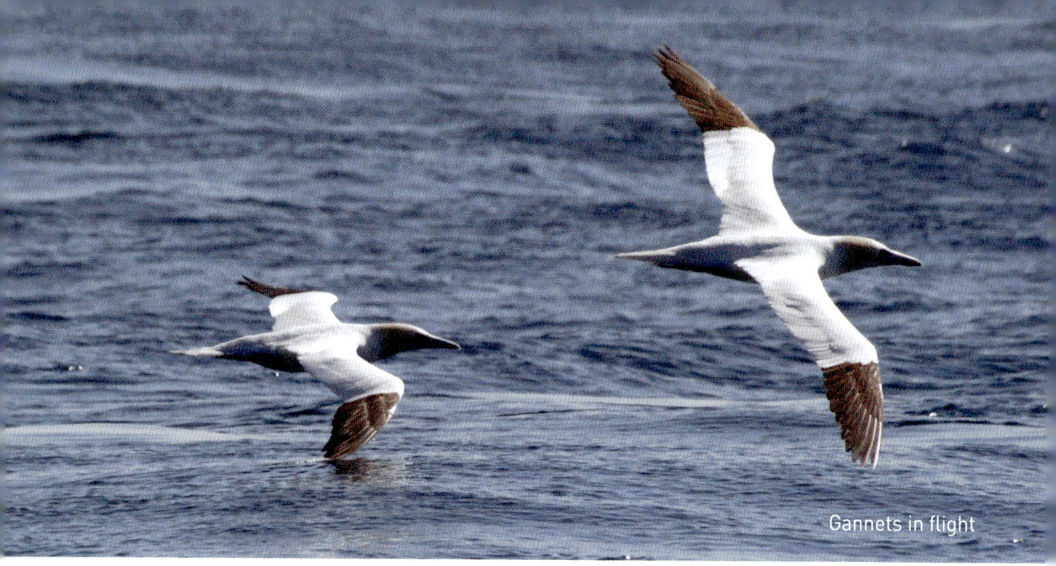

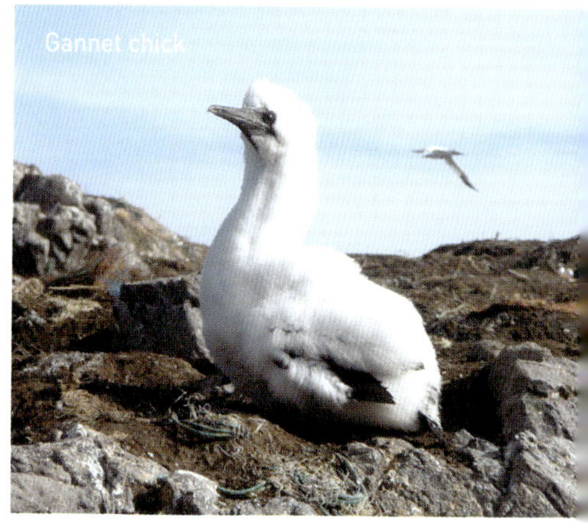
Gannets in flight

porpoise all appeared to go for the same fish, and both gannets squawked on their way down as if to say 'mine'. It resulted in a flurry of feathers and fins as they came up squabbling.

Gannets may come back to Grassholm as early as February and will lay their eggs mid April, incubating them for 43 days. Unlike the auks, which incubate eggs on top of their feet, the gannets will incubate theirs underneath. When the chick is ready to hatch they transfer it to above their feet, and occasionally during this tricky manoeuvre inexperienced females may crush the chick. It takes an incredible further 90 days before the



 Ramsey Island and beyond

chick is fully-fledged and ready to leave the nest; they will finally start leaving the island in early September. When they first hatch, gannet chicks are black, leathery and slightly prehistoric looking, until they turn into white powder puff balls, with their juvenile plumage eventually turning dark brown. This latter colour has the disadvantage of not being camouflaged for hunting, but it is thought to protect them from the unwanted attentions of naturally aggressive adults, as it marks them out as youngsters. Despite being doting parents, gannets are hostile neighbours and life in the colony often involves a lot of squabbling, particularly during take off and landing which, despite their aerial prowess, is a pretty clumsy affair with a distinct lack of spatial awareness.

It will take the juvenile birds up to four years to completely lose their dark brown juvenile colouring, and it is easy to pick out immature birds returning to the colony, as they will have dark speckles running through their plumage. The gannet chick chooses when it is ready to fledge and the parents will continue to feed it right up to the point when it leaves the nest. This is unlike many seabirds, where the adult dictates when they have to leave home and some, like the shearwater, will be abandoned to a period of starvation. This probably accounts for the fact that the young gannets, weighing

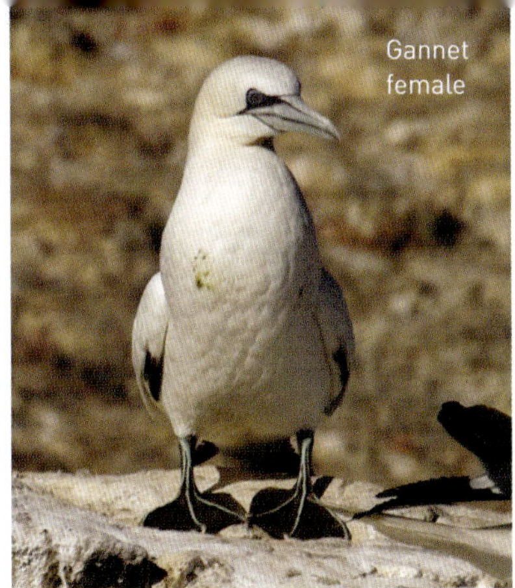



in at about 4kg, are too fat to fly when they first leave their native colony. An ungainly scramble and tumble, often causing chaos with the neighbours on the way, will take them to the water's edge where they will take the plunge and bob about, looking slightly bemused in their new environment. Once on the water they will start their migration to the coast of western Africa, paddling initially, where they are likely to spend their first couple of years before returning to their native colony. Their puppy fat will sustain them for about a week whilst they learn to catch fish and master their diving technique with no parental guidance. Some fledglings will reach African waters in less than a fortnight.

It is very difficult to tell the males from the females, although, close up, females have blue veins on their feet.

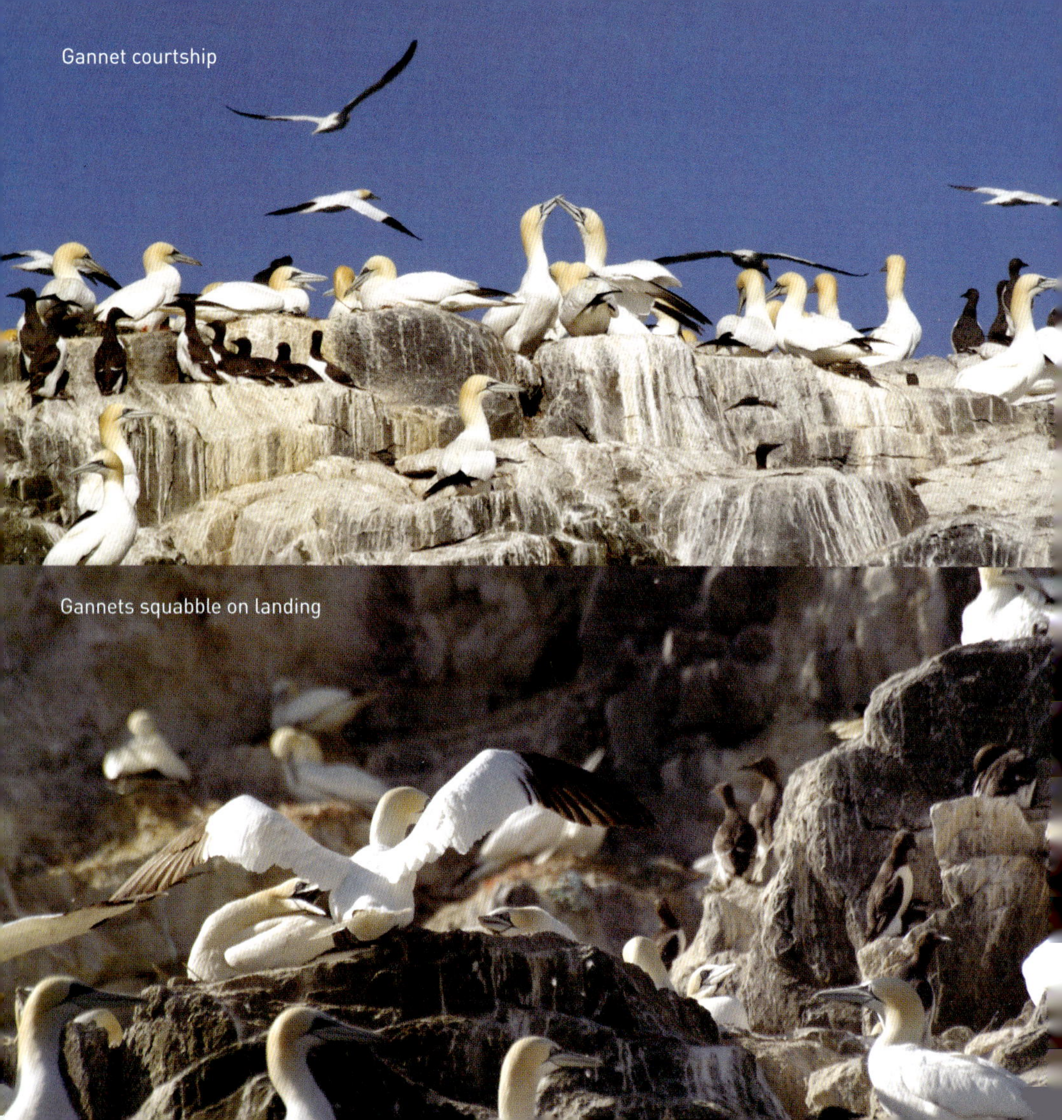

Gannet courtship
Gannets squabble on landing

# Fulmar Petrel

Fulmar – *Fulmarus glacialis*, from the Norse meaning *Foul Gul.*

The fulmar is one of my favourite seabirds; they are a member of the petrel family, also known as tube-bills, and are distantly related to the albatross. Fulmars are something of a success story in the UK where, in the last century, numbers have increased dramatically following a change in fishing practices and the introduction of factory ships creating a large increase in discards at sea. Fulmars will eat small fish, squid and crustaceans but also carrion, and it is this, combined with the fact that they are no longer hunted, which has led to their population increase. They are thought to have an incredible sense of smell that enables them to detect rotting flesh and fish oil from up to 15 miles away, a dubious accolade!

The fulmar is designed first and foremost as a seabird, and is extremely well adapted to life on the ocean wave. They have a straight winged, economical, gliding flight, similar to that of the albatross, and it enables them to cover great distances at sea, largely by gliding and expending very little energy. They have been known to leave their nests and fly 1,500 miles to the Mid Atlantic Ridge to feed before returning to relieve their partner from incubation duties. Like other members of the petrel family they

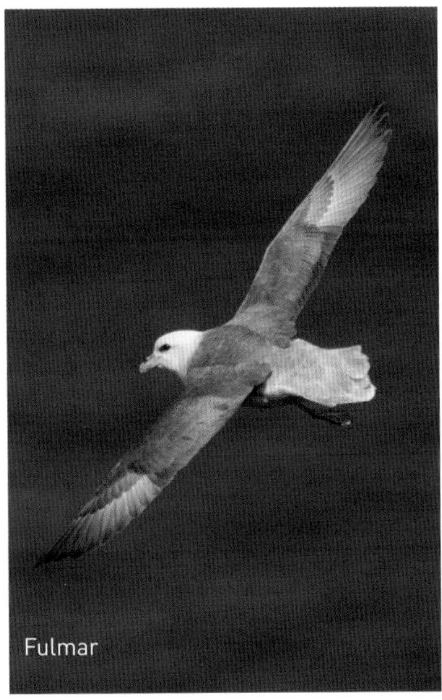

Fulmar

utilise the updrafts off the waves, using the ground effect to produce a super-efficient flying technique. They also have their feet located a long way back on their bodies, right under their tails, where they are ideally placed for taking off from the surface of the water. As they paddle themselves across the sea's surface they look as though they are walking on water, earning them the name petrels, after St Peter for his similar ability. The downside

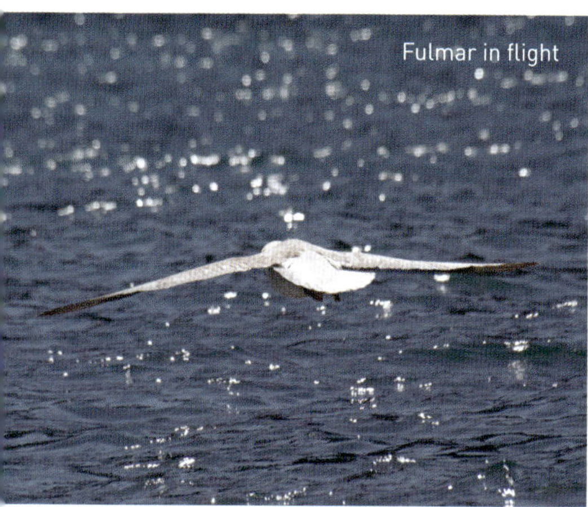
Fulmar in flight

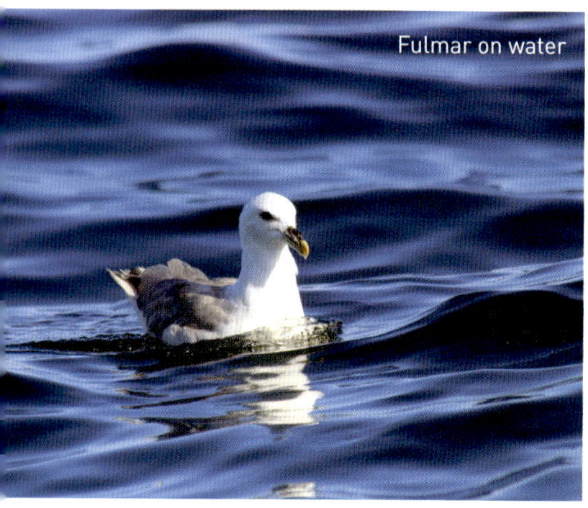
Fulmar on water

of this is it makes them very clumsy on land and, whilst not the clumsiest of the petrels, when it comes to landing on their nest sites they tend to resemble more of an organized crash landing than anything else, often requiring a number of fly-bys and several attempts. As a result they choose very open, grassy ledges on the cliffs as nest sites, making landing marginally easier. You would think that this accessibility would leave them open to predation; however, the fulmar has overcome this problem with a very effective self-defence mechanism in the form of projectile vomiting. They are capable of projecting their stomach contents at any predators foolhardy enough to come within a one metre range. It is a sticky, foul smelling, oily gloop that is virtually impossible to get off fur, feathers, or clothes for that matter. It also contains stomach acid, and any predatory bird that finds itself on the receiving end may well be rendered flightless. It won't be able to clean its feathers and the acidity will also rot them, so it is pretty much game over for the predator. I know of one cat that investigated a fulmar's nest and the fur that had come into contact with the vomit turned brown and fell out. Unsurprisingly, the fulmars tend to be given a wide berth by furred and feathered predators alike. Occasionally, a hungry young bird of prey will make the mistake of thinking they are an easy meal; I have rescued two peregrines and a young buzzard, all of which had fallen foul of a fulmar and all had ended up in the sea, drowning. They were all sent off to have their feathers professionally cleaned and then re-released on the island, hopefully a little wiser. When fulmars were hunted, particularly on St Kilda, they were prized for their ability to produce this oily substance, which was used for lamps, and it wasn't unheard of for the island's residents to turn the whole bird into a lamp by sticking a wick in it. In addition, the fulmar's vomit was believed by the Victorians to cure tooth abscesses!

Another interesting adaptation of the fulmar that enables it to spend long periods at sea are the twin nasal tubes on its beak (a feature of all the petrels and albatross called *procellariiformes*, or tube noses). These enable them to filter salt from the sea water and gain some fresh water from it, so, in effect, an inbuilt desalination plant. This ability is particularly useful when you consider that when young fulmars fledge they will head out to sea and not come back to land for six years, until they are sexually mature and ready to breed themselves, spending all that time out at sea.

Fulmars, like many seabirds, are a long-lived species and have been recorded at ages over fifty. Of our visitors, they have one of the longest breeding seasons, with eggs being laid in May and youngsters not leaving till early September.

## Shearwater

The Shearwater's latin name, *Puffinus puffinus*, is somewhat misleading as it has nothing to do with puffins but is a name they got in the Middle Ages when they were prized for their plump fatty nature and called puffins or puffings.

Over half the world's population of the Manx shearwater nest on Pembrokeshire islands, with the majority of these (456,000) nesting on Skomer and Skokholm and 6,225 on Ramsey.

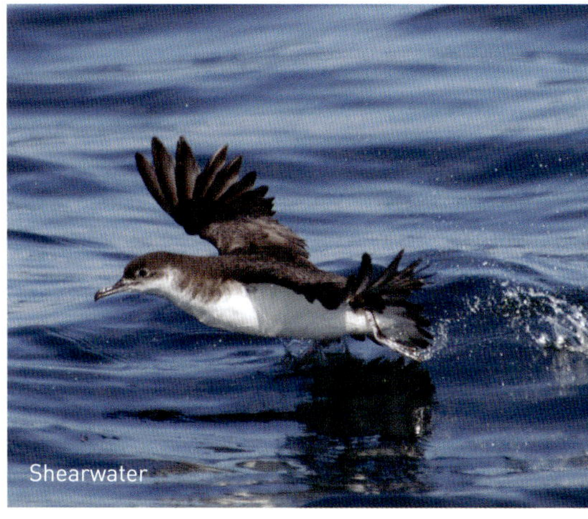

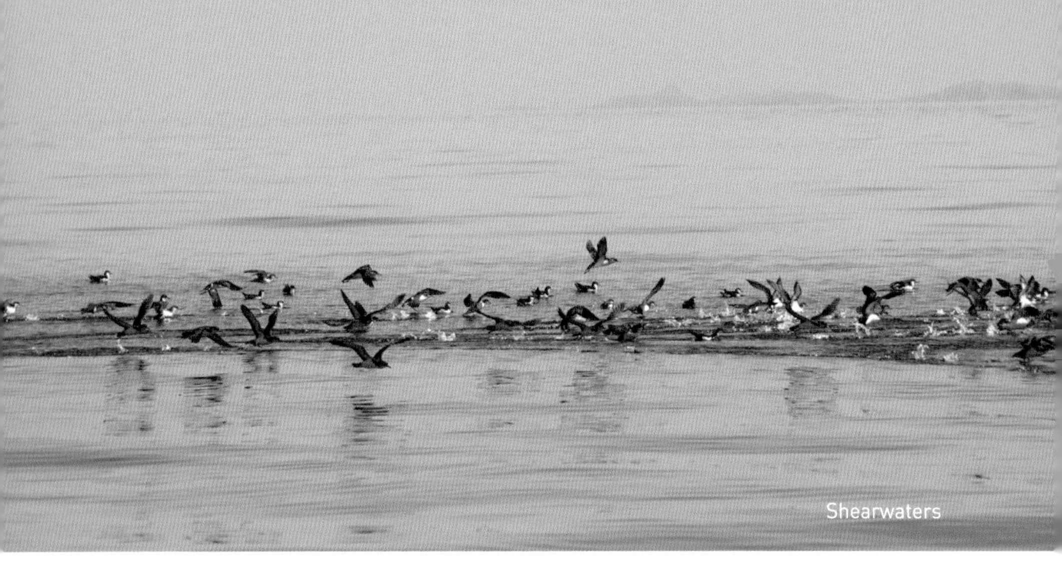



To put into perspective the importance of Pembrokeshire as a breeding site for these birds, the UK is home to 90% of the entire world population of Manx shearwater. Ramsey's population is comparatively small against its neighbouring islands and this is attributed to the fact that it is the only island which had rats, and being burrow-nesters the Manx shearwater are very vulnerable to ground predation. This is supported by the dramatic increase in shearwater numbers after the rat eradication, from 897 pairs in 1999 to 6,225, when the last full census was done in 2022. A full census is done every four years and, with that number of essentially nocturnal burrow-nesting birds to count, is no small undertaking.

Shearwaters are clumsy on land due to their feet being situated so far back on their bodies, even more so than their cousin the fulmar, but unlike the fulmar they don't have any defence mechanism to compensate, which is why they nest in burrows on remote islands with no ground predators. A bird so graceful in flight, on the ground it is often reduced to an ungainly shuffle, resorting to pulling itself along with the elbow of its closed wings. Without a cliff or an incline they struggle to get airborne at all, and youngsters that have been storm-blown or disorientated by the lights of the land, which is not an uncommon occurrence in the autumn, are often found stranded inland, unable to take off. The shearwaters are visitors to the Pembrokeshire islands, usually arriving around late March to early April, though they won't lay their eggs until early May and it is thought that after mating the female will head offshore again for about a fortnight to feed whilst the egg develops. When it is laid, the egg will be a massive 15% of the body weight of the adult. Once the egg has been laid it will take fifty-one days to incubate, with the parents taking it in turns to sit on the egg whilst the other goes out to feed. After it has hatched it will be a further seventy days before the chick is ready to leave. Due to being so vulnerable to predation by the larger gulls, such as the greater black-backed gull, shearwaters are largely nocturnal on land, and after heading towards the islands en masse at the end of a day's fishing, they will raft up just off the islands in their thousands, waiting for darkness to fall. It is only then, under the cover of darkness, that they will brave the flight to their burrow. The bird in the burrow will call to the home-coming bird to enable it to locate its burrow amongst the thousands of others, and if you are ever lucky enough to stay on one of the Pembrokeshire islands

at night during the summer the whole island will reverberate with the calls of the shearwaters. It is a quite surreal but wonderful experience. If you happen to be in the flight path of a shearwater and its burrow you are quite likely to get flown into. On particularly light nights the shearwaters may not return to the islands at all. At sea the shearwaters feed largely on small fish such as sand eel, sprats and herring, plankton, squid and crustaceans, and although they will often feed on the surface the birds can also dive for their fish, using their wings and feet to swim down. They can cover hundreds of miles on a fishing trip alone.

When it is time to leave, the shearwaters embark on a massive migration to the waters off the coast of Argentina. Research done on Ramsey from 2009-2012 involving geolocators being attached to a number of shearwaters has shown they tend to migrate in a clockwise direction around the Atlantic, broadly speaking heading down the eastern Atlantic on their way south and up the western side on their way north, by using the trade winds. It will generally take them two to four weeks to do this trip. The adults will leave for Argentina eight or nine days before the chick, leaving a fat, often still partly down-covered chick in the burrow, still expecting its next meal to be delivered! After a few days, realisation will eventually dawn that food is no longer forthcoming, and over two or three nights the chick will make its first few tentative forays out of the burrow, where it will flap its wings to strengthen them before retreating to safety again. When it does finally leave it will do so at night and, without a backward glance, will embark on the same journey to South America as its parents. It is still something of a mystery how they manage this amazing feat of navigation on their own with no adults to show them the way. Recent research has proven they use their sense of smell for navigating across oceans and they can smell DMS (dimethyl sulphide) emitted by their prey, krill, in concentrations of less than 1 part in 10 billion.. To get a perspective on the sort of distances these birds cover, the oldest recorded shearwater was ringed in 1957 and still alive in 2008, making it at least 51 years old. It was calculated by ornithologist Chris Mead, taking into account not only its migrations but also foraging trips, to have covered somewhere in the region of five million miles in its lifetime.

One experiment carried out to test the navigational skills of a Manx shearwater from the island of Skokholm was to transport the bird to Boston, where it was released. It took it a mere twelve and a half days before it was back in its burrow on Skokholm, having covered a distance of 3,000 miles.

As well as the geolocator work, on-going monitoring of Ramsey's shearwater populations includes annual ringing of chicks in a particular study plot, which the wardens have been doing since 2010. This again is something I have been lucky enough to be involved in, having volunteered to help a couple of years in a row. It involves catching the chicks in late August/early September as they emerge from their burrows at night prior to leaving, weighing them, grading them according to how much down they still have, ringing and releasing them. Wardens Greg and Lisa have already seen some of the young birds they ringed coming back to the island.

## Storm Petrel

These, the smallest of the petrel family and in fact the UK's smallest seabird, are also an RSPB success story when, in 2008, after the rat eradication, five breeding pairs were recorded on Ramsey. This is the first time they have ever actually been recorded breeding on the island. Storm petrels will typically nest in boulder screes, walls, under large boulders or even in burrows like the shearwater. The breeding sites were found when the wardens were surveying potential nest sites on the west side. The method for discovering storm petrel nests

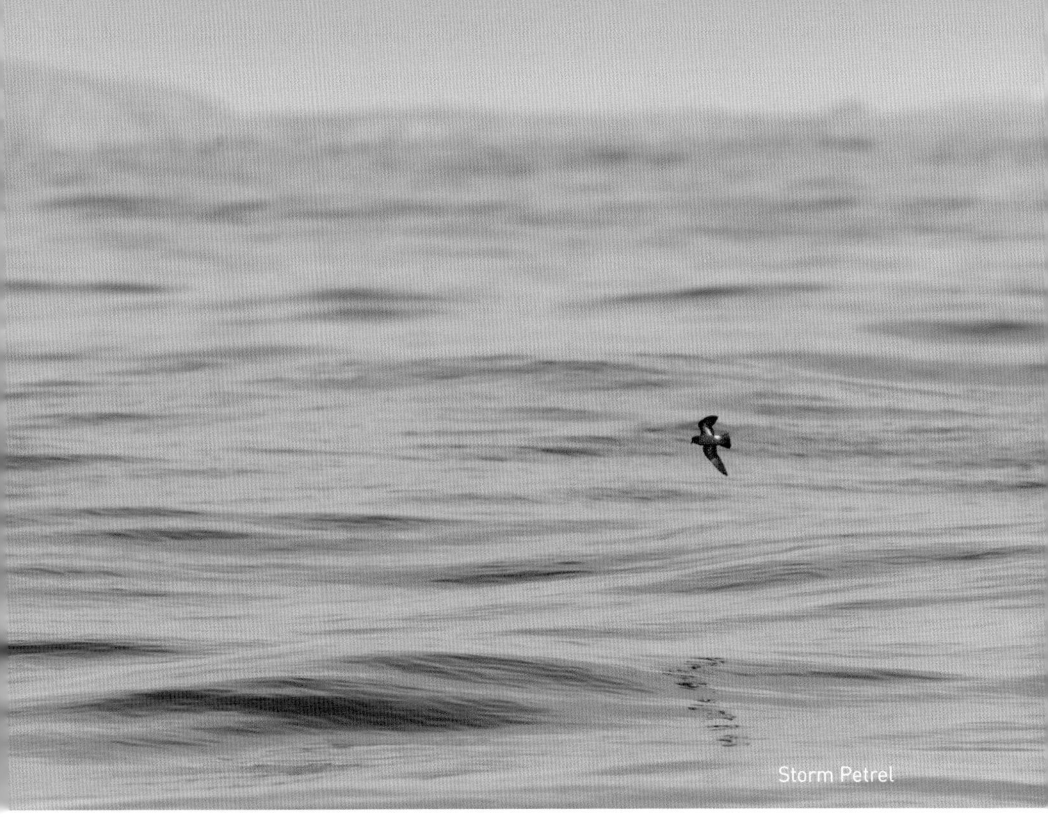



is to play recordings of their calls outside likely looking sites and listen to hear if there are any returning calls. The same technique is also used for establishing what shearwater burrows are occupied, although Dewi, Greg and Lisa's sheepdog, has also become quite adept at sniffing out occupied burrows and usually helps Greg with these surveys.

Other storm petrel populations in the area include 163 pairs on the Bishops, 300-400 pairs on Skomer and 5,000 on Skokholm, which is the largest population in Wales.

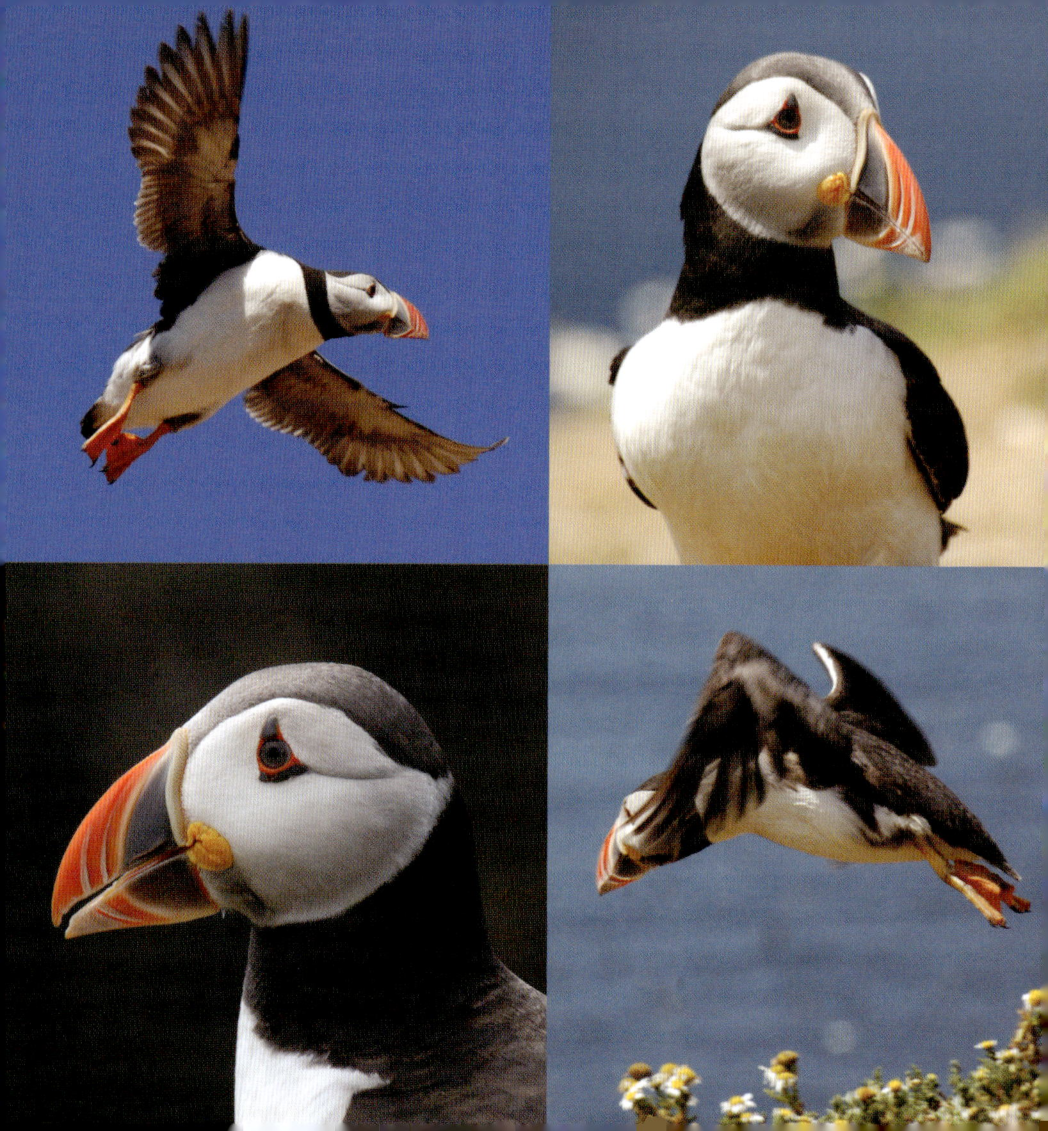

## Puffins

Whilst species such as the shearwater and storm petrel are very much a success story for the RSPB, when it comes to Ramsey the puffin is proving to be somewhat more elusive. They are ground or burrow nesters prone to predation but, unlike the shearwater which continued to breed on Ramsey despite the invasion of rats, puffins have not bred on the island for more than 100 years. They were last recorded breeding there in 1894. Since the eradication of rats, the RSPB have been hoping that puffins will once again breed on the island. In an attempt to entice potential breeding birds onto Ramsey, wardens Greg and Lisa decided to try introducing decoys, a method which had been successfully pioneered on Eastern Egg Rock Island, off Maine, as well as Ailsa Craig Island, off Scotland. So every year since 2009 during the puffin breeding season, a 200 strong colony of plastic puffins can be seen gracing the cliffs by Aber Garlic on the north west of the island. The thinking behind this is that puffins, being naturally gregarious birds, prefer to breed where there are already other puffins, which poses a bit of a catch-22 situation for the likes of Ramsey. This was always going to be a project that may take several years to succeed, if indeed it is successful, as puffins breed at about 5 years old and it is the young non-breeding birds that the RSPB are initially hoping to attract. Whilst there had been increasing sightings recorded of puffins on the water in the area around the decoys, it was not until the introduction of a sound system playing puffin 'love music' that puffins were actually recorded landing on Ramsey for the first time in over a century. The solar-powered sound system was first trialed in 2013, and was in place for a number of breeding seasons. It was early on during the trial period that puffins were first seen on low tide rocks below the decoys, which suggests that the sound system could be a valuable addition to the project. They have also since been spotted amongst the decoys themselves. Hopefully in the not too distant future we will see puffins back breeding on Ramsey.

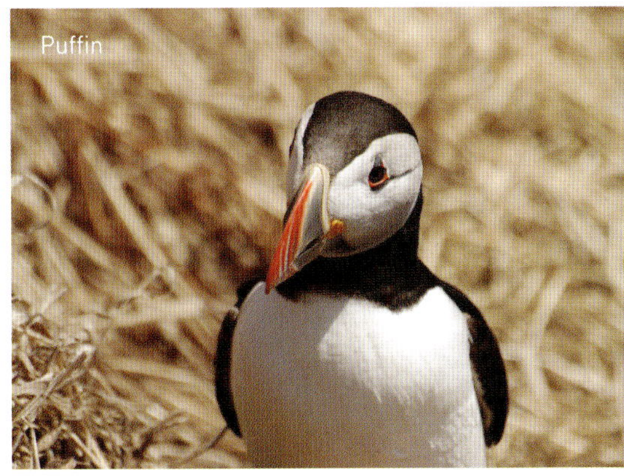

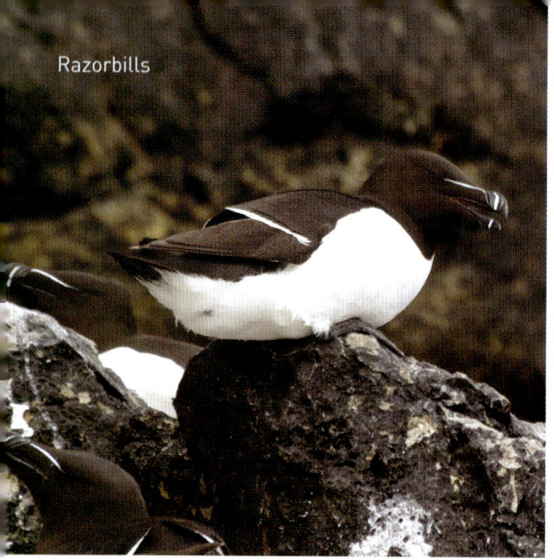

## Auks –Guilemots and Razorbills

The auks, which include guillemots, razorbills and puffins, are somewhat reminiscent of the penguin, with their incredible ability to dive gracefully under the water to astonishing depths of up to 210m. They use their wings to propel themselves under the water rather than being masters of flight, and both in habits and appearance they are like the Northern Hemisphere's equivalent of penguins, being infinitely more at home in the water than in the air. They have short wings in relation to their body size, which are much more effective underwater than in the air, and whilst they have not lost the art of flight they are not particularly aerodynamic creatures. Take off from the water often resembles something akin to a wind-up bath toy. In flight they have to beat their wings incredibly fast to stay airborne like the puffin, which beats its wings 600 times a minute, and whilst they are surprisingly speedy fliers, reaching speeds of up to 50mph, they require significantly more energy to stay airborne than other species of birds.

Guillemots and razorbills will lay a single egg, usually in May, which will hatch after a 30-day incubation period. The egg is quite oddly shaped, being far more pointed at one end than the other, the pyriform shape makes it more stable on the ledge and less likely to roll as there is more egg in contact with the ledge. Little known facts about guillemot eggs – their shells have a hydrophobic surface made up of cone-like nanostructures, which also gives the shell a 'self-cleaning' quality as water beads and drops off, taking dirt and salt with it. Also, the markings on each female's egg are very different, helping mums-to-be to identify their egg on a crowded ledge. Both species lay their eggs directly onto narrow rock ledges on the sea cliffs of Pembrokeshire, though they choose different areas of cliff on which to breed. Razorbills will tuck themselves into little nooks and crannies and around cave entrances in a bid to deter predators,

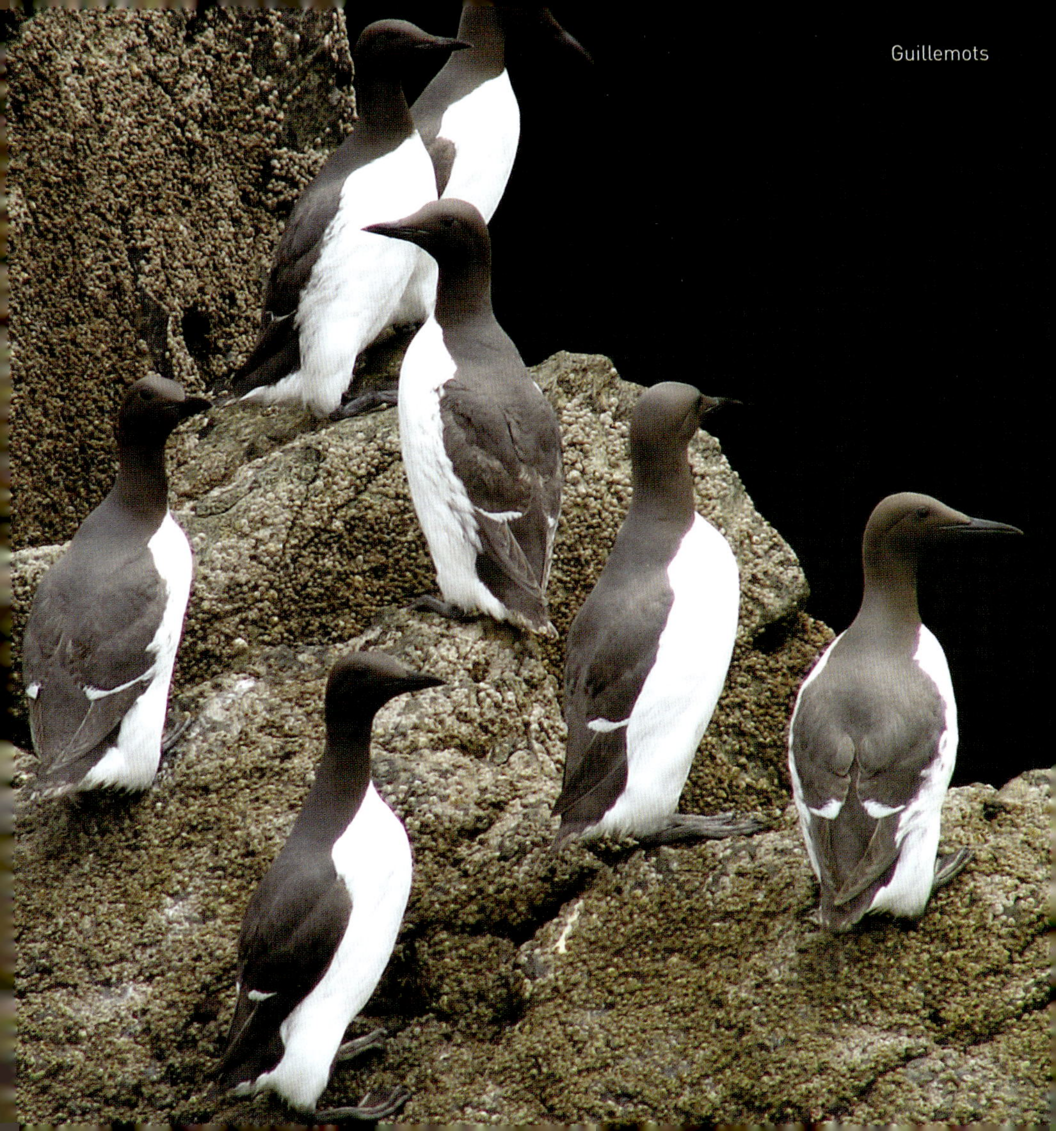
Guillemots

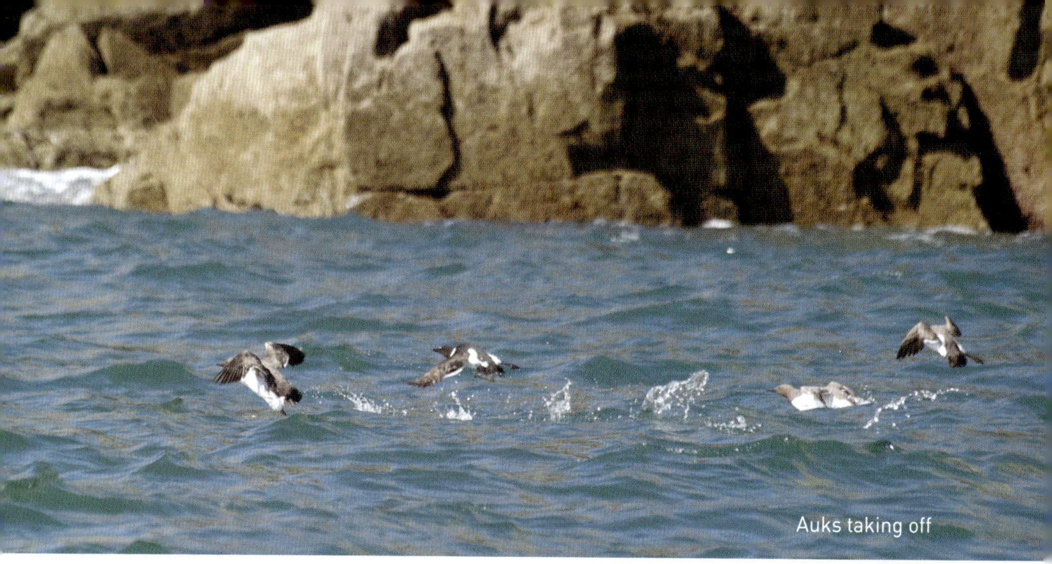



whereas guillemots prefer the high cliffs of the western side of the island, where they employ a 'safety in numbers' approach: cramming as many birds as they can get onto a long, narrow ledge on the sheer cliffs in the hope that large-winged predators such as gulls, ravens and peregrines will struggle to land on them. They then face the cliffs, incubating the egg on their feet, and presenting an army of backs to predators. This only works up to a point, and gulls and ravens are an ominous presence during the breeding season, patrolling the cliffs looking for any opportunity to break through the guillemots' defences.

Ravens are not above pulling an adult off the ledge by a wing, or anything they can get hold of for that matter, to get at the eggs and chicks beneath. The guillemots, however, are not easily intimidated and will stand their ground, stabbing at predators with pointed bills. This is despite the fact that some of the larger predators, such as the greater black-backed gulls, are quite capable of eating the adult birds themselves, as well as the chicks and eggs. It's very much nature red in tooth and claw round the island at that time of year!

Interestingly, one pair of ravens is capable of taking several hundred auk eggs in a season, and they will hide those surplus to requirements for leaner times, very much like a squirrel. I have seen them retrieving eggs they have hidden earlier in the year as late as September.

Three weeks after hatching, the young auks, still only a third of the size of the adult bird and little more than bundles of fluff, are apparently ready to leave the island. This involves an enormous leap of faith, quite literally, as they have to launch themselves off cliff ledges which are often a couple of hundred feet high, hence their name, 'jumplings'. The father will come down onto the water and call to the chick, who will jump off, or, if a little hesitant, it may get a helpful nudge from mum. Once airborne it will discover it can't fly, and will tumble, glide and occasionally bounce its way down to the water. Father and chick will then need to locate each other before swimming out to sea together. This often involves a lot of shouting, and the chicks can make an incredible amount of noise for so small a creature. It will be a couple of months before the chicks grow their full flight feathers and are able to fly, but as these birds are better designed for life on the water this does not pose too much of a problem. They are particularly vulnerable to predation when leaving the cliffs, so the sooner they get offshore and away from predators the safer the chick will be. The females will stay on the ledges until the last chick has

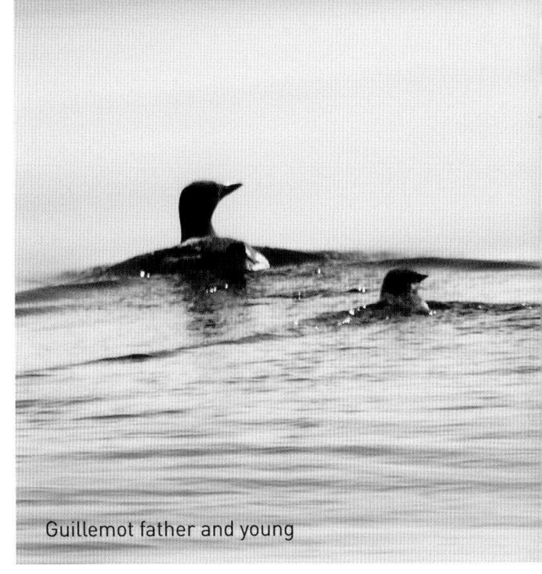

Guillemot father and young

fledged, maintaining the numbers to offer protection for the remaining chicks. It also allows them to secure their breeding territory for the following year. One day in mid-July we will come round to the west cliffs and find all the auks have left almost overnight. Their winter is spent at sea, returning to the island the following spring, though occasionally some will be seen on the cliffs during the winter months. Whilst guillemots and razorbills look similar, there are a number of distinct differences, in particular colour and beak shape.

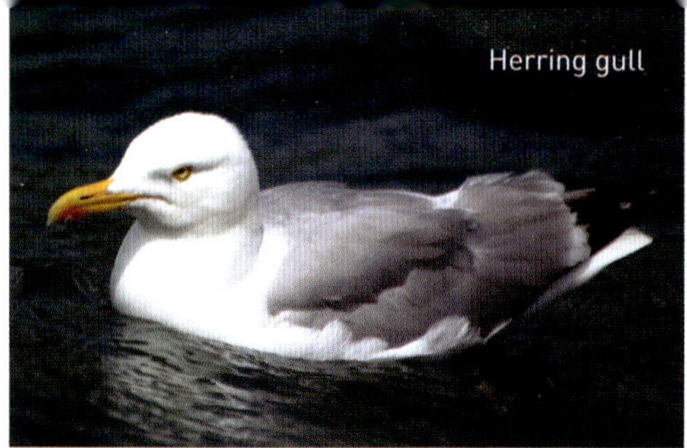

Herring gull

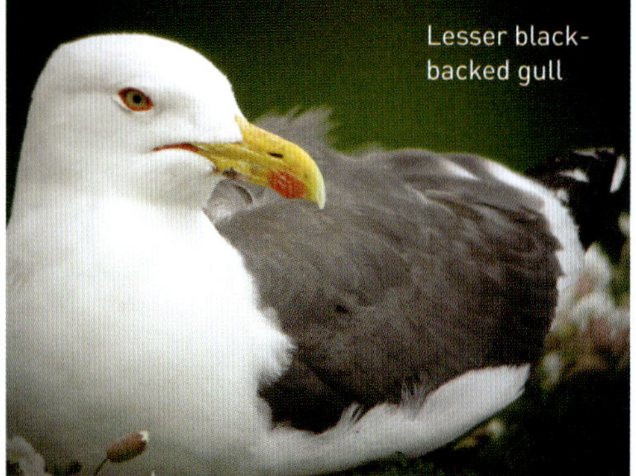

Lesser black-backed gull

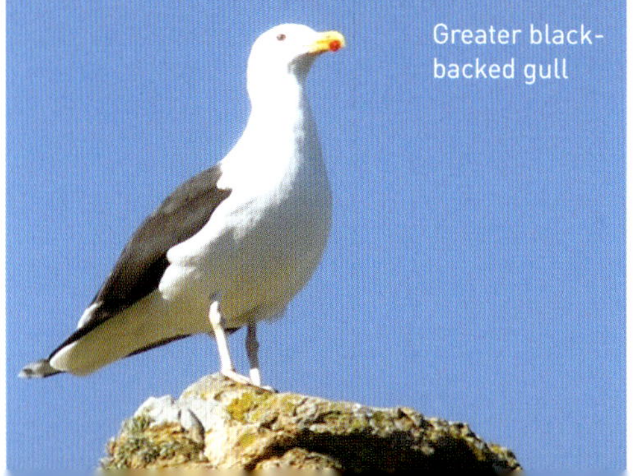

Greater black-backed gull

## Gulls

There are three resident species of gull on Ramsey. The herring gull and lesser black-backed gull are the same size and differ only in that the lesser black-backed gull has a darker slate-grey back and yellow legs. Both are common sightings around the island and somewhat opportunists on the feeding front. They will occasionally predate on the smaller seabirds but much less so than the larger greater black-backed gull.

The greater black-backed gull tends to draw the most attention as, with a five foot wingspan, they are the largest gull in the world and one of the top predators on the island. Despite not having talons or a hooked beak, they behave more like a bird of prey. They predate heavily on the small visiting seabirds and will take chicks, eggs and adult birds. I have seen one eat a young rabbit whole, and to give an idea of their ferocity there has been more than one report of them attacking small dogs such as Yorkshire terriers.

## Kittiwake

The kittiwake is the smallest of the British gulls to breed on Ramsey, and one of the only visitors to build a proper nest. This enables them to raise two or occasionally even three young, unlike the auks which, for obvious reasons, can only raise one chick. Nests are an elaborate affair, made

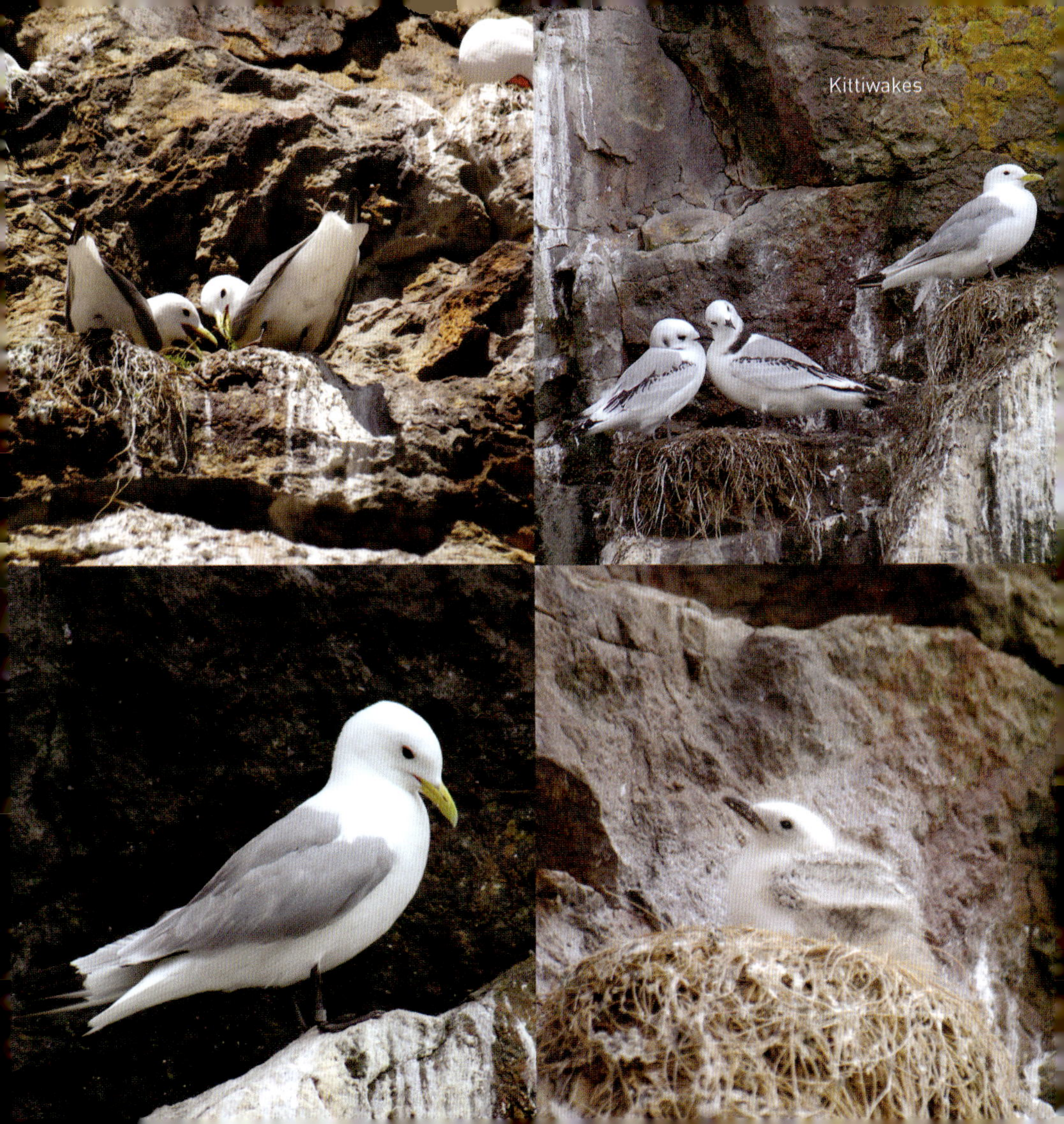
Kittiwakes

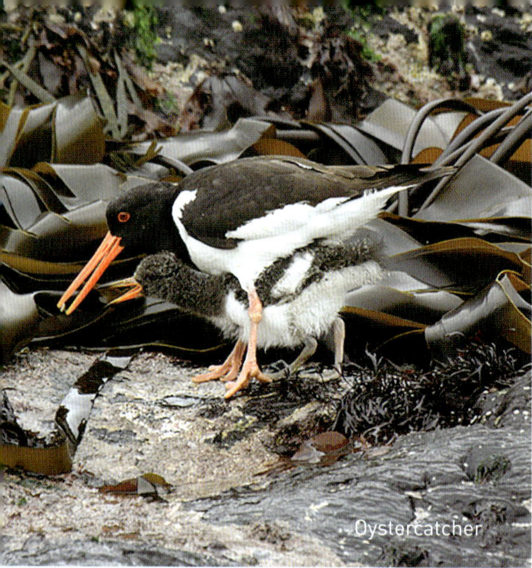


don't even have the decency to fly off with their dinner and will often just devour a kittiwake chick on its nest.

## Oystercatcher

The oystercatcher is something of a misnomer, as they rarely eat oysters. They are waders that feed predominantly on cockles, mussels and other bivalves, barnacles, limpets and, inland, will even feed on worms. These pretty but noisy birds have acquired some interesting local names. They are called *Piodin Y Môr*, Welsh for 'magpie of the sea', but some of the older generations of fisherman used to call them *Aderyn dim byd*, or the 'nothing bird', because it sounds as though that is what they are saying. If they heard them then the fishermen would believe their catch that day would be bad. They have long, heavy beaks and these beaks give a clue as to what feeding method they employ. If they have a sharp pointed bill, they favour jamming their beak into bivalves and cutting the muscle, a risky business, as if they get it wrong and the bivalve clamps shut on their beak they can end up drowning. There is one recorded incident of this happening where an oystercatcher body was found with the tip of its beak stuck in a clam! The other method is hammering their way in to the crustaceans, which leads to a blunt tip to their beaks. The baby oystercatcher will

of wet grasses, seaweed and often mud, which they stick to the rock ledges with guano and saliva. They are a true 'seagull' in the sense that they only come to land to breed, spending their winters at sea, and will never be found far from the coast. We have a few small colonies on Ramsey, but in the time I have been working around the island there has been a noticeable decline in the numbers of breeding kittiwakes, and some colonies have been almost entirely abandoned. They are heavily predated on by greater black-backed gulls and also by peregrines, both of which are quite capable of taking adults and chicks. The peregrines on the island

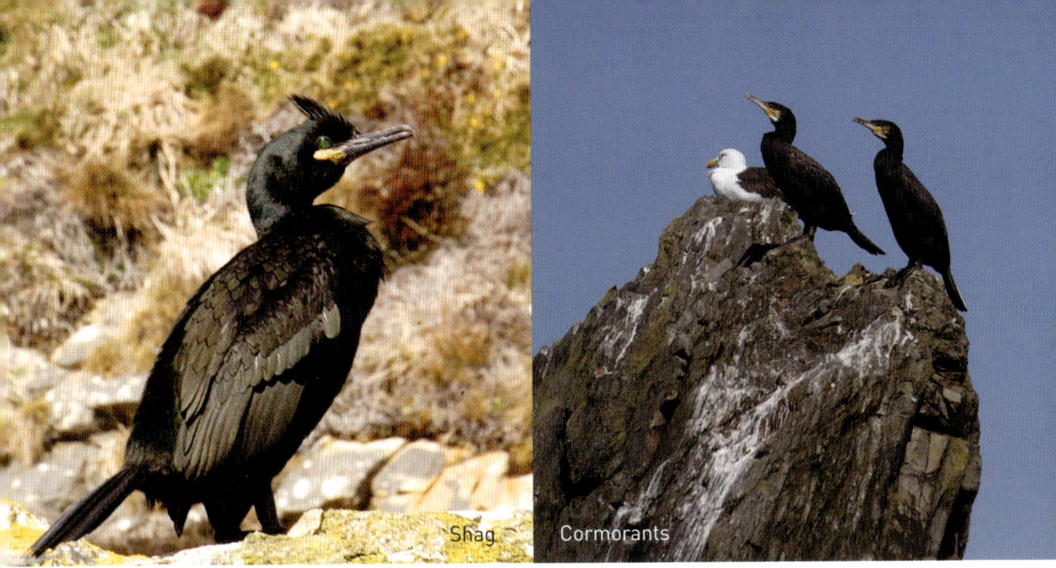



learn the best method from the parent bird, who they will follow around over many weeks and copy the technique they see Mum and Dad employing.

Once an Oystercatcher chick hatches, adult birds distract predators by making huge amounts of noise and flying away from the chick. They are not above feigning injury to convince a predator they are an easy target, thereby protecting their young.

## Shags and Cormorants

The shag and the cormorant are closely related and both can be seen on the Pembrokeshire islands, although whilst the shag is exclusively a coastal bird, the cormorant will often also be found on inland waterways, lakes and estuaries.

Both birds are deep-diving, and shags have been recorded at depths of 50m by divers off the North Sea oilrigs. They use their feet to propel themselves underwater, and unlike most seabirds they have the curious adaptation of only semi-waterproof feathers to help them reach these depths. Their feathers absorb water, which has the effect of acting like a weight belt on a diver and allows them to reach great depths with relative ease. The downside of this is that if their feathers become too waterlogged they

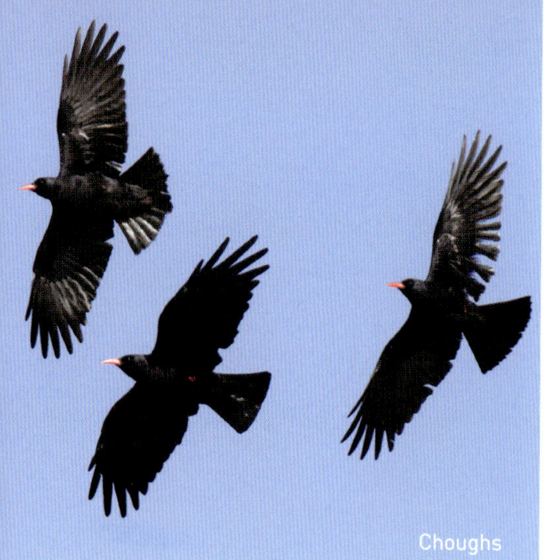
Choughs

## Chough

The choughs are among the rarest species of bird in the UK and they are listed on the IUCN (International Union for Conservation of Nature) red list, along with a number of other conservation directives. The chough population on Ramsey was one of the reasons the RSPB were interested in buying it. In 2015, a national survey showed 335 breeding pairs of chough in the UK, and populations here had suffered significant decline both due to persecution and loss of habitat. As a result of conservation measures put in place both by habitat management on a number of RSPB

risk drowning, so every couple of dives they have to stand out on the rocks and hang their wings out to dry.

Whilst from a distance these two species can be almost indistinguishable, close up they have a number of distinctive differences. The shag has a bottle green hue to its plumage; hence, its welsh name of *Mulfran Werdd*, or 'green cormorant'. It also has a shaggy crest on top of its head when in breeding plumage, which is where the name shag comes from. Cormorants, as well as being larger than the shags, have white patches on their hips during the breeding season, white cheek patches, and a flatter head profile.

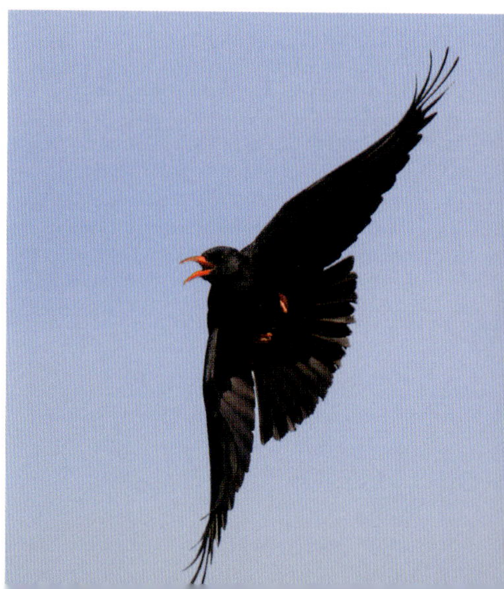

    Ramsey Island and beyond

reserves and agri-environment schemes such as Tir Gofal, they are making a comeback, and are recognised as an important species by the RSPB as they are dependent on a threatened ecosystem.

The chough is a striking member of the crow family, with a scarlet bill and legs. It is this that has given them their Latin name, *Pyrrhocorax pyrrhocorax*, meaning 'fire crow', and also led to their persecution in Cornwall, where in the past the superstitious belief prevailed that they were responsible for starting fires with their flame-coloured beaks and feet. The choughs on Ramsey nest in inaccessible crevices and ledges in the rock, on the high sea cliffs and often in sea caves. This being the case there is no shortage of suitable sites.

Choughs are not only found on Ramsey but can be seen along much of the Pembrokeshire coast, which provides an ideal habitat and is a bit of a stronghold for them. They have a very distinctive acrobatic flight, often seen tucking in their wings and plummeting into impossibly narrow fissures in the cliff face where they nest. They can be differentiated from other corvids in flight by splayed wing primaries that look like the fingers on an open hand, as well as rounded wing tips. They also have a very distinctive call, and you will often hear them before you see them.

Most years, Ramsey is home to between nine and eleven breeding pairs of chough, and as they feed on insects and small invertebrates just below the surface of the soil and in dung, they need short grass to be able to feed effectively. Maintaining suitable habitat for them is part of the land management plan of the RSPB. What this means for Ramsey's wardens in terms of habitat management is to ensure that certain areas of the island where the chough feed are adequately grazed, and in fact quite a lot of farming still takes place on Ramsey. The resident rabbits are useful in terms of keeping the grazing down, but due to lack of predators the population goes through cycles. Numbers will increase dramatically to a point where much of the island has been grazed to within an inch of its life, and even the tops of gorse bushes have been topiaried by the rabbits. At this point the population becomes unsustainable and allows diseases such as myxomatosis to recur, causing rabbit numbers to plummet. Myxomatosis was originally introduced to the island deliberately in 1958, and the crash in population it causes has a tendency to go in approximately four-year cycles. As a result, depending on the rabbit population the wardens may need to graze more or less animals, and spring will often find them busy lambing their flock of sheep with the help of Dewi, the

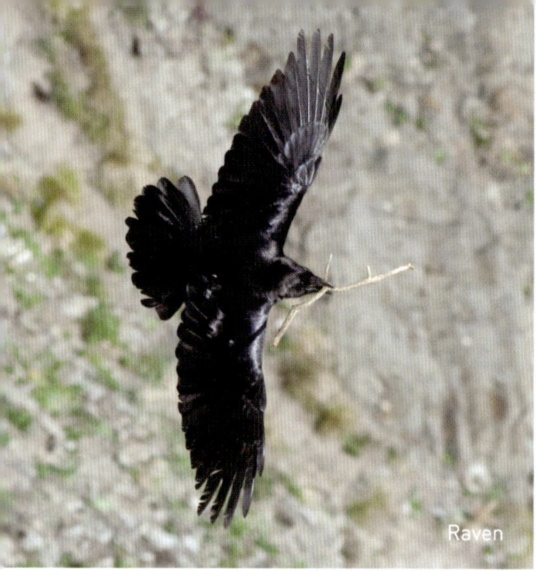
Raven

sheepdog. In addition to varying numbers of sheep there are also the small herd of deer and four welsh mountain ponies that contribute to the grazing.

## Ravens

Most years four pairs of ravens nest on Ramsey, though on the occasional autumn day it is not unusual to see as many as forty flocking together. Ravens are a fascinating member of the corvid family, which are known for their intelligence, and the raven is no exception. They are often to be seen above the sea cliffs, showing off in aerial displays that include inverting their wings to fly upside down, which they appear to do just for fun. There is an often-told story that the original ravens in the Tower of London came from Ramsey, and that if the ravens were ever to leave the Tower then London would fall. Whilst there is little actual evidence to support this, the legends surrounding the Ravens and the Tower are many and varied; one of the earliest is contained in the early Welsh myths of the Mabinogi, compiled around the twelfth or thirteenth century. The tale in question tells of how, following the battle between Britain and Ireland caused by the mistreatment of the British Princess Branwen by the Irish King Matholwch, her brother Bendigeidfran, one of very few survivors on either side, ordered his head to be cut off and buried underneath the white hill where the Tower stands today, facing France and protecting Britain from foreign invasion. The same Bendigeidfran is also associated with Grassholm.

Ravens are one of the top predators on the island, feeding extensively on the chicks and eggs of visiting seabirds, so much so that the hatching of their young coincides with the visitors laying their eggs so they can feed their young with auk eggs and chicks. They will also eat rabbits and aren't above feeding on carrion.

## Peregrines

Another of Ramsey's birds to feature in Britain's history books is the peregrine falcon, whose latin name, *Falco peregrinus*, means 'pilgrim' or 'wanderer'. This is particularly apt as they can be found in every area of the world apart from New Zealand and Antarctica, making them possibly one of the most successful species of bird on the planet. Ramsey has two or three breeding pairs most years, and as they are highly territorial and quite aggressive towards newcomers this is possibly as many as the island can sustain. The peregrine is the fastest living creature on the planet, having been clocked at speeds in excess of 240 mph in their stoop after prey, an awe-inspiring sight unless you are a pigeon, their favourite food. To stop the air pressure damaging their lungs at this speed they have small bony tubercles in their nostrils to direct the airflow, and enable them to still breathe whilst diving. A number of the more astute pigeons round Ramsey have taken to hanging out in the relative safety of sea caves, and a couple of pairs even breed in Ogof Hen, one of the longest sea caves at the northern end of Ramsey.

They hunt a variety of species of birds and catch their prey on the wing, hitting them at incredible speeds. Death is almost instantaneous and pigeons explode in a burst of feathers, leaving the peregrine with its dinner practically ready plucked.

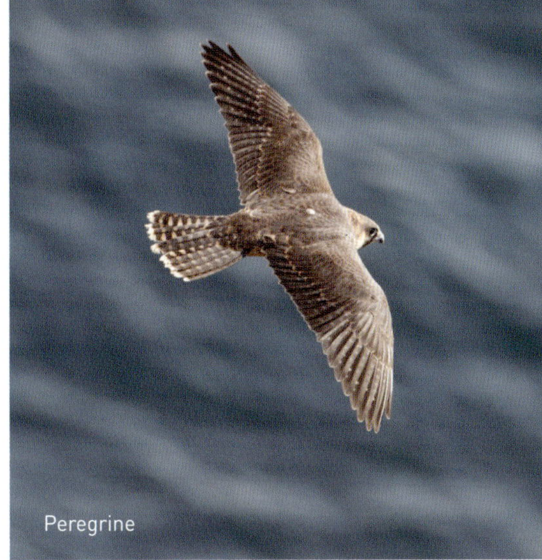
Peregrine

Technically, at least according to the books, they are not supposed to hunt over water, though I have seen them trying to hunt shearwater. This was probably a young, inexperienced bird trying its luck, as shearwaters generally fly too close to the water to make recovery of prey possible, even if the hunt had been successful, which was unlikely. Young birds when they are learning to hunt will have a go at pretty much anything, even a child's kite, as some of the island's previous residents found out. The males are about a third smaller than the females, as with many birds of prey, hence the traditional name 'tiercel' for a male falcon,

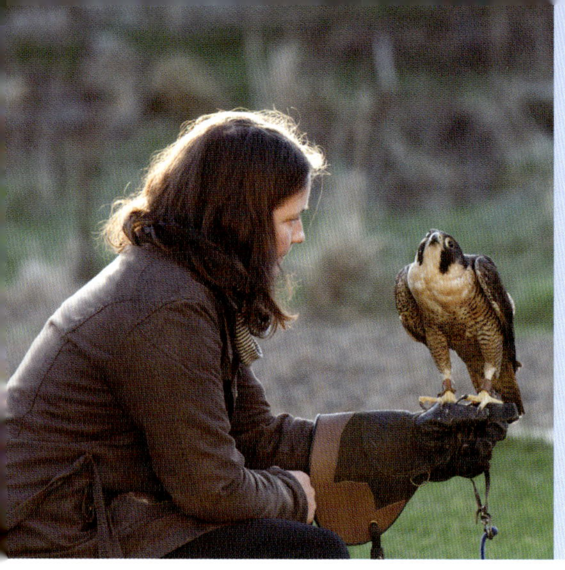

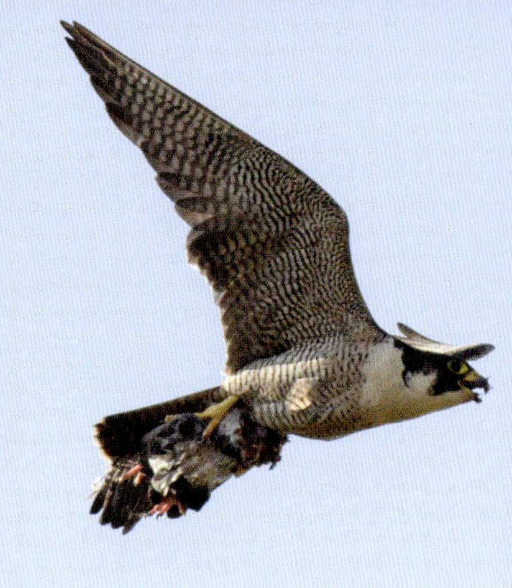

although this name is also attributed to an early belief that only one in three eggs would hatch a male bird. The fame of the Ramsey peregrines dates back to the twelfth century and the reign of King Henry II as recorded by Giraldus Cambrensis in his *Description of Wales*. He describes how, on his way over to Ireland, King Henry stopped at Ramsey, having seen a peregrine fly over and being keen to put it to the test against his Norwegian goshawk, a much larger bird of prey. The Ramsey peregrine, according to the story, struck the hawk, which fell dead at the king's feet. Henry was so impressed that he demanded that from then on every year eyasses (young falcons) from Ramsey were to be captured and sent to the Royal Mews, that he might hunt with them. At that time peregrines were protected by royal decree, so only kings and nobles were permitted to use them for falconry. It is also rumoured that when Richard the Lionheart was incarcerated in Austria, two Ramsey peregrines were requested to make up part of the ransom sent to free him.

**Above left:** Conversations with a peregrine.

**Above right:** Peregrine with pigeon.

## Migrants

There are many more occasional and very unusual sightings recorded on Ramsey due to its far westerly location, unfortunately too many to mention here. But below are some of the more regular migrants who have been known to pass through on their way either north or south.

The purple sandpiper is a small wader, which normally passes by the UK on its way to and from its breeding grounds in the Arctic Circle. These are of particular interest as, unusually, a small group of up to twenty birds will often overwinter on Ramsey. They are a good gauge of the seasons, as summer has definitely arrived by the time the last one leaves for the north, and likewise the first to arrive back after breeding is a sure sign of autumn's arrival.

Other birds we see most years include skuas, sooty shearwaters, terns and phalaropes, to mention but a few. Increasingly, red kites are often to be seen gracing the skies above Ramsey, and this is due largely to their recent successful reintroduction in other parts of Wales. Ospreys have also been spotted, and historically there was even once a pair of golden eagles on Ramsey.

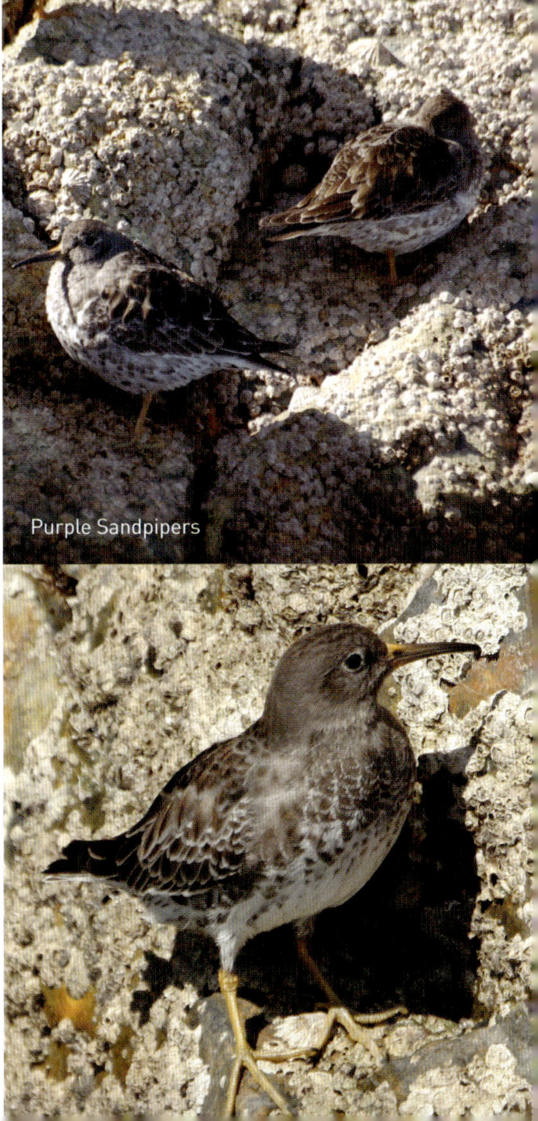
Purple Sandpipers

# RAMSEY ISLAND RSPB NATURE RESERVE BREEDING BIRDS 2021
## (INCLUDES THE BISHOPS AND CLERKS WHERE INDICATED)

### 39 species confirmed breeding

| | | |
|---|---|---|
| Canada goose | *Branta canadensis* | 1 pair (as 2020) |
| Mallard | *Anas platyrhynchos* | 3 pairs (2 pairs in 2020) |
| Northern fulmar | *Fulmarus glacialis* | 305 AOS |
| Manx shearwater | *Puffinus puffinus* | No survey (4,796 AOB in 2016) |
| Storm petrel | *Hydrobates pelagicus* | min 7 AOS Ramsey |
| | | 163 AOS B&C (2017) |
| European shag | *Phalacrocorax aristotelis* | No survey (6 pairs in 2018) |
| Common buzzard | *Buteo buteo* | 2 pairs (as in 2020) |
| Peregrine falcon | *Falco peregrinus* | 3 pairs (as in 2020) |
| Oystercatcher | *Haematopus ostralegus* | 24 pairs (18 pairs 2020) |
| Herring gull | *Larus argentatus* | No survey (235 AON in 2018) |
| Lesser black-backed gull | *Larus fuscus* | No survey (100 AON in 2018) |
| Great black-backed gull | *Larus marinus* | No survey (22 AON in 2018) |
| Kittiwake | *Rissa trydactyla* | 51 AON (85 in 2020) |
| Common guillemot | *Uria aalge* | 5395 individuals |
| Razorbill | *Alca torda* | 2160 individuals |
| Atlantic puffin | *Fractecula arctica* | 55 individuals (N. Bishop only) |
| Wood pigeon | *Columba palumbus* | 6 pair (3 in 2020) |
| Little owl | *Athene noctua* | 1 pair (1 in 2020) |

| Short-eared Owl | *Assio flammea* | none (1 pair in 2020) |
| Skylark | *Alauda arvensis* | 2 pairs (7 in 2020) |
| Barn swallow | *Hirundo rustica* | 6 pairs (5 in 2020) |
| House martin | *Delichon urbicum* | 8 pairs (10 in 2020) |
| Meadow pipit | *Anthus pratensis* | 99 pairs (89 in 2020) |
| Rock pipit | *Anthus petrosus* | 37 pairs (30 in 2020) |
| Pied wagtail | *Motacilla alba* | 14 pairs (3 in 2020) |
| Wren | *Troglodytes troglodytes* | 52 pairs (50 in 2020) |
| Dunnock | *Prunella modularis* | 8 pairs (9 in 2020) |
| European stonechat | *Saxicola torquata* | 25 pairs (34 in in 2020) |
| Northern wheatear | *Oenanthe oenanthe* | 93 pairs (121 in 2020) |
| Blackbird | *Turdus merula* | 22 pairs (21 in 2020) |
| Song Thrush | *Turdus philomelos* | 1 pair (0 in 2020) |
| Whitethroat | *Sylvia communis* | 5 pairs (8 in 2020) |
| Sedge warbler | *Acrocephalus schoenobaenus* | 1 pair (as in 2020) |
| Chiffchaff | *Phylloscopus collybita* | 1 pair (as in 2020) |
| Jackdaw | *Corvus monedula* | no survey |
| Chough | *Pyrrhocorax pyrrhocorax* | 9 pairs (10 in 2020) |
| Carrion crow | *Corvus corone* | 8 pairs (5 in 2020) |
| Raven | *Corvus corax* | 4 pairs (3 in 2020) |
| Linnet | *Carduelis cannabina* | 48 pairs (50 in 2020) |
| Reed bunting | *Emberiza schoeniclus* | 1 pair (0 in 2020) |

AON = Apparently Occupied Nest

AOS = Apparently Occupied Site

AOB = Apparently Occupied Burrow

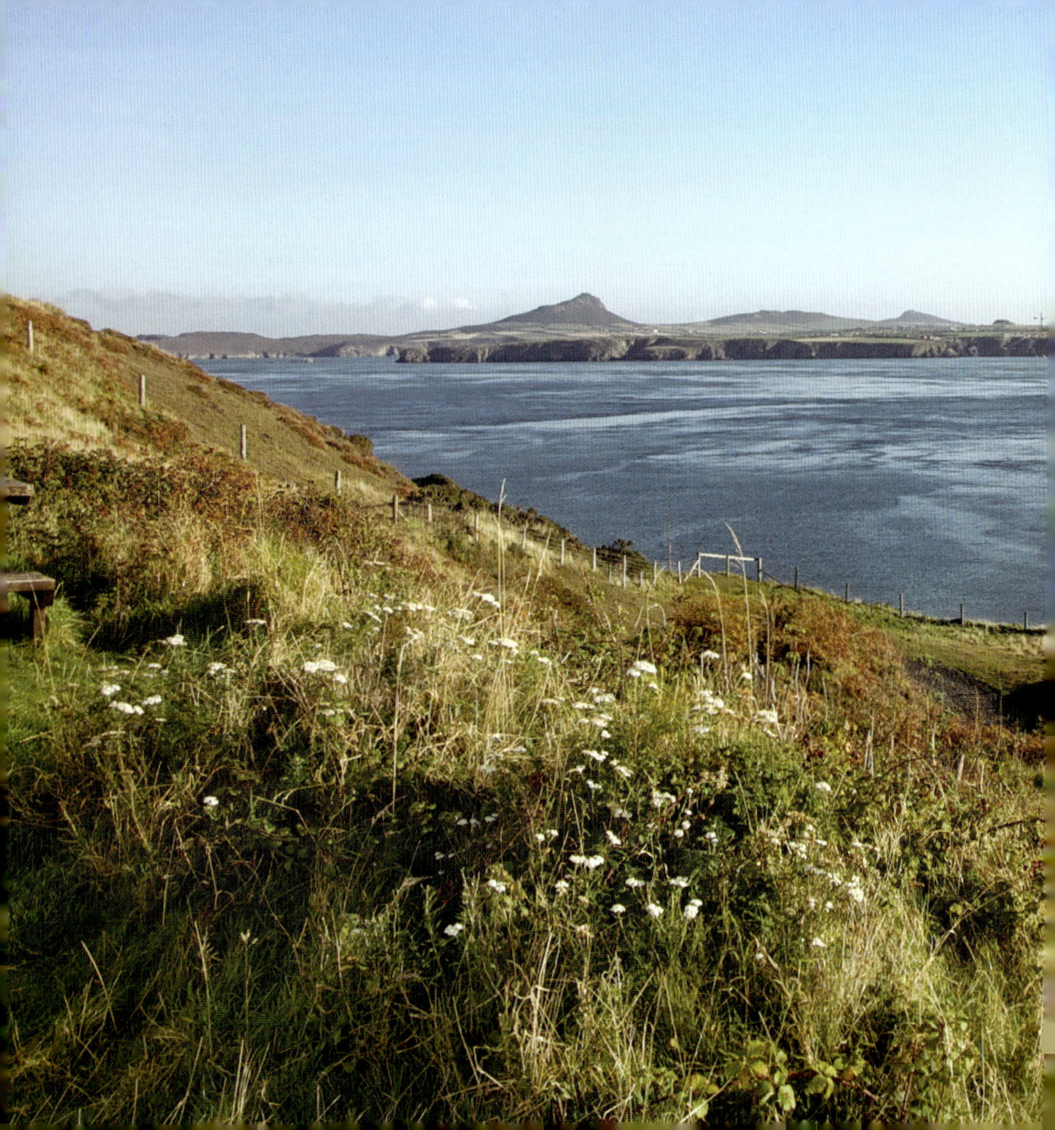

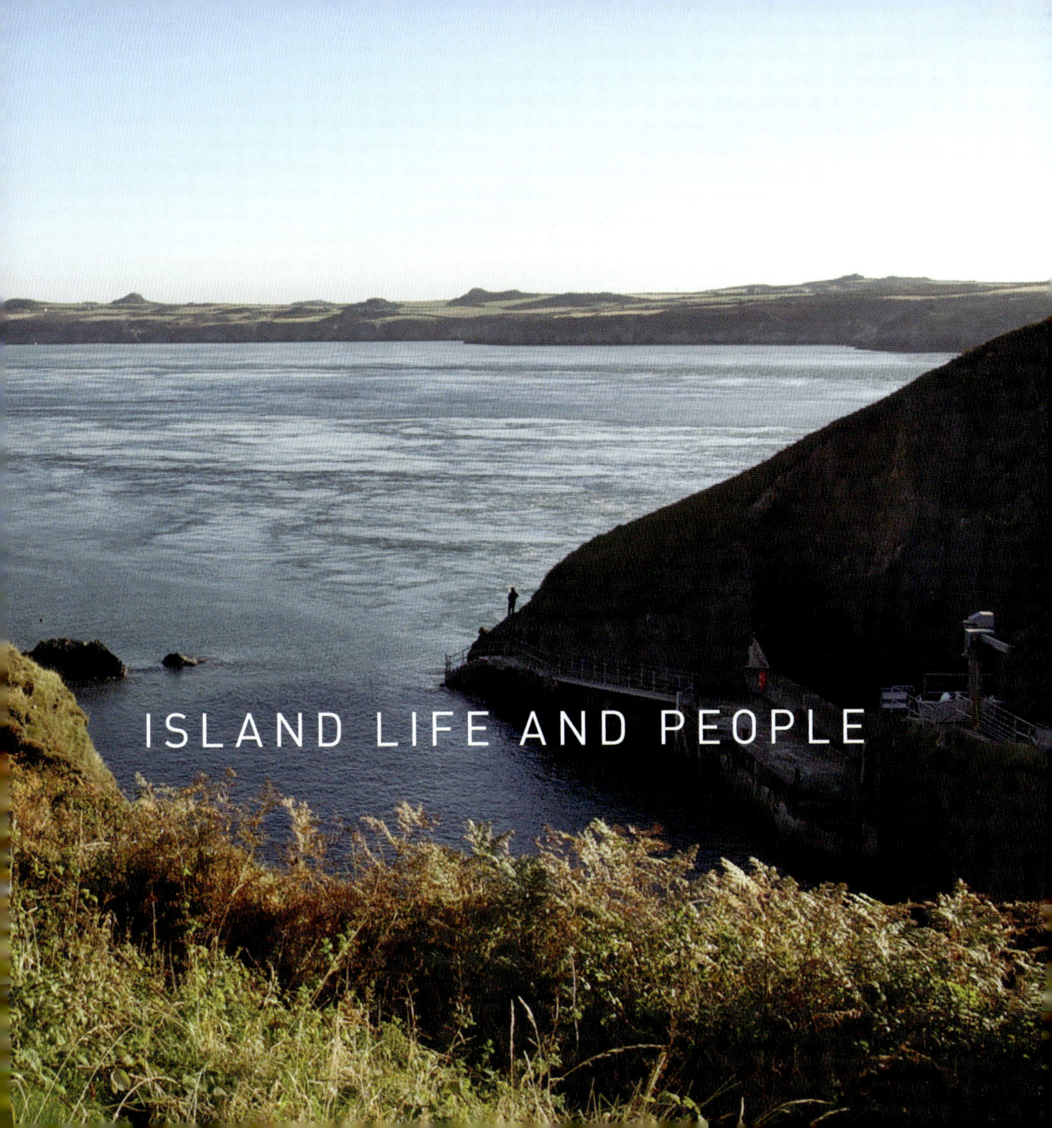
ISLAND LIFE AND PEOPLE

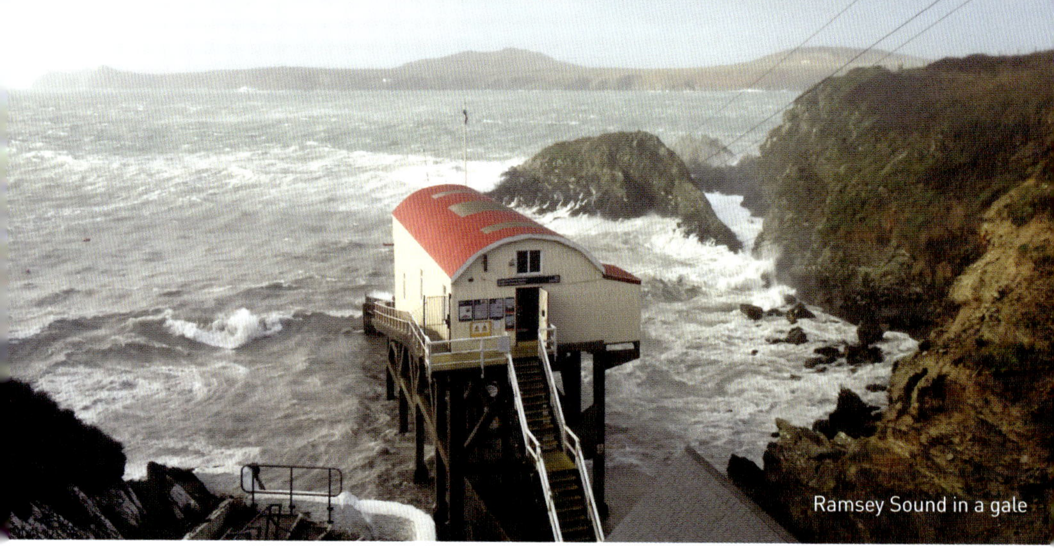



It takes a special type of person to be able to cope with the isolation associated with life on an island, and, as Wynnford Vaughan Thomas eloquently stated after spending merely a month on Ramsey having sailed there from Milford, "The sea can be a savage guardian of the loneliness of these islands" (*Sounds Between*, p11). It is also not an easy life in many respects, as day to day tasks like shopping can suddenly become a major expedition, or even rendered impossible, particularly in bad weather.

Over the years I have met many of the people who have lived and worked on Ramsey, and many have become friends.

Latterly it has been RSPB wardens, usually couples, though some have braved it alone on the island. Island life has often come to an end with the arrival of children, when practicalities such as getting to school become an issue and the possibility of medical emergencies with small children highlights the isolation. Most recently Greg and Lisa managed the island together for 14 years along with their working border collie Dewi who grew up on Ramsey. This is the longest stint since the RSPB took over the island. In 2018 Lisa moved to work for the Wildlife Trust of South and West Wales, managing the islands of Skomer and

Skokholm, with Greg continuing as Site manager of Ramsey. Nia Stephens took over as warden in 2021.

Life is pretty varied. The summer brings thousands of visitors a year, as the island is open to the public from Easter until the end of October. You can land between 10am and 4pm, spend the day wandering its seven miles of paths and enjoy the abundance of wildlife and stunning sea vistas it offers to the day visitor. With two landings a day, visitor management is a big part of the job in summer, giving visitors an introduction to the island, as well as information about where they can and can't go. There is an information centre to be looked after, as well as a shop serving tea and coffee, although visitors do need to bring their own lunch.

During the summer season they have a volunteer system, where you can come and stay on the island to help out for a couple of weeks. This is very popular and is always booked up well in advance, with many volunteers having become regulars. Speaking from experience, nothing can beat exploring the island or just sitting on its cliffs or hills enjoying the solitude it offers after the doors are closed to the public at the end of the day.

Jobs also include farming, one of the main elements of this being the herd of up to 200 sheep. Greg had not only to learn shepherding skills, but also

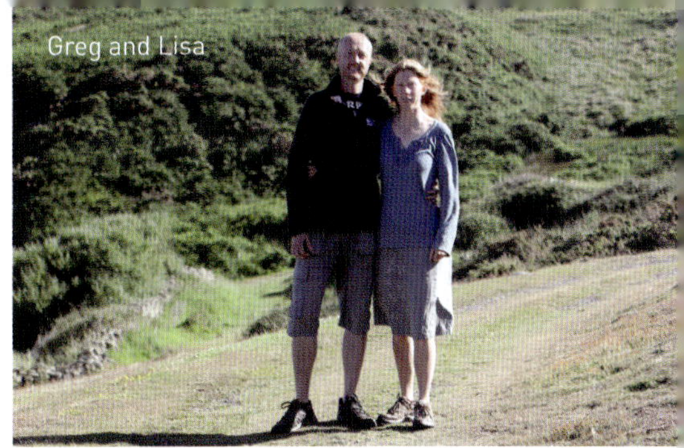


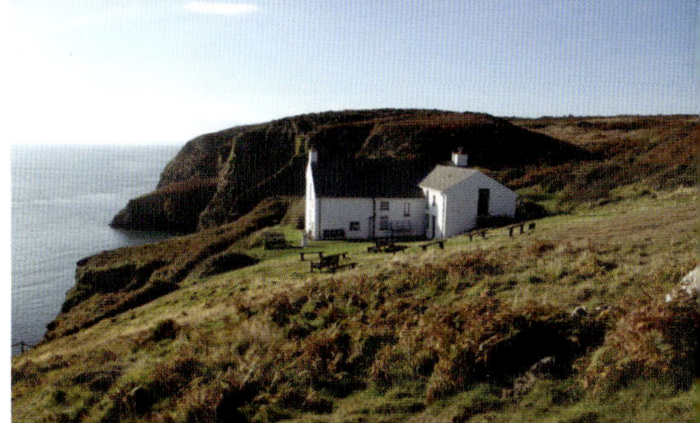

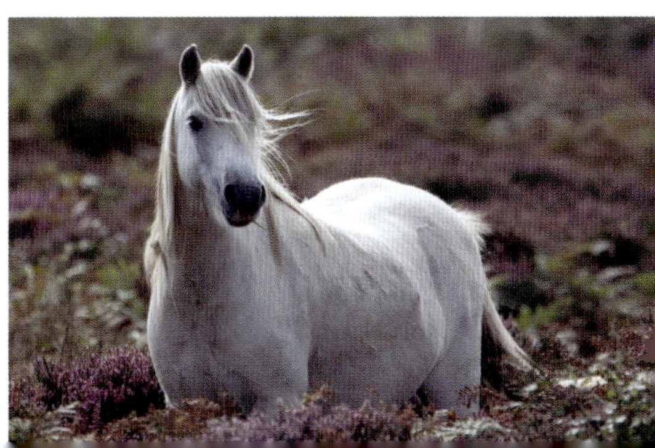

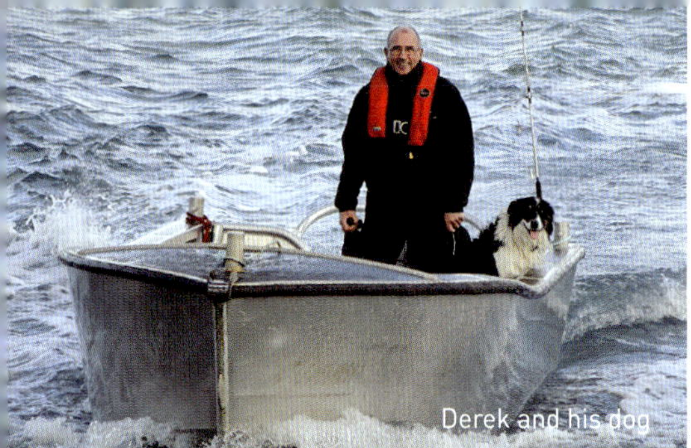



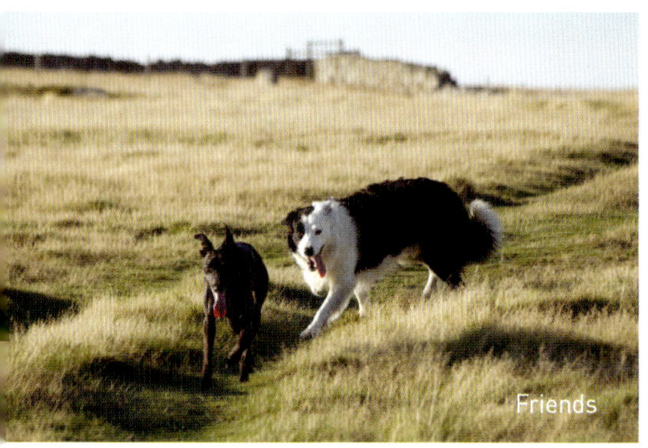



a local boatman, farmer, stone waller and general handyman extraordinaire, to name but a few of his talents. His jobs on Ramsey stretch to far more than just delivery. On the animal front there are also the Welsh mountain ponies and deer to be managed, and in 2015 Greg and Lisa even turned their hand to ploughing, again with Derek's help. This was the first time the island has been ploughed for about 18 years. The ploughing was in a bid to grow turnips as winter fodder for the sheep, and this will mean they won't have to bring over extra fodder with the increased work, expense and biosecurity hazard that that brings with it. Their turnip growing skills proved successful and Greg and Lisa were really hoping that their sheep like turnips, or their winter meal times could have resembled an episode of Blackadder in attempts to find 101 uses for a turnip.

## Welsh Blacks

2009 saw an interesting new addition to the island's inhabitants, when the grass had become too long and Greg and Lisa decided to try their hands at farming the Welsh Black cattle for which Pembrokeshire has become well-known. Whilst bringing seven relatively small calves over on local boatman Derek's small landing craft didn't seem too challenging, the return journey three

train Dewi, who joined the wardens on the island as a ten week old pup, and spring will often see them up at all hours lambing. Initially this was all done under the watchful eye of mainland-based farmer Derek Rees and his sheepdogs, although Greg and Dewi now have it down to a fine art. Derek Rees has the delivery contract for the island and is

years later, when the cattle were four times the size, was a different story. It began with prayers for settled weather, followed by the use of seven different items of machinery (JCB, tractor, two different trailers, the island crane, and, of course, a suitable, and by now larger, landing craft). A huge sigh of relief later saw the cattle safely back on the mainland. On one much earlier incident, during the tenancy of the Arnold brothers, a young heifer was being taken across the Sound by boat, which resulted in the animal sticking one of its horns through the side of the craft. It had to be sat on and lashed down with its horn still sticking through until they reached the safety of the shore. Even with today's technology, it is easy to see why the animals often used to be swum across the Sound. It certainly highlights some of the issues of island farming and why, ultimately, commercial farming on Ramsey proved questionable.

Farming, however, is only part of the land management that keeps the wardens busy. They also maintain the heathland, which is of national importance and, along with the ponds, is home to some extremely rare plants, such as the three-lobed water-crowfoot, floating water-plantain and wavy-leaved St John's-wort. As well as maintaining the existing ponds, they have also dug a couple of new ones. Regular bracken bashing has

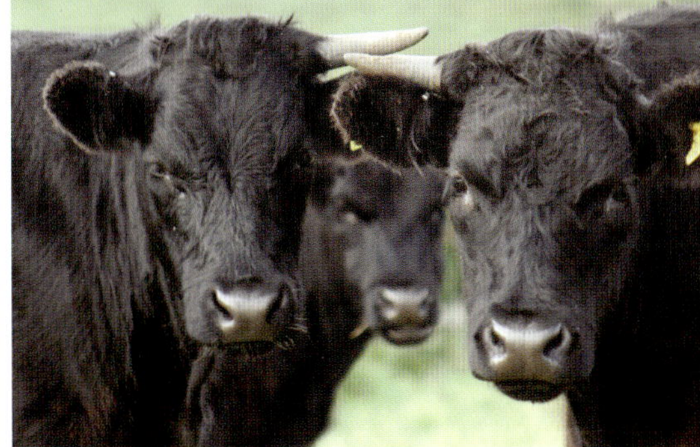

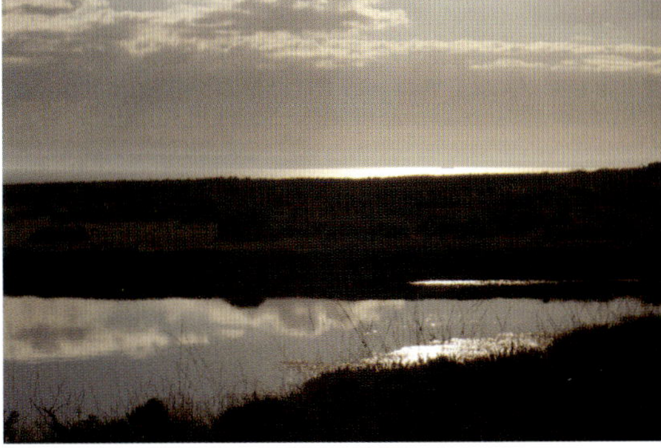

to take place to keep on top of bracken growth; this is always a good job for the volunteers!

Other jobs include bird counts, research projects, such as shearwater ringing, seal surveys, report writing (usually a winter job), as well as general maintenance of the farmhouse, the volunteers' bungalow and the farm

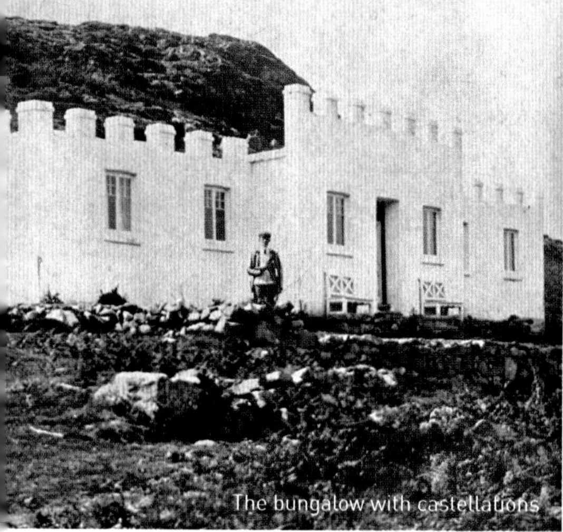

The bungalow with castellations

buildings, including composting toilets for the visitors. They also manage the offshore islands of Grassholm and the Bishops and Clerks with their associated seabird colonies.

Greg lives in the old farmhouse, which dates back to the early nineteenth century and is thought to be at least the third house built on that site. Apart from the farm buildings above, the only other building on the island is a bungalow built on the site of a cattle shed in 1908, at the same time as the bungalow at St Justinians. It was previously a cottage dating back to the seventeenth century. Today, the bungalow offers very basic accommodation to the volunteers who stay on the island, but when it was first built it was somewhat grander in appearance, painted white with castellations across the front.

Despite being physically cut off from the mainland they do have some of the luxuries of modern life, such as a television and fridge/freezer, and life has definitely been made easier by the relatively recent additions of solar panels and a wind turbine, which has reduced their reliance on the generator by about 70%. This is not only great on the sustainability stakes but on a practical note means a lot less cans of diesel to be manhandled.

Once November arrives, Ramsey closes for the winter and whilst the wardens now return to the mainland for the winter they still visit regularly to manage the livestock and keep an eye on things. Whilst they enjoy welcoming visitors to the island, promoting their work and sharing an understanding of the conservation required to maintain this jewel in the crown of the National Park, they also relish being able to close the doors. Having visited them in the winter, there is definitely a special quality to wandering around the island on your own, looking back to the mainland and enjoying the peace and solitude that is so hard to find in today's busy existence. It makes all the extra effort that goes into living there worthwhile, and it is, in some respects, a simpler existence. Despite having their own boat and regular visits from Derek with winter deliveries, it was not unusual for the island to get cut off from the mainland in bad weather, as the Sound often becomes impassable. The longest stint they had to do without supplies or seeing another soul was seven weeks in the winter of 2013/2014, where a succession of ferocious storms with little let up in between meant that it just wasn't possible to cross the Sound safely in a small boat. On occasion, the St Davids lifeboat has stepped into the breach and delivered supplies, mail and one year a Christmas turkey, whilst out on exercise.

Malcolm Gray, first started working on the boats at St Justinians in the mid-60s at the age of fourteen, when he used to crew for all the boatmen working there; local characters including Dai the Mill, Willy Bach, Jenkin, and Terry and Phil Davies, earning himself the princely sum of 10 shillings per day – £4 a week. Malcolm has many a fascinating story of his time on the water, and when I told him I was planning to write a book about Ramsey and would like to include his voice, his response was that if he were to write a book about it, it would be called "Salt with everything!", a sentiment with which, having spent 25 years working around the island, I would largely agree.

Very much a local character himself these days, Malcolm was the previous coxswain of the St Davids lifeboat, and

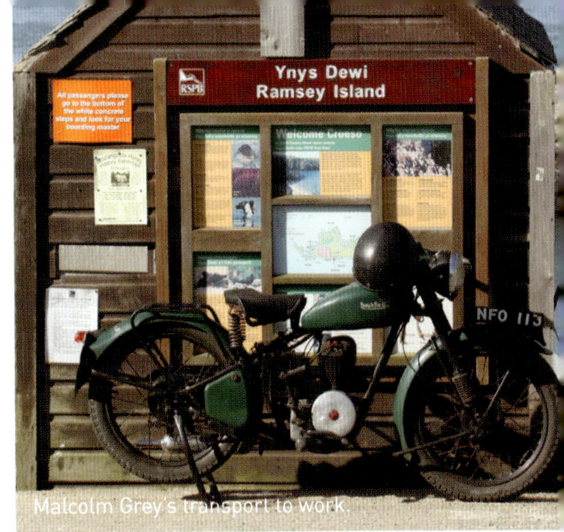



Malcolm Grey's transport to work.

has crewed on the last four lifeboats on station at St Justinians, the first being the Joseph Soar (1963), then the Charles Henry Ashley, followed by the Ruby & Arthur Reed, and finally, for Malcom, the Garside, which left the old boat house in September and has been replaced by the new Tamar, Norah Wortley, housed in the new station which opened in 2017.

Malcolm describes how every Wednesday during that time, Dai the Mill, who had the contract to deliver the stores to the South Bishop lighthouse, would call him in and say, "We're going deep sea today", and given the type of boat they were going in it probably felt like it. In order to drop off the stores they had to come into the north-east gut of the island,

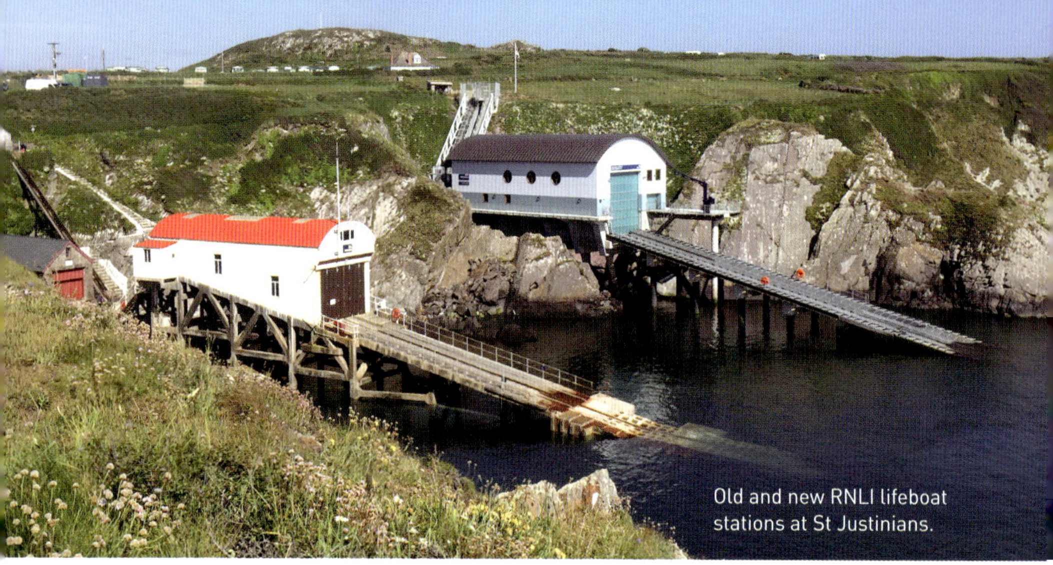

Old and new RNLI lifeboat stations at St Justinians.

tie the bow of the boat in and lift stores from a davit and hook as best they could, picking their moment as the boat rode the swells.

When out fishing on the Horse Rock they would actually run the boat up on the rock in order to fish it, as otherwise the tide would keep carrying them away from it, not having the sort of horse power to play with that we have today. Back in those days, the local boat owners obviously didn't have the same technology, including simple things like tide tables, crucial in an area so affected by the tides. Knowledge was handed

down from generation to generation, and Malcolm is one of the last of those. One example he gives is how he only needs to be able to see the moon and he can tell where the tide is in relation to high or low water, to within about 15 minutes, without any need for a tide table. Sadly, many of these skills have been lost to younger generations because we don't need them. The old-timers would have had an intimate knowledge of the tidal movements in the Sound, such as which lines to take and what back eddies could be used to maximise their use of the flow. I remember my father telling me how, if you knew it well enough, you could tell where you were in the Sound even in the fog by reading the surface of the water around you, as it is that changeable.

If planning to go to Grassholm they used to have to work the swell, and the rule of thumb was whatever the swell on the slipway at St Justinians you could multiply it by 1.5 for the back of Ramsey, by three for the Bishops and by nine for Grassholm. Malcolm assured me that back then, when the main weather patterns were prevailing south-westerlies, this calculation was never far off. This is one of the many tips I learned when I first started sailing out to Grassholm, and I feel privileged to have had the opportunity to learn something of the intricacies of the local waters from those whose experience was second to none.

When I asked Malcolm about the Smalls, in the early days he knew it only really from lifeboating, and described going out there as a monumental thing and very much his nemesis, because it brought so many horrible memories. It used to take four to five hours to get there on the earlier lifeboats, and even in the newer boats he said it wasn't a good place to be in bad weather.

One of the changes that Malcolm has seen in his time is a massive reduction in basking sharks. They used to be a very common sight, particularly on the

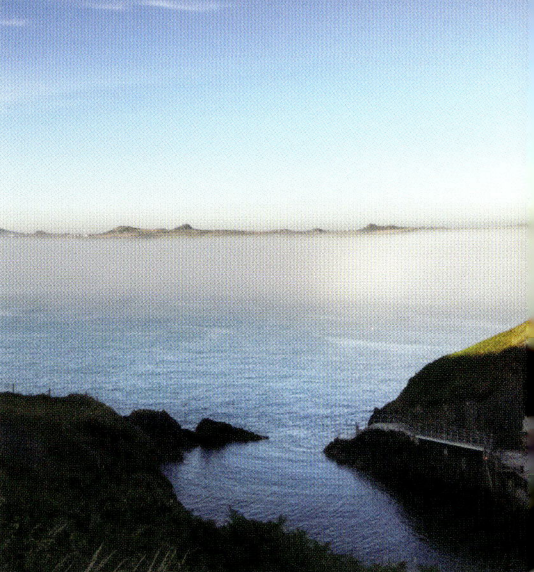

run out to Grassholm, whereas now, although we do still see them, they are seen far less frequently. He even recalls one occasion when Dai the Mill was trying to come alongside the harbour wall on Ramsey, and every time he got close the boat pulled away again. He couldn't understand it, but when he looked down there was a basking shark between the boat and the harbour wall. He had to move off to allow it to swim out of the harbour before he could come alongside.

**Above:** The Sound swathed in fog.

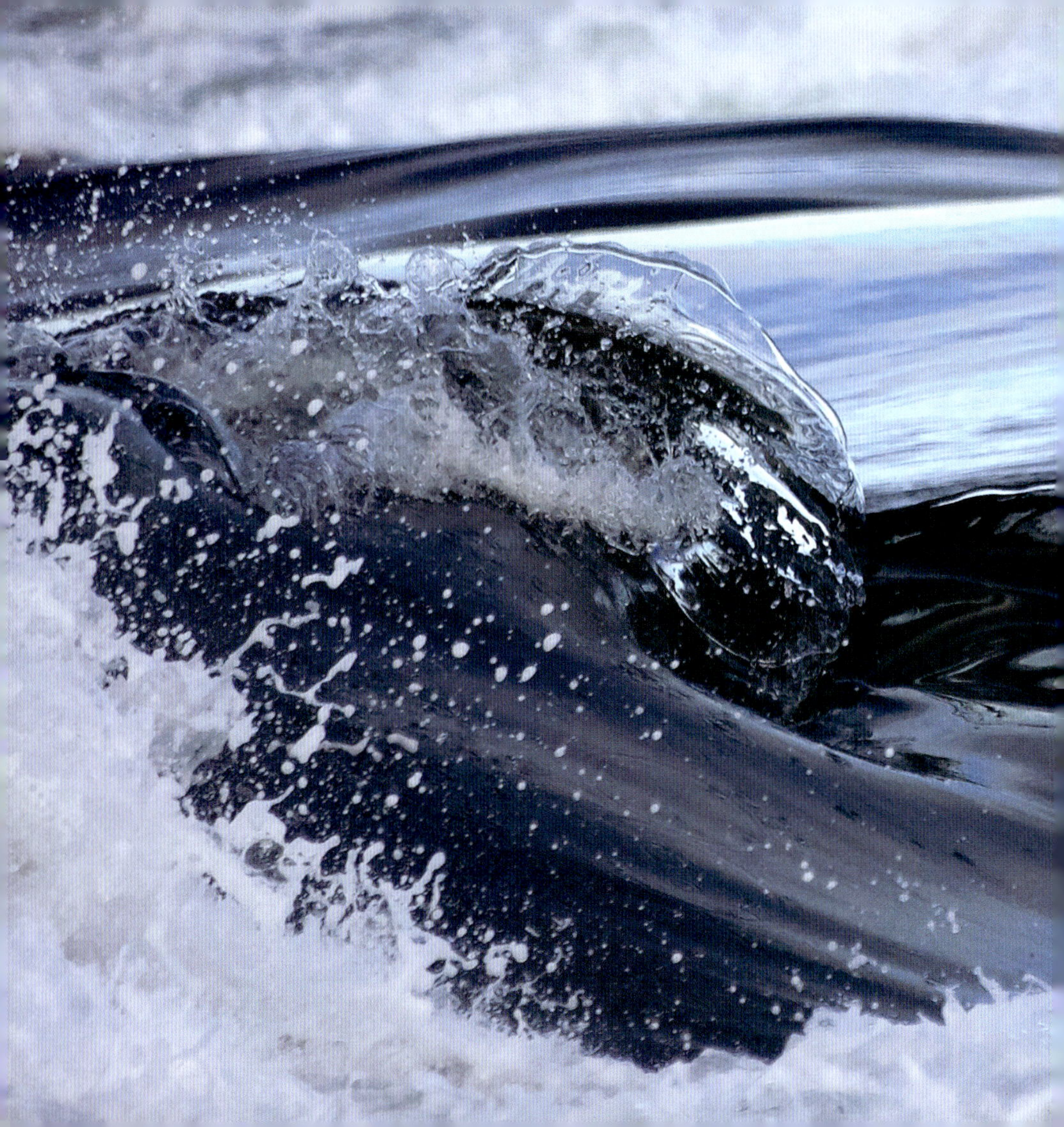

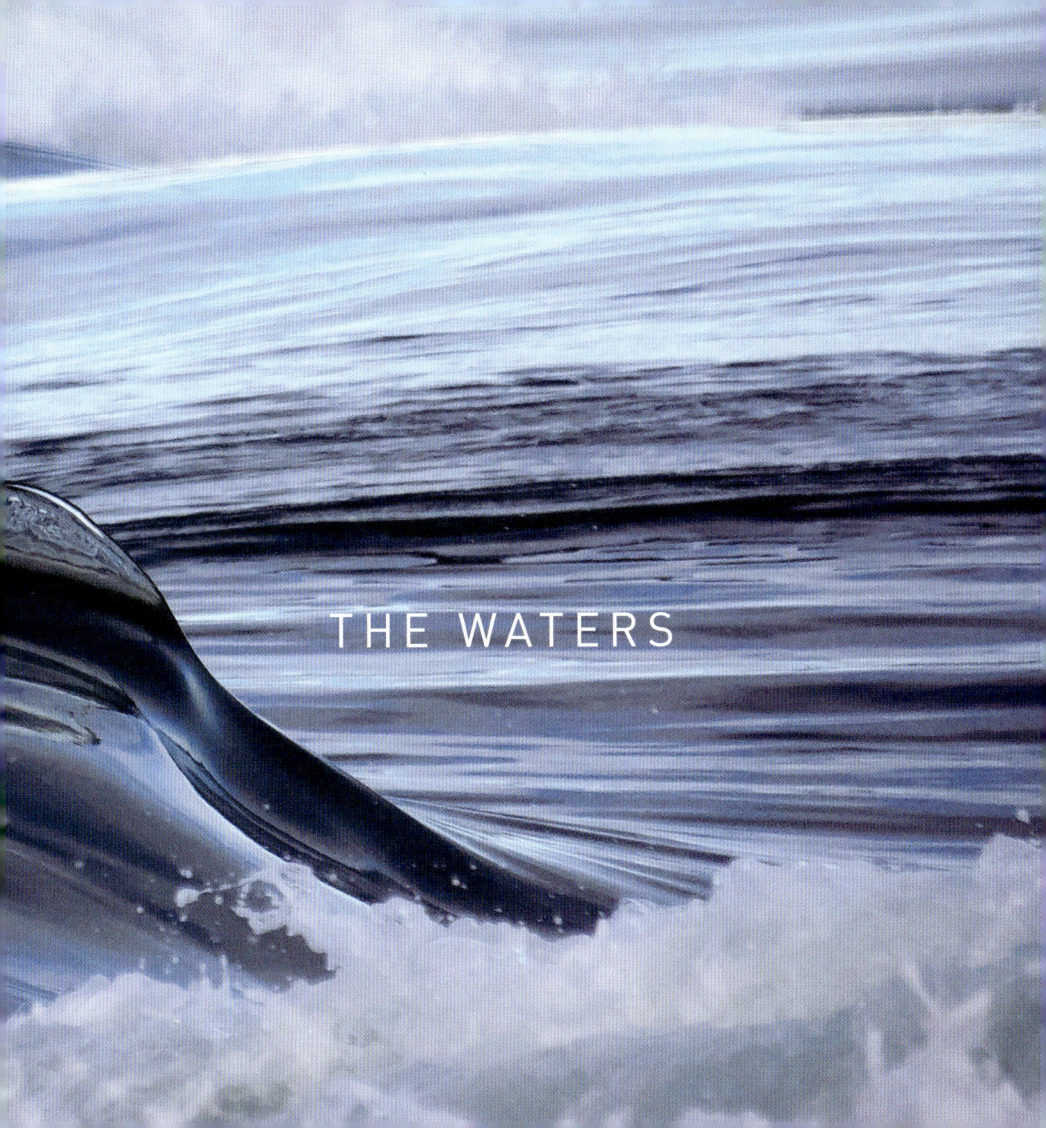
THE WATERS

## The magic of the waters and their changing moods

The waters off Ramsey have an ever-changing quality which is very hard to put into words; they change daily, even hourly, with the weather, the tides, the light. They also change with the seasons, and come September or even late August you can wake up one morning to a subtle change in the air, the light, something hard to define that tells you autumn has arrived. The sea reiterates this message, in a way even more difficult to define. The quality of it changes, there is a shift in the energy of the swells, and its movement holds the promise of the winter storms to come. Sometimes you notice the change on the water before it reaches the land, the harbinger of winter.

Sitting as it does so far out to the west, Ramsey and the St Davids Peninsula are often subject to their own little microclimate, which can bear little relationship to what is happening further inland even a couple of miles away. You can watch entire weather fronts approaching as the day turns from glorious sunshine to ominous skies, almost in a matter of minutes. Spending so much time on the water soon teaches you to read the signs written in the sky, such as mare's tails or mackerel sky that can foretell strong winds to come on an otherwise glorious summer's day. Seeing shearwaters flying through the Sound at lunchtime is a sure sign (if you were in any doubt) that you should be tucked up safely ashore with a hot drink until the summer storm has passed! Shearwaters only ever venture that close to shore during the day in very bad conditions, usually strong winds, accompanied by horizontal rain or drizzle.

The waters of Ramsey Sound and the outlying islands are home to some of the most ferocious tidal currents in the UK, which, whilst making them an adventure playground for kayakers and the like, also makes for some of the most perilous waters around the British coastline. It's not for nothing that St Davids Head, lying just to the north of the Sound, earned the name of *Octapitorum promontorium* or the 'Promontory of the Eight Perils', so called by the second century Egyptian geographer Ptolemy. It is the tides, combined with its exposed situation on the westernmost part of the Welsh coastline and therefore open to the Atlantic swells built up over thousands of miles of fetch, which lead to the dramatic seascapes for which the area is renowned. Ramsey, the outlying islands and their adjacent coastline are the first land those storm waves encounter. Those craggy, scarred cliffs bear the full brunt of the sea's enormous force which, even on a calm day, has an underlying power but which, when urged on by gale force

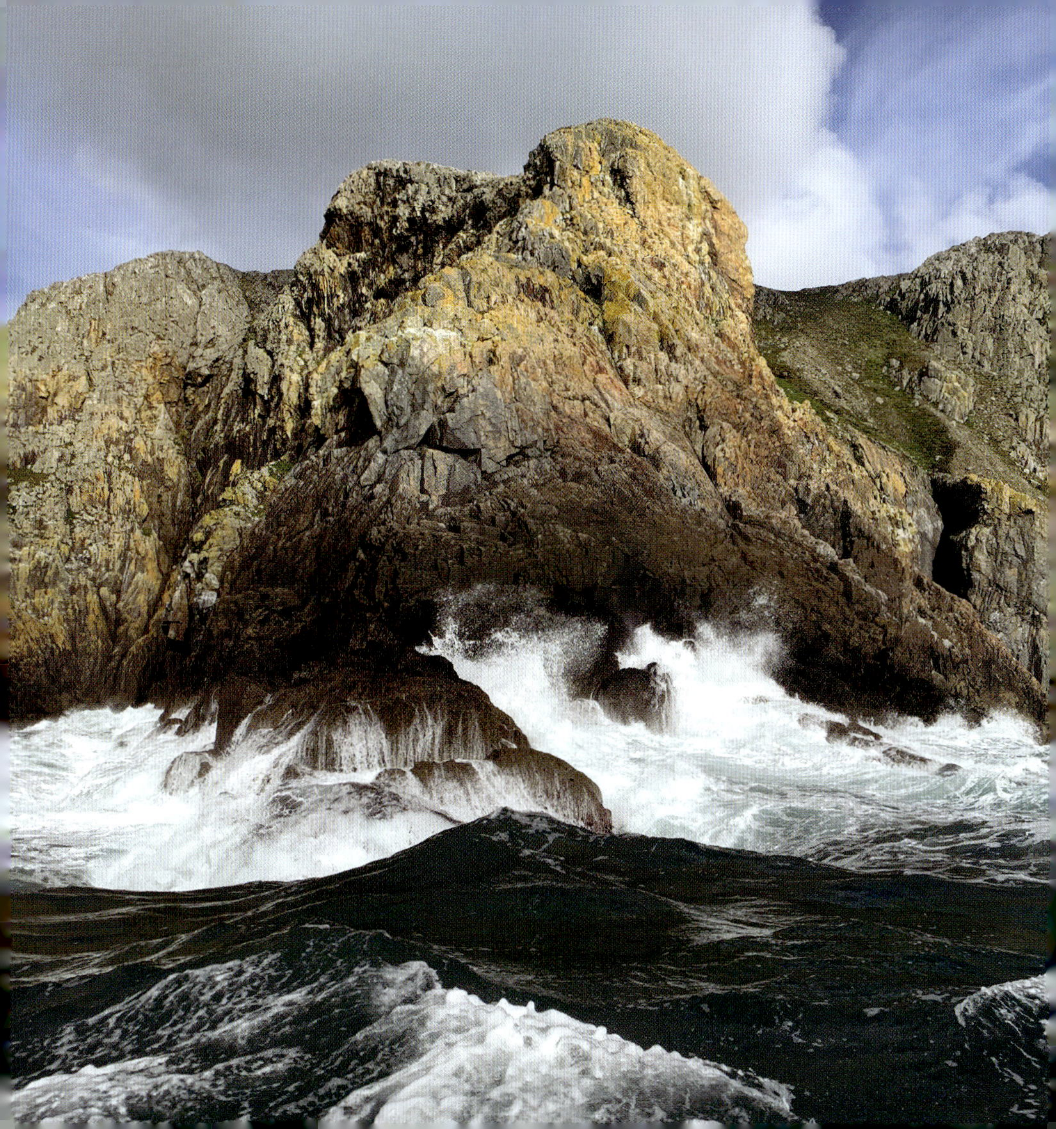

winds, can create truly spectacular waves capable of hurling spray over the 130m tall western cliffs of Ramsey.

## Tides

The exceptionally strong tides that run through Ramsey Sound are caused by the topography of the area exaggerating the gravitational pull of the moon and sun. In its daily sojourn north and south, the flooding and ebbing tide is constricted on a large scale by the Irish Sea and St George's Channel, and then on a more local level by the sweep of St Brides Bay and the position of Ramsey in that tidal current. As the vast body of water funnels through the narrow channel of the Sound, it is squeezed between island and mainland, causing it to speed up. Then, to add insult to injury, a reef of rocks known as the Bitches stretches one third of the way into the Sound from the island, creating a natural barrier or dam holding back the tide. As a result the tides do not behave as you would expect them to. The restriction is so great that not only do the tides speed up considerably, reaching up to 18 knots in some places, but there is an anomaly in the tide times whereby the flood tide will run for approximately three hours after high water, which is when you would expect it to change direction, and the ebb runs for two and a half to three hours after low water. There may

be some variation on this depending on whether you are on spring or neap tides. The tidal range in Ramsey Sound is almost eight metres on a spring tide, while neaps may be less than five metres. Neaps will allow for up to twenty minutes slack water, where there is little or no movement, whereas on spring tides the water will literally stop flowing in one direction and immediately start flowing in the opposite direction. In fact, in some places in the Sound at the change of tide on spring tides, it can be flooding in one place and ebbing in another. All of this adds up to local knowledge being pretty much essential for the safe navigation of this area.

The bathymetry of the Sound (right) in particular is incredibly dramatic, and if you drained all the water out, this is what you would see. It's hard to imagine such a dramatic landscape existing beneath your feet when you are out in a boat, although it goes a long way to explaining the complex, ever-shifting currents. It is this ancient landscape, created between ten and twenty million years ago which creates hundreds of opposing currents, with the water changing direction and speed numerous times as you cross the Sound, forming not only back tides and eddies but also vertical columns of moving water. The speed of these currents also varies enormously depending on location and the state and size of tide. In the middle, the Sound drops off to a deep underwater canyon whose charted depth is 67m, though deeper soundings of almost 100m have been recorded more recently. It shallows at either end, with hill masses sometimes known as 'monadnocks' (an erosion resistant isolated hill or rock outcrop) to the east and west. This complex landscape was partly carved out by ice movement from the last Ice Age, and it is thought that a meltwater channel beneath the ice may have caused the deep closed canyon down the middle of the Sound. Most geologists think that much of the surrounding coastal landscape today was created by marine erosion, and parts of the coastal platform in this area are thought to be a wave-cut platform created at a time when sea levels were much higher.

The shallowing at either end of the Sound causes great upwellings of water, as the tide is forced to the surface in vertical currents. Nowhere is this more evident than around the Horse Rock, an infamous pinnacle rising from the depths of this canyon, which is only visible above the surface at low water spring tides. Situated, as it is, in the middle of the Sound in almost a straight line between the harbour of Porthstinian and Ramsey's harbour, it can make for a dangerous crossing and has been responsible for numerous shipwrecks.

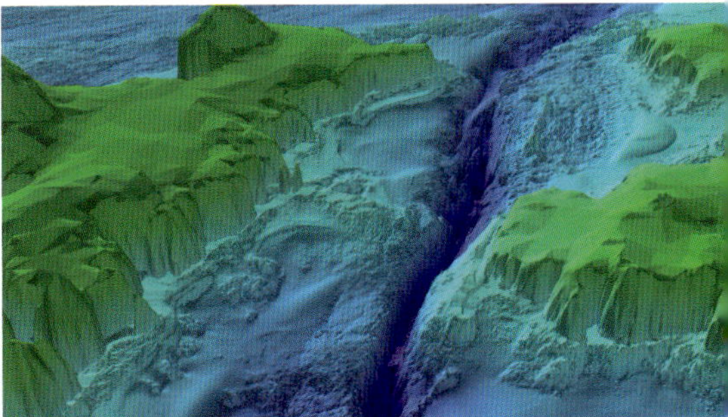

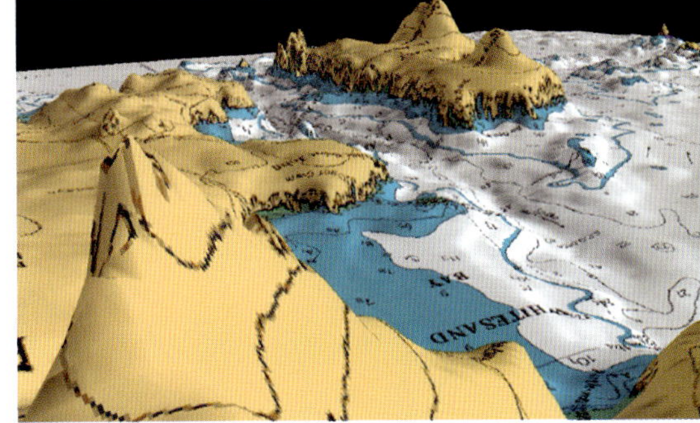


Conditions over the Horse will tend to be worse on the flood, as the north-going tide encounters this rock rising up out of deep water. The result is a mesmerizing, boiling mass of upwelling and whirlpools which has proven deadly for both kayaks and boats alike over the years. In a kayak, it is possible to get sucked under here and spat out several hundred yards further down tide. In addition, if you add a northerly wind blowing against the northbound tide, it can build up spectacular overfalls (unpredictable breaking waves) in almost a matter of minutes with the turn of the tide. This can transform what looks like a relatively benign stretch of water with a northerly wind and ebb tide into a maelstrom of huge, breaking waves when the tide turns to flood. With no apparent change in weather, this sudden change in sea conditions can be somewhat disconcerting if you are not familiar with the area.

The conditions all this creates with wind over tide can make the whole area a serious hazard for boats, hence the large number of shipwrecks, few of which have stayed on the bottom to be explored as they tend to break up quickly and get swept away.

A relatively recent example of the dangers posed by this stretch of water happened back in 2000, when a passenger rhib with an extremely experienced skipper was playing on the Horse during a 'white water' trip. At the time of the incident there was a big spring flood tide running and a strong southerly wind, when the boat fell foul of the overfalls and was capsized in the breaking seas, throwing all the passengers and crew into the water. The unpredictable nature of overfalls is such that, as reputedly happened here according to the MAIB (Marine Accident Investigation Board) report, a hole can just open in front of you which the boat falls into. On this unfortunate occasion, as she surfed down a wave it is thought that the turbulent water caused her to sheer to port, combined with a breaking wave lifting the port quarter of the vessel and turning her over. Fortunately, on this occasion disaster was averted by the quick actions of the skipper of her sister vessel who, once alerted to the situation and despite still having a boat full of passengers, quickly went and safely recovered all the casualties from the water. To give an idea of the speed of the tide at the time, by the time the lifeboat was launched the upturned hull of the rhib was found drifting north of St Davids Head, more than 3 miles away. This is a sobering reminder that, even with today's technological advances, state of the art boats and many years of experience, the sea is a fickle mistress with a capricious nature, and her power and unpredictability is not to be underestimated. It should, however, be noted that many thousands of boat trips have been run around the Pembrokeshire islands over the last few decades and this is the only incident that has ever resulted in a boat turning over, which shows an exemplary safety record.

## The Bitches and Whelps

The reef of rocks running out into the Sound from the east side of the island are generally known as the Bitches, a shortening of the translation from the Welsh meaning 'bitches and whelps' after a female dog and her pups. A mistranslation of this has also given rise to it being called the 'Bridge of Ghosts', which despite its dubious origin seems like an apt name for such a notorious reef, given the many lives it has claimed over time. The Bitches has been a major hazard for shipping over the years, particularly dating back to the days of sail, when boats did not have engines powerful enough to motor against such tides as would be encountered there. There have been many recorded shipwrecks here, and almost certainly many more that have gone unrecorded. Even today, most sailing vessels are not fast enough to sail or motor against the tides through the Sound and have to use them instead, planning their passage accordingly.

The tide on the Bitches runs south for approximately six hours on the ebb tide, then changes direction to run north for six hours on the flood tide. As the tide builds, being at its strongest during the middle third of the tide, the rocks will start to act as a dam, holding the tide back and creating a weir effect, whereby the difference in water level can be as much

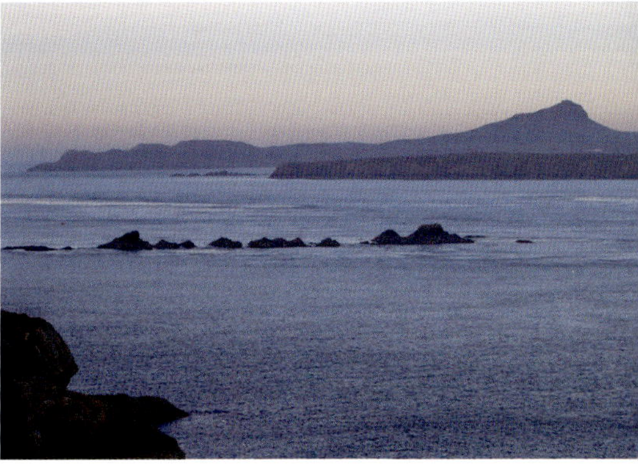

as 1.5m from one side to the other. The resulting rapids as the tide pours over the top of the reef create big standing waves and stoppers reminiscent of a river in full spate. It is a strange sight to behold at sea, and with the speed of the water reaching an incredible 18 knots over the reef it is easy to see why it has been the cause of so many disasters. Such is the power of the tide here that the noise the rapids make on a still evening during spring tide can be heard from the Cross Square in St Davids. It is precisely these conditions that today attract kayakers to the area on spring tides. The standing wave can be over 1.5m on larger springs, and with sufficient skill can be surfed in a kayak, or even a surfboard if you are feeling brave. Such is its renown in kayaking circles

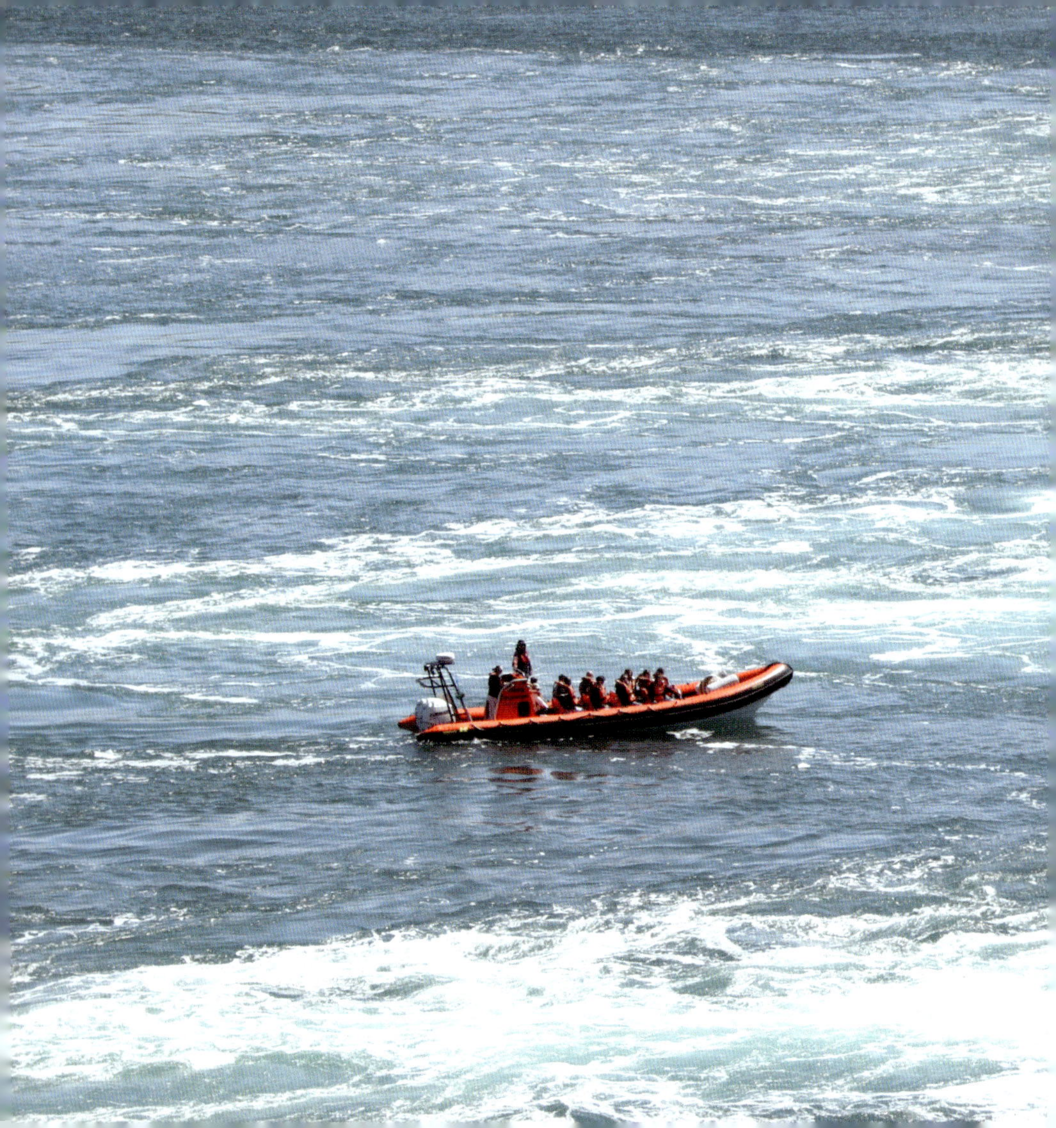

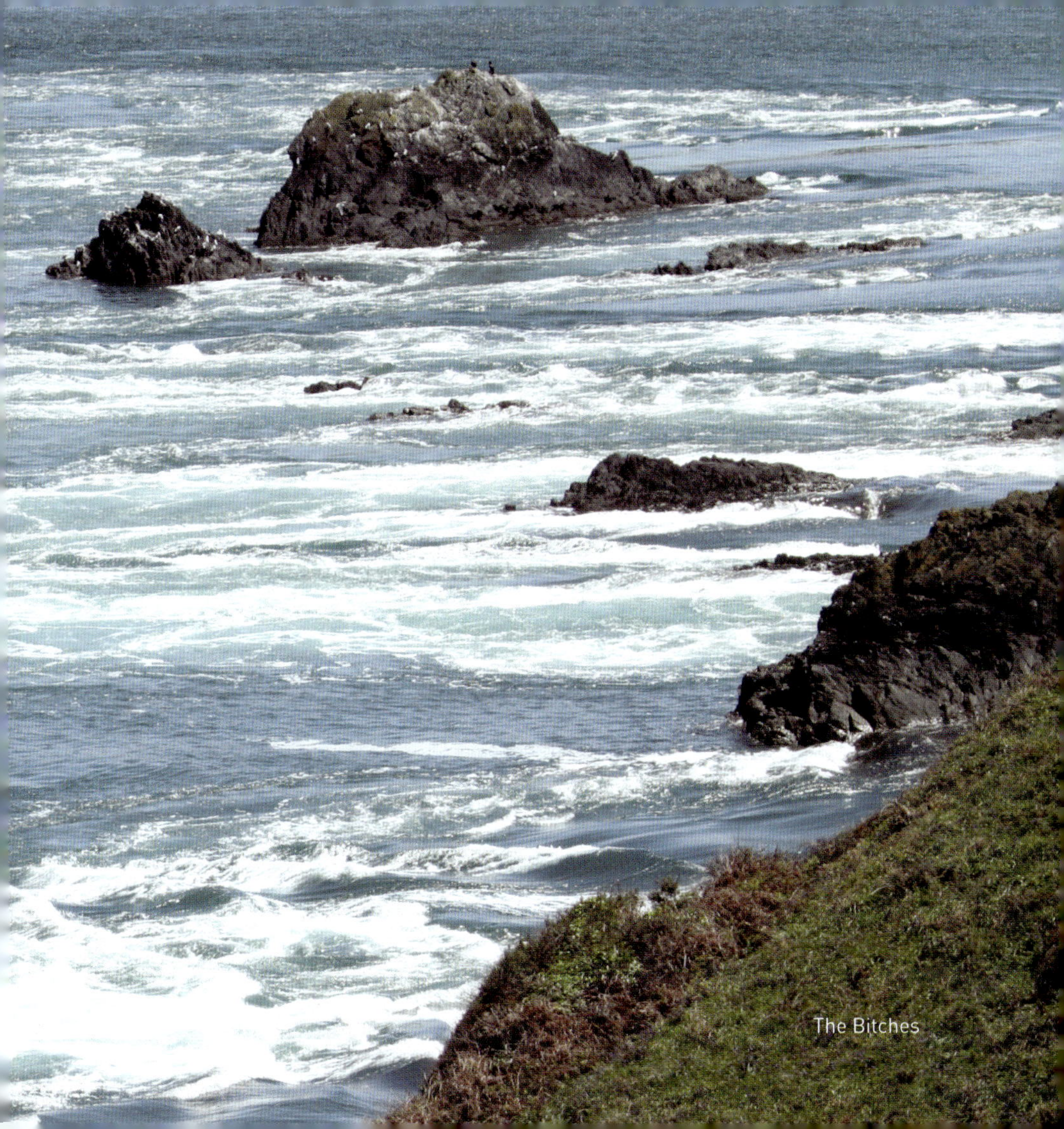
The Bitches

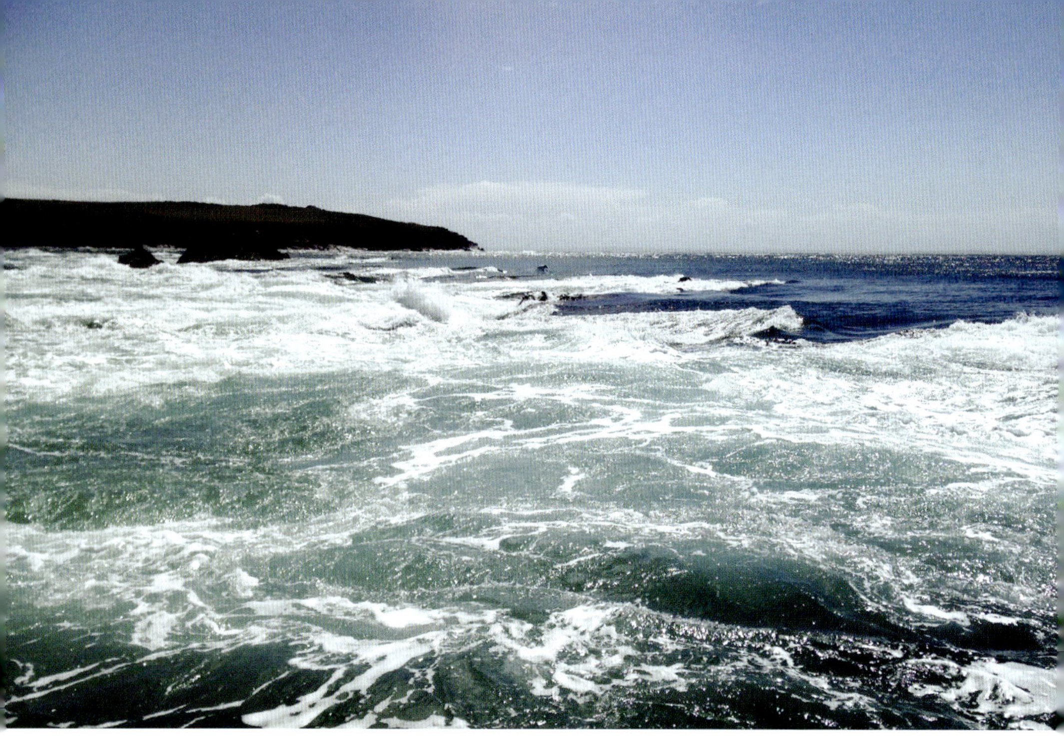

that international white water kayaking championships have been held on the Bitches in the past. It is not, however, for the fainthearted or inexperienced kayaker, as unlike a river rapid it often has an Atlantic swell, exaggerating the effect of the waves. In wind against tides conditions, the paddle across the Sound from St Justinians, a journey which is tricky in fair conditions, can become perilous. The turbulent water and whirlpools found around Horse Rock are a particular hazard for kayakers on the flood and are to be avoided at all costs.

## The Wrecking of the Gem

One of the more famous wrecks that we know of on the Bitches happened back in 1910, resulting in the loss of the then St

Davids lifeboat, the Gem, and the lives of three of her crew.

It was a stormy night on October 12th 1910, when a trading ketch, the Democrat, was riding at anchor in the area known as the Waterings, having delivered a load of culm to the island earlier in the day. This is an area marked on the chart as a safe anchorage on the eastern side of Ramsey and, as the weather was unfavourable, the Captain decided to anchor for the night until conditions improved. During the night the wind picked up to a gale from the northeast and, finding themselves on a lee shore and worried the anchors would drag and they would be carried onto the rocks, the crew of the Democrat alerted the mainland of their plight by burning some flares. On seeing the distress signal, an answering rocket was fired from the mainland and the St Davids lifeboat was launched with a crew of fifteen. Lifeboats in those days did not have engines, being powered instead merely by oars and sail, and due to the strength of the wind that night the Gem went out under oar power alone. The crew battled with tide, wind and heavy seas in the dark before finally reaching the Democrat and dropping anchor themselves, in an attempt to come alongside to rescue her crew of three. On their third attempt, they finally managed to get the crew safely aboard the Gem. The Board of Trade wreck report

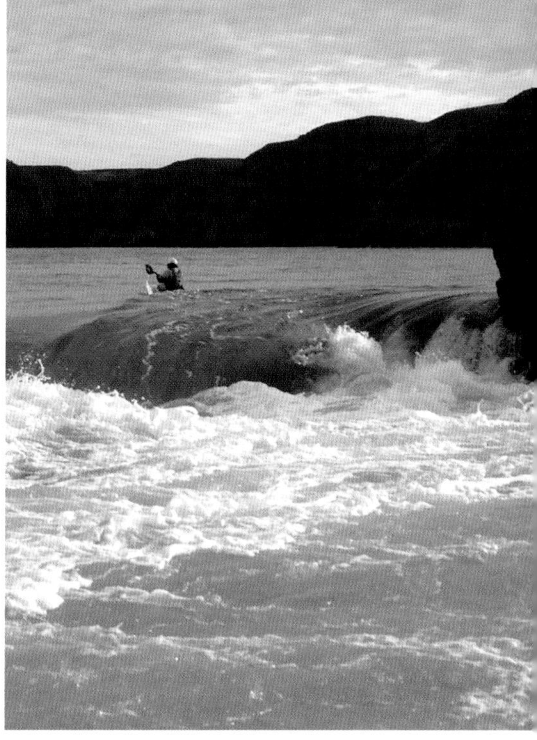

suggests that due to the severity of the conditions at this point the coxswain's intention, having rescued the crew, was to pull north of the Democrat and anchor for the night. Even this, however, was no mean feat; battling wind and tide and, by this point, fatigue, it proved to be one they could not win. The boat became unmanageable as wind and tide carried them ever closer to the Bitches.

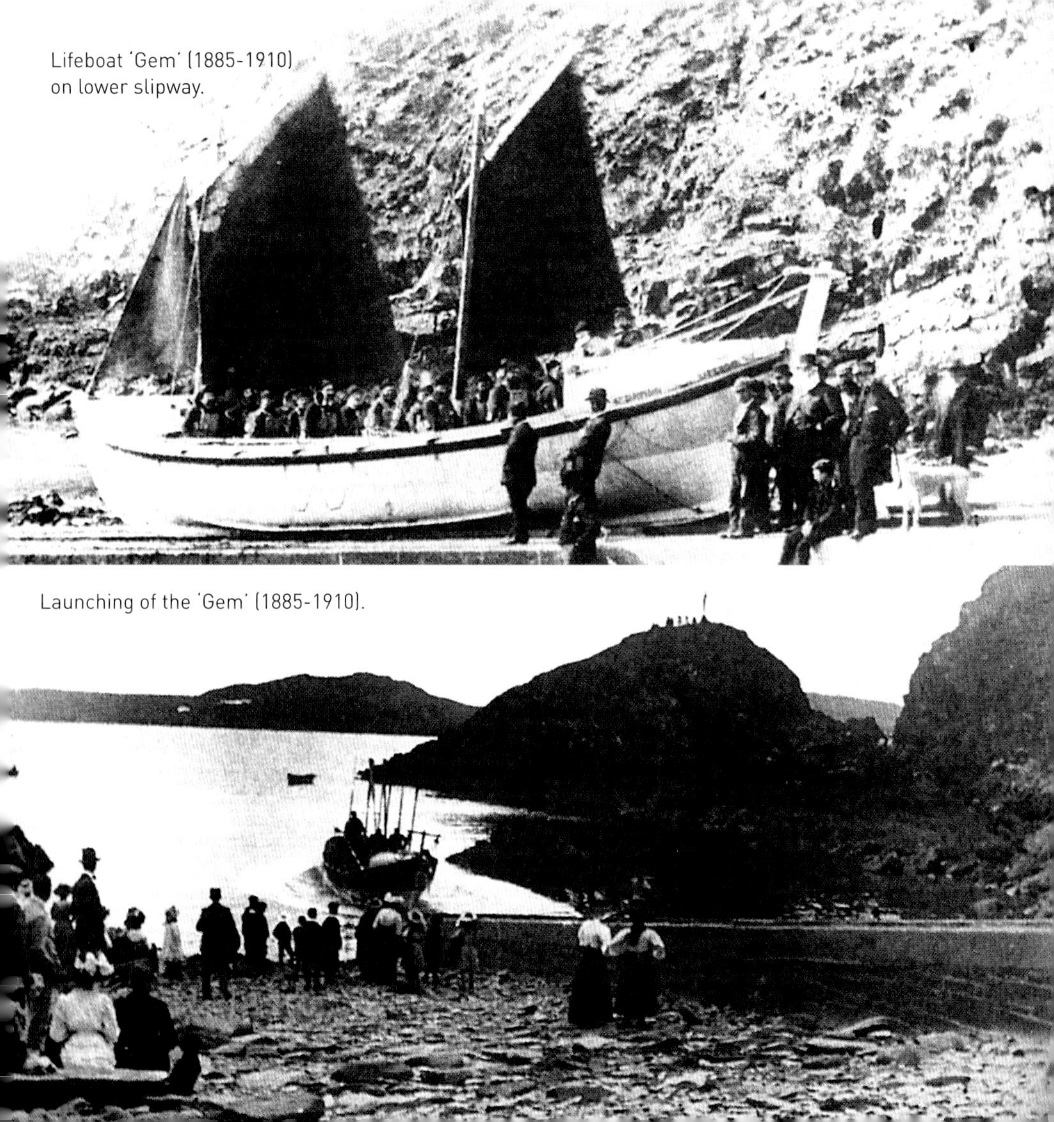

Lifeboat 'Gem' (1885-1910) on lower slipway.

Launching of the 'Gem' (1885-1910).

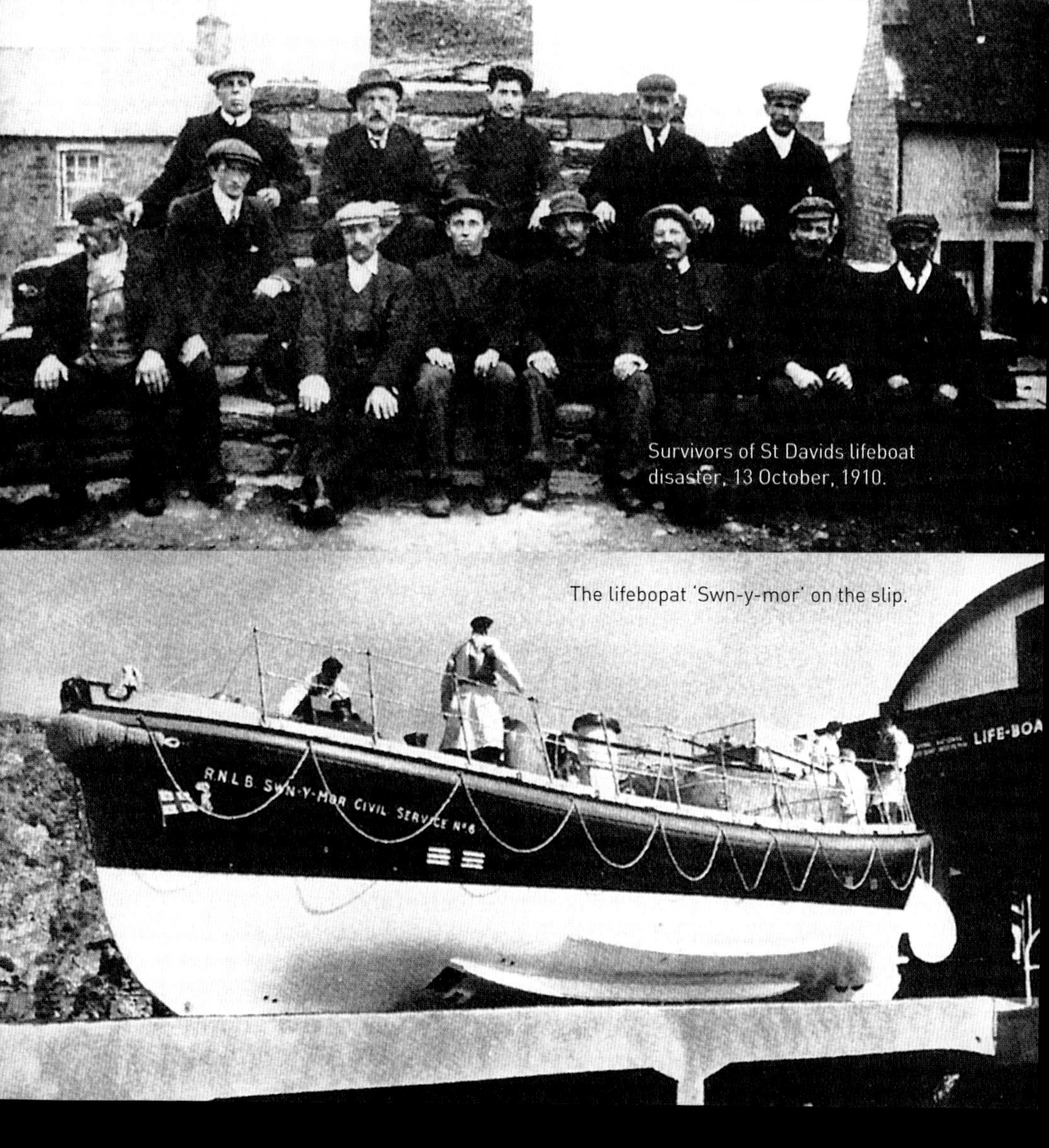

Survivors of St Davids lifeboat disaster, 13 October, 1910.

The lifebopat 'Swn-y-mor' on the slip.

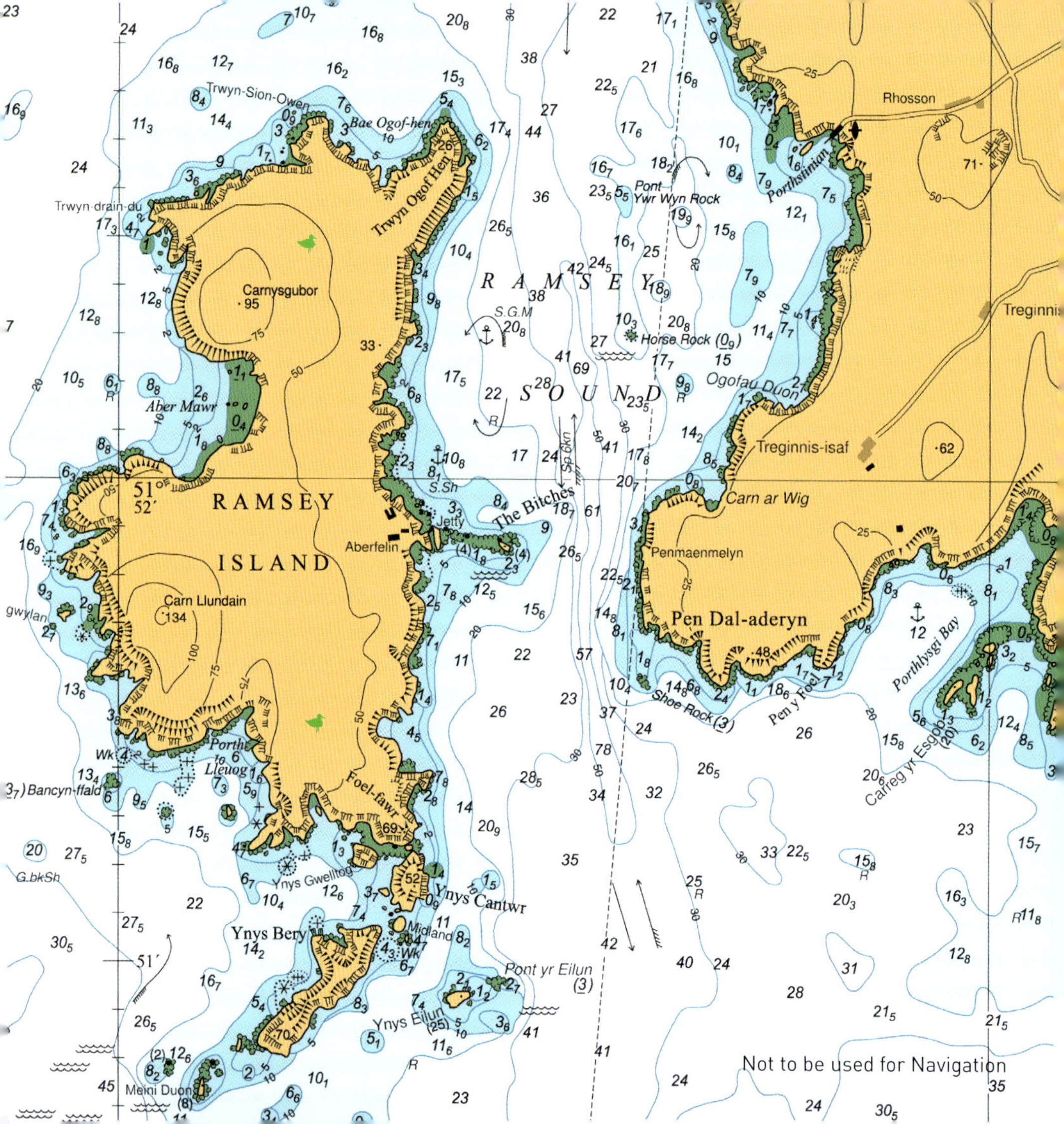

RAMSEY
ISLAND
RAMSEY SOUND
Trwyn-Sion-Owen
Bae Ogof-hen
Trwyn Ogof Hen
Trwyn-drain-du
Carnysgubor
·95
Aber Mawr
Carn Llundain
·134
Porth
Lleuog
Foel-fawr
Bancyn-ffald
G.bkSh
Ynys Gwelltog
Ynys Cantwr
Ynys Bery
Midland
Wk
Ynys Eilun
Pont yr Eilun
(3)
Meini Duon
gwylan
S.G.M
Pont
Ywr Wyn Rock
Horse Rock (0₉)
Ogofau Duon
S.Sh
Jetty
The Bitches
Aberfelin
Rhosson
Porthstinian
Treginnis
Treginnis-isaf
·62
Carn ar Wig
Penmaenmelyn
Pen Dal-aderyn
Shoe Rock (3)
Pen y Foel
Porthlysgi Bay
Carreg yr Esgob
(20)
Sp.6kn
Not to be used for Navigation

In a last desperate bid to save her, the coxswain attempted to steer the Gem through one of the gaps in the reef in the pitch black. The attempt failed and the Gem struck the rocks, throwing some of the men into the sea whilst others jumped for safety. The Gem was wrecked, and in total fifteen men made it to the relative safety of the Big Bitch. Tragically, three of the Gem's crew, including the coxswain, were drowned that night, whilst the rest weathered out the night clinging to the rocks until first light brought the possibility of rescue. They set fire to some oilskins to alert those on the mainland of their predicament and let them know the Gem would not be returning. At noon the next day a young lad of sixteen, a fisherman called Sidney Mortimer, launched a rowing boat from the neighbouring harbour of Porth Clais and, with two members of the coastguard, rowed round into the Sound in the aftermath of the storm to attempt to rescue the stricken crew. This he safely achieved in a number of runs. It was then they discovered the coxswain John Stephens and crew members Henry Rowlands and James Price had been lost. Their bodies were found washed up on Aber Maharan, a cove to the south of the Bitches, two days later, not far from the wreck of the Gem itself.

As there was no sign of the Democrat the following morning, it was assumed she had broken her anchor during the night as feared and been wrecked. The cruel irony of the story was only realised three days later, when the Democrat was found south of Milford, unmanned and intact, floating like a ghost ship, and the reality that three brave men voluntarily risked and ultimately lost their lives that night to rescue the crew of a vessel that went on to survive the storm was discovered. In recognition of his bravery, Sidney Mortimer was awarded the RNLI silver medal and two years later, at the age of 18, became coxswain of the new St Davids lifeboat. He remains the youngest coxswain ever appointed to this day.

On telling this story to a boat full of passengers a couple of years ago, it turned out that one of the them was a relative of Will Thomas, one of the lifeboat crew on that fateful night. She explained that he had been one of the only smokers on the crew, and as a result always tried to ensure he kept his matches dry. It was due to this that they were able to set fire to their oilskins to signal for help.

The Bitches are a formidable sight in daylight on a calm day. Looming out of the dark or the fog with a gale raging, totally at the mercy of the elements, they must have been a terrifying prospect. It is worth noting that in 1910, in addition to not having motorised lifeboats, the clothing and safety equipment of the crew would have been very basic compared to today's

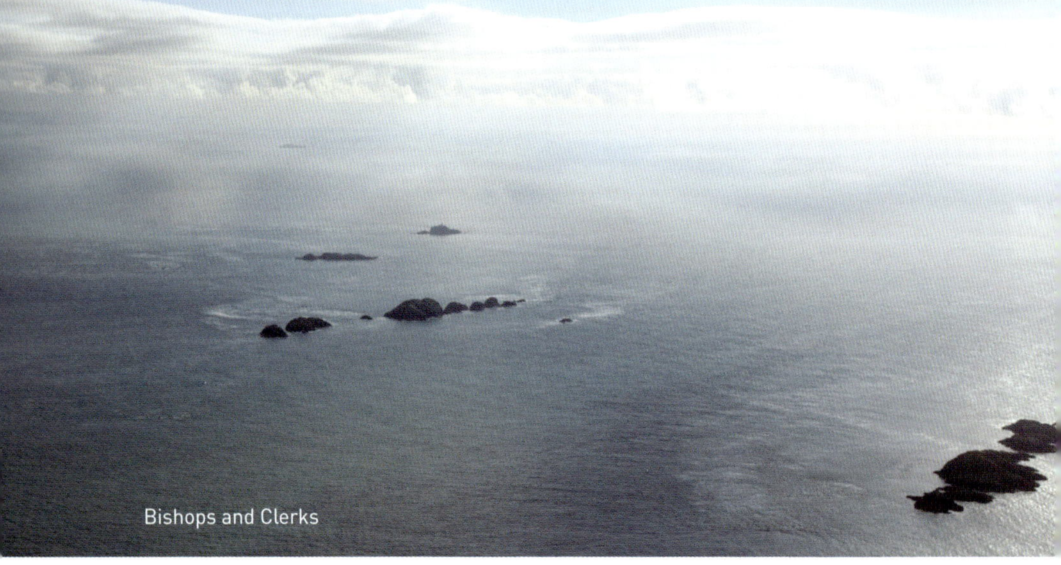

Bishops and Clerks

standards, including cork lifejackets, which is what the crew were wearing, as noted in the report.

This tragedy resulted in the replacement lifeboat at St Davids being a motorised one, one of the first in Wales. Today's coxswain, David John, when interviewed on the subject at the 100-year anniversary of the disaster, was quoted saying, "The bravery of those men, who went out during gales and high seas, in little more than a wooden rowing boat, is truly astonishing."

## Bishops and Clerks

The Bishops and Clerks are the treacherous stretch of rocky islets and reefs which lie to the west of Ramsey, many of which are submerged or semi-submerged. They are also subject to the strong tidal races and overfalls, which make the area a notorious hazard for shipping and the site of thirteen known wrecks. They are comprised of four main reefs: North Bishop, Carreg Rhosson, the Daufraich (Welsh for two arms) and the South Bishop, or Emsger. In addition, there are three semi-submerged rocks called the Llechau Isaf, Llechau Uchaf and Carreg Trai. The very name the Bishops and Clerks came about as the result of a shipwreck mentioned in the *Milford Haven Telegraph*, January 3rd, 1866, in the 'Old Families of Pembrokeshire Section'. This tells of how, some 300 years ago, a fleet of merchant ships on their return from Spain were 'wrecked upon the fatal rocks, now known as the Bishop and his Clerks'. The only three survivors, Miles Bishop and James and Henry Clerk, after whom the rocks were then named, were found clinging to the North Bishop.

When you sit amongst them, even on a calm evening, and watch the raw power with which the tide races through, creating drop offs which look like they shouldn't be possible in the sea and producing a sound which can be heard from the mainland, it is not difficult to imagine the terror these rocks have inspired in unwary mariners over the centuries. They have inspired many a local historian to pass comment on them, one of the earliest perhaps being the Elizabethan antiquary George Owen. Given the ecclesiastical history of the area, it is perhaps not surprising that the name Bishops and Clerks soon began to be associated with the Church, and descriptions include that of George Owen, who described them in one of his books as "The Bishop and these his Clerkes preache deadly doctrine to their winter audience, such poor seafaring men as are forcyd thether by tempest, onlie in one theing they are to be commended, they keepe residence better than the rest of the canons of that see are wont to do".

Another shipwreck captured the imagination of the early 19th century local historian Richard Fenton. In his *A Historical Tour Through Pembrokeshire*, he recounts how in 1780 some Swedish mariners were shipwrecked on these rocks and tells the tale of the dramatic rescue that followed. Blanch Williams of Treleddyn, a local farm that overlooks the Bishops, having seen the plight of the men through her telescope, single handedly rowed out to one of the smaller rocks, possibly Carreg Trai, and despite the "boisterousness of the weather", which sounds like a bit of an understatement, proceeded to rescue them and take them back to her house to recover.

In 1839, the South Bishop Lighthouse was built to mark their south-western extremity and warn shipping of the navigational hazard posed by the rocks.

## South Bishop

Also known as Emsger, Norse for isolated rock. The lighthouse was built in 1834, converted to electric operation in 1959, and in 1971 the addition of a helipad made landing on the island for maintenance considerably easier. The tower stands 11m high, is 44m above mean high water

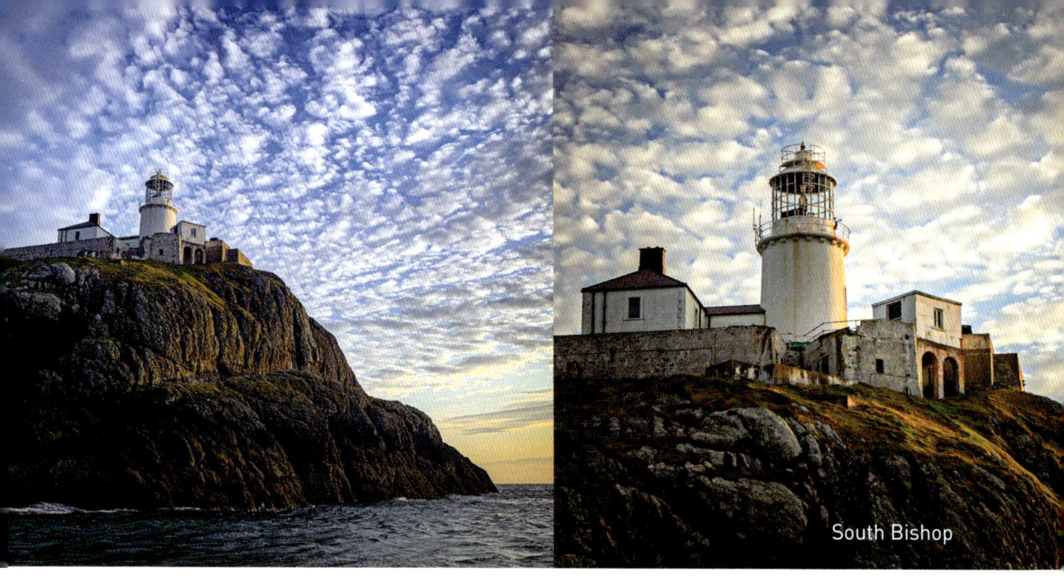

South Bishop

and was automated in 1983. The light has a range of sixteen miles, and yet only uses a 70 watt MBI bulb. Growing up in a house overlooking the cliffs above Whitesands, we would often hear the fog horn warning of incoming fog. This has been replaced with a fog signal with a supposed range of 2NM, although I have been out at the South Bishop in the fog and almost bumped into the island before we heard the fog horn. Built as it is in the path of migrating birds, many were drawn to the light and flew into the lantern, until collaboration between Trinity House and the RSPB led to special bird perches being built around the lantern,

considerably reducing the amount of deaths caused. As offshore lighthouses go, the South Bishop is one of the more hospitable, boasting a three-bedroom house as well as a walled garden and unrivalled sea views!

Being a lighthouse keeper out on the South Bishop, whilst considerably more spacious and comfortable than the Smalls, was still not without its trials and tribulations. You only have to look at the rough-hewn steps in the rocks that serve as a landing place on this exposed rock to realise that getting on and off the South Bishop would have been a tricky business even in calm weather.

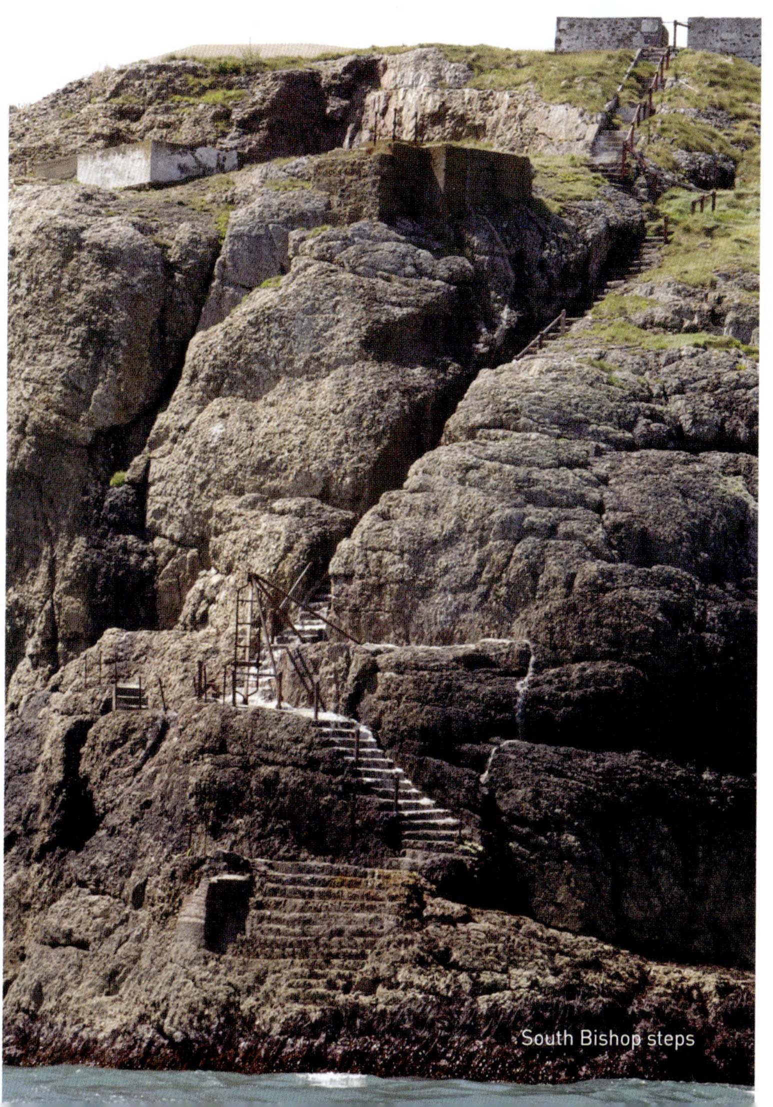

South Bishop steps

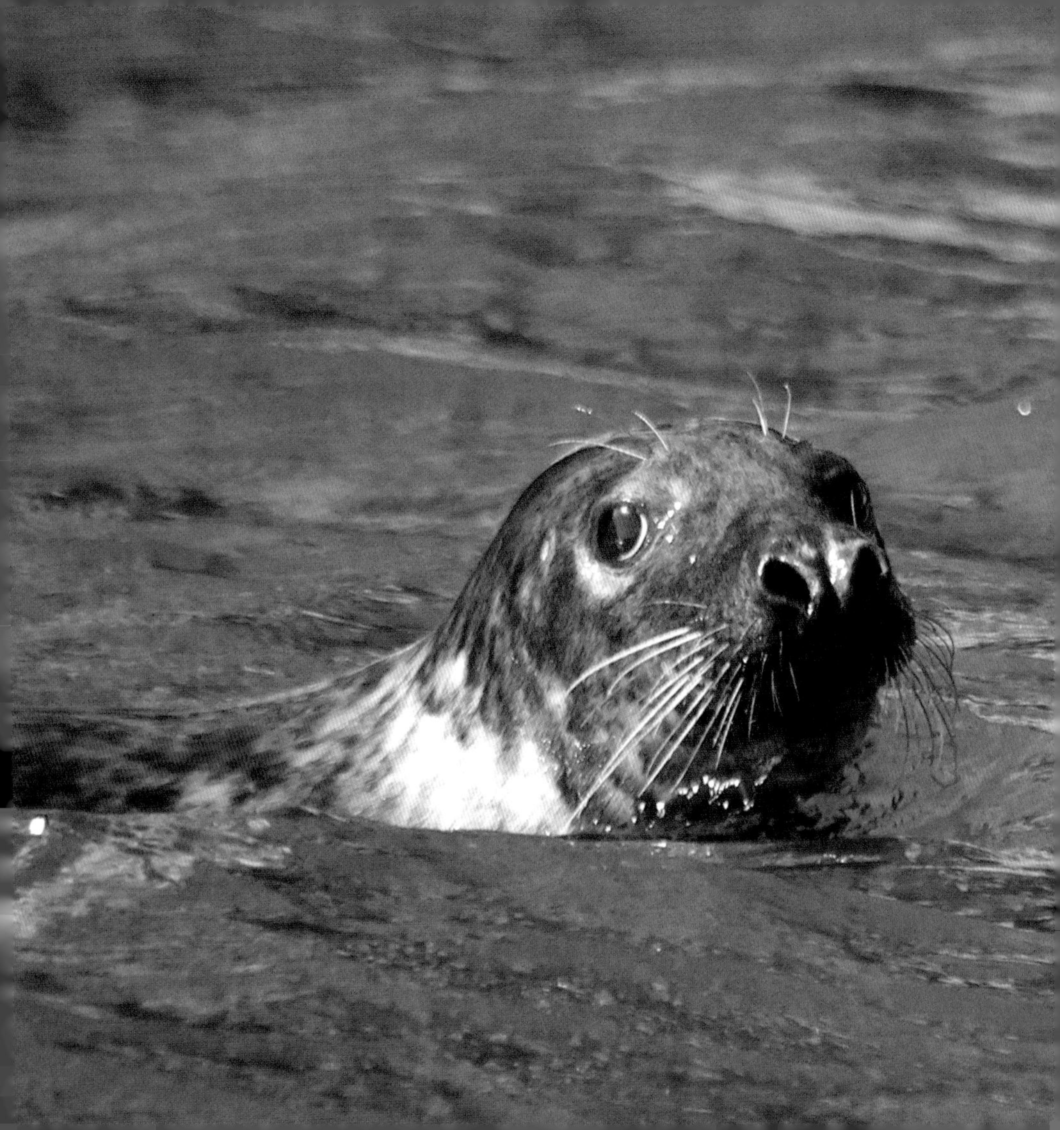

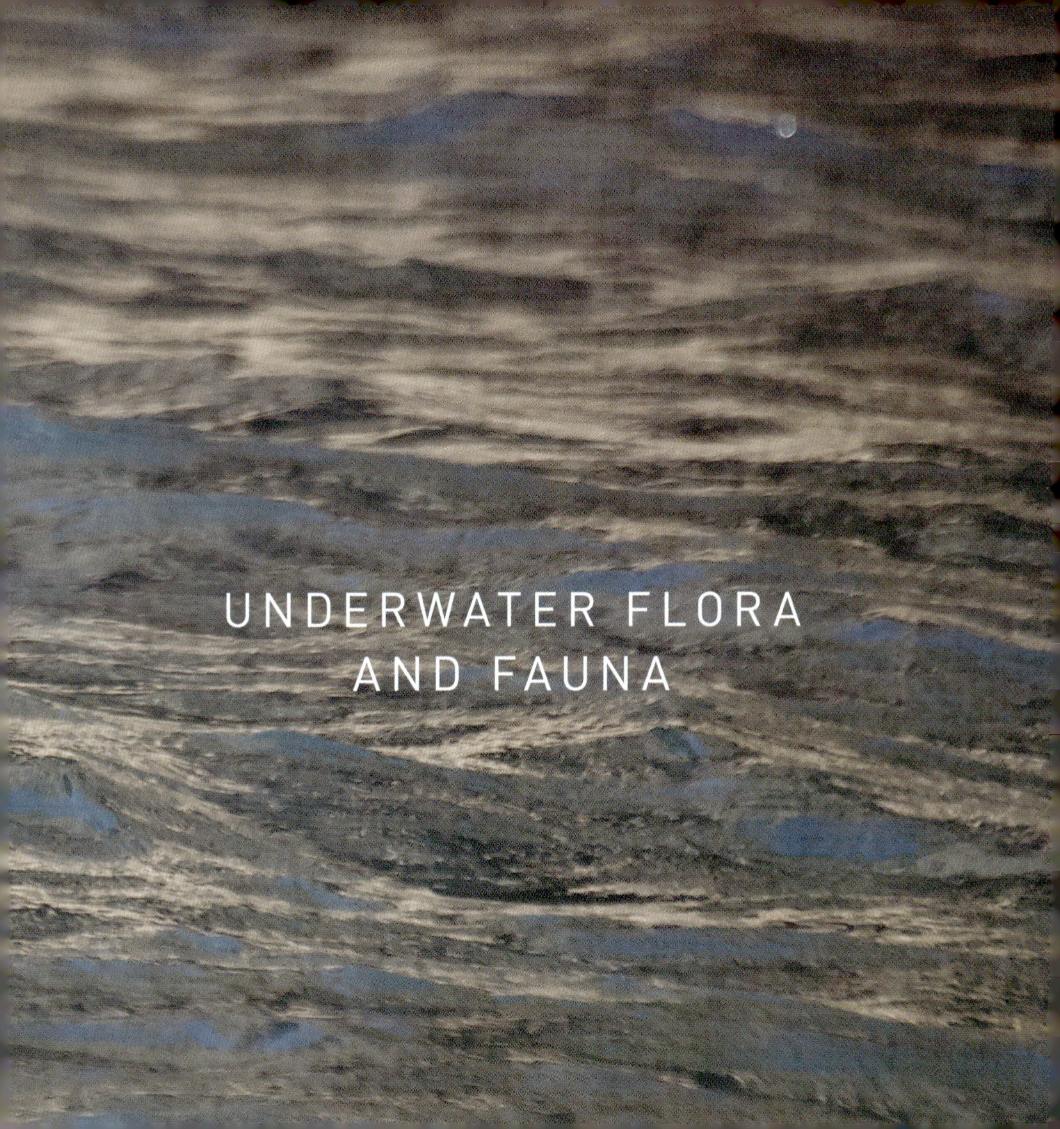
UNDERWATER FLORA
AND FAUNA

There are a number of factors that contribute to the rich underwater flora and fauna to be found in the waters off the north Pembrokeshire islands. One of these is the presence of the Celtic Deep, a depression on the seabed which drops off to depths of 100m to the north, increasing to a maximum of 200m towards St George's Channel. The seabed here, called the Celtic Shelf, forms part of the continental shelf of Europe.

The southern tip is 112km north-west of Trevose Head in Cornwall, while the northern tip is 84km off the coast of Pembrokeshire, covering an area of 348 square km. It is an area of important frontal activity in summer, and large aggregations of copepods have been recorded here. These can be used as a biodiversity indicator to determine the health of the marine food chain, and it is these that make it such a good foraging ground for both the marine mammals and seabirds that gather here to feed during the summer months.

In addition, the fast-flowing tidal races which run around our coastline and islands combine to result in the rich feeding grounds which support our diverse, if fragile, underwater ecosystem. They are home to an amazing wealth of marine life, from tiny phytoplankton to the fin whale, the second largest mammal on our planet.

## Atlantic Grey Seals

Latin – *Halicorus grypus*, hook nosed sea pig.

Ramsey boasts the largest breeding colony of Atlantic grey seals in southern Britain. Throughout most of the year it is home to a small population of approximately 100, often juvenile, seals. Twice annually these numbers will increase significantly, as the adults come to the area to moult from December to February/March, and to breed in late August to November.

During the breeding season in particular, numbers can increase to in excess of a thousand seals around Ramsey alone. As the British Isles are home to almost 50% of the world's population of these seals, a colony of this size is of both national and international conservation importance.

Atlantic Grey Seals are a feature of the SSSI and also protected by the Marine SAC. Surveys carried out on the island by the RSPB over the last few years have regularly recorded counts of between 500-700 pups born each autumn. Figures would suggest there has been a significant increase in the number of seal pups born on the island since a full survey involving marking all the pups with dye was carried out some 25 years ago.

The wardens are also carrying out photo ID on the Atlantic grey seals, and are building up a database of individuals

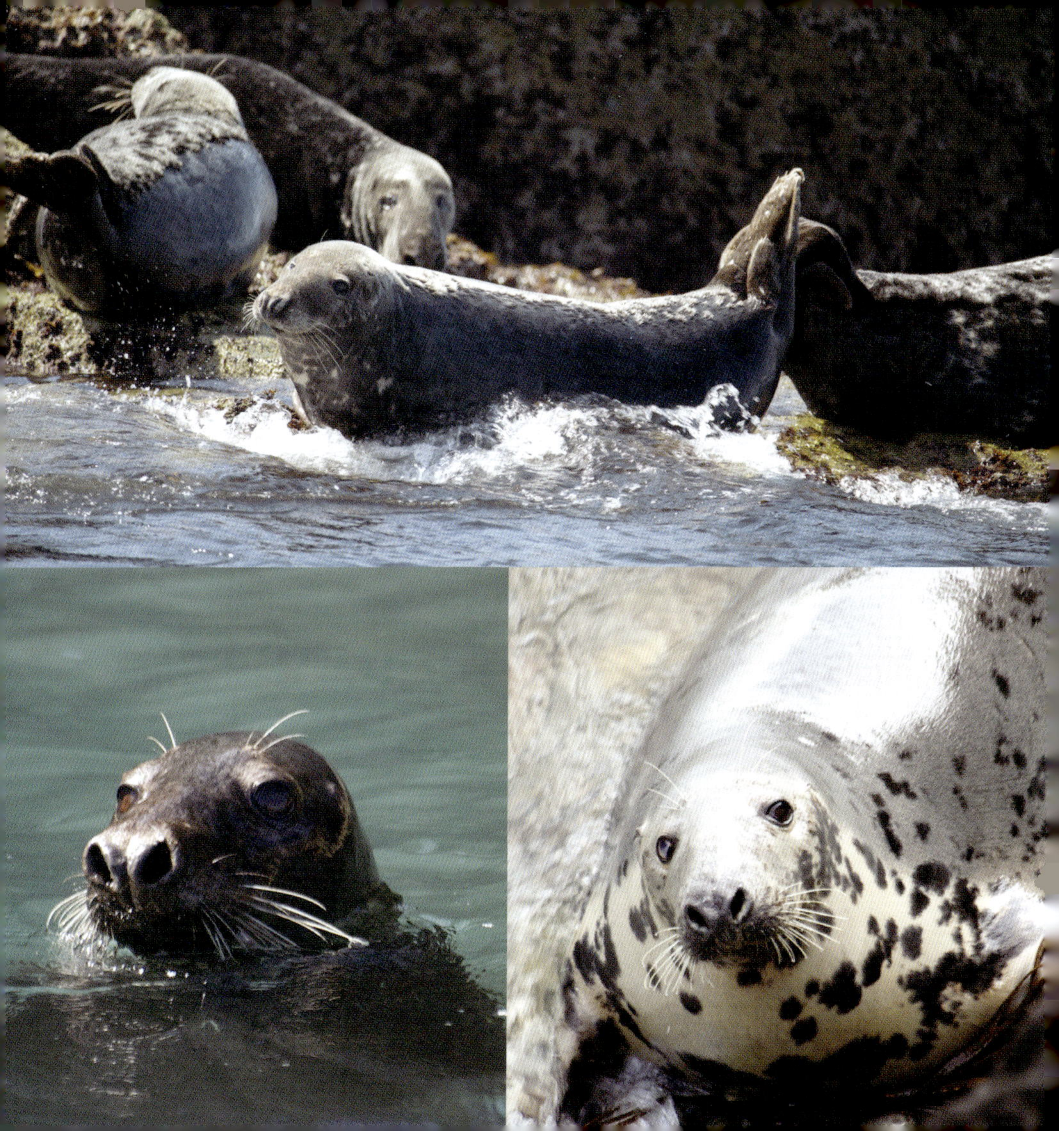

which is being compared with results from similar projects around the UK, to find out to what extent individual seals move around its shores. The fact that the markings on an Atlantic grey seal's coat are as individual to each seal as our fingerprints are to us, and do not change as the seal grows and moults, makes photo ID a good way of identifying them. Some markings are obvious to the human eye, whilst others are more subtle and require computer software to make the match.

The average lifespan of an Atlantic grey seal is between 25 and 35 years, though the oldest recorded female was 46, and an adult bull seal can reach 310kg/40 stone and 2m in length, females being somewhat smaller. Females outlive bulls by anything up to ten years, and this is generally attributed to the fact that during the breeding season each cove will have a dominant bull for the duration of the season. He will have to patrol his territory and fight to defend it from potential rivals if necessary. They rarely fight to the death, but on occasion I have seen fights with evenly matched males last over an hour, leaving both parties torn and bloodied. Each breeding cove may have anything from two to ten females in a territory, and larger territories such as Aber Mawr on the north-west coast of Ramsey may have several dominant bulls, as there can be sixty cows on that beach.

The bulls play no part in the raising of the pup, in fact the females won't tolerate them anywhere near their pups. It is possible they may not be the father of the pup on the beach if they were not the dominant bull in that cove the previous year.

During the breeding season the seals give birth to their pups on the beaches around the island. These pups are typically 90-105cm in length and weigh 10-18kg. The female will feed her pup for a sum total of three weeks before weaning and abandoning the youngster. In this short amount of time the pup will triple its birth weight, gaining an average of 2kg per day, fed on one of the richest mammal milks known to man, at about 60% fat. Meanwhile, the female rapidly loses condition, dropping 4 kg per day and shedding as much as a third of her body weight. It is a massive transfer of fat from mother to young. Neither males nor females will feed much during the breeding season, as for different reasons they will not leave the breeding cove; the bull because he doesn't want to leave his territory unprotected, and the cow because she won't leave her pup which needs regular feeding. The pups are born with a white, fluffy, non-waterproof coat, which they will moult out in their third week when they are weaned. For the first few weeks of life the pups generally spend very little time in the water as, in addition to a non-waterproof coat, they are not good swimmers and do not have sufficient body fat to keep them warm in the sea. They will, however, be encouraged into the water by the mother from about a week old, where they will be given swimming lessons. Sometimes pups are born in caves, on beaches or rock ledges that are washed out at high tide, and have no choice but to swim twice a day. Most seem to cope with this, as long as it doesn't coincide with too much rough weather coming through.

Females will generally return to the same cove year after year and we will often recognise individual animals returning to a particular cove. There is some evidence to suggest they will return to the cove that they themselves were born on.

Once weaned, pups are abandoned by the mother, who heads back out to sea to start feeding again. She mates with the dominant bull in the cove before she goes; however, she has lost so much weight feeding the pup that she is in no condition to become pregnant. To overcome this, seals have a clever system of delayed implantation, whereby the fertilised egg will not implant in the womb for about 3 months, after which a hormone is released which will re-start the pregnancy. This allows the female time to head back out to sea and build up her fat reserves, creating a full, year-long

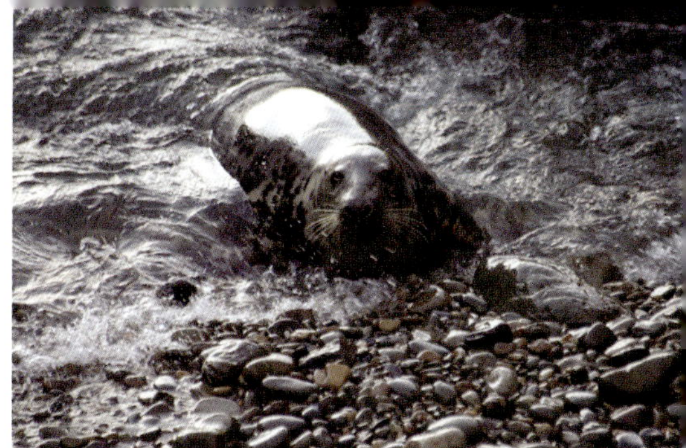

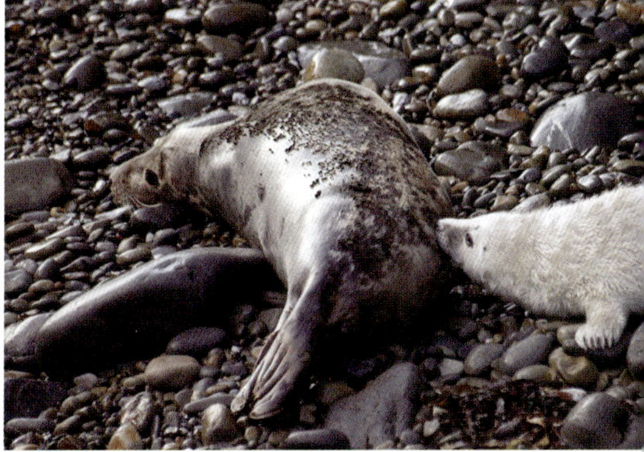

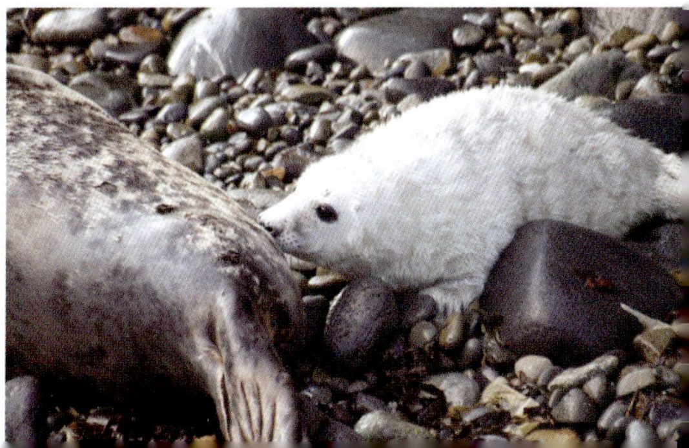

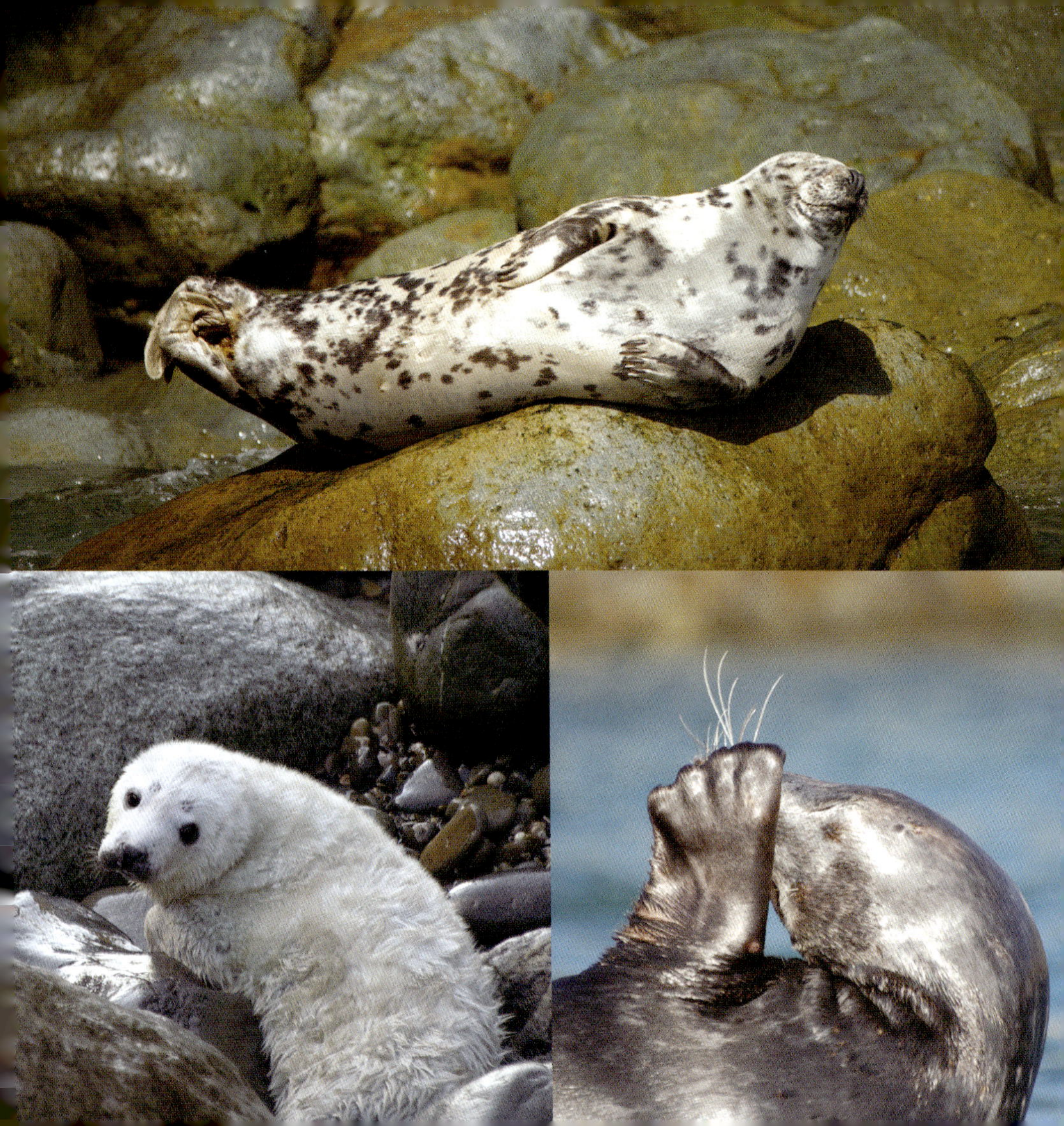

cycle, and ensuring that pupping occurs at the same time annually. Aside from the moult, it is the only time of year where all the seals come in to the island at the same time.

The pup, meanwhile, is left to fend for itself, and will eventually take to the water, where it will have to hone its swimming skills and learn to hunt without parental guidance. During this time it will survive off the fat reserves it has gained from its mother's milk. Weighing in at about 45kg, they are so fat when they are abandoned that they should have sufficient reserves to see them through this learning process. For the first few months pups are very vulnerable to bad weather and, as the breeding season coincides with the equinoxial gales, the weather is one of the main causes of fatalities amongst them. Grey seals disperse to feed, some staying close to their breeding sites whilst others travel long distances. Pembrokeshire seals have been recorded around Cornwall, France, Spain and Ireland. Radio tracking has shown them to travel 800 miles in 25 days.

The seals are intelligent animals and have become very accustomed to boats, frequently swimming very close to get a good look, and I often wonder who is watching who. Their natural curiosity and playfulness will occasionally lead to the youngsters playing with lobster pot buoys, wrapping themselves up in the rope and pulling the buoys under the water. Sadly, the interaction between seals and both marine and domestic plastics can end in disaster, and it is not unusual to see a seal with rope, netting or frisbees round their neck, which as the animal grows creates a constriction, cutting into their skin and blubber.

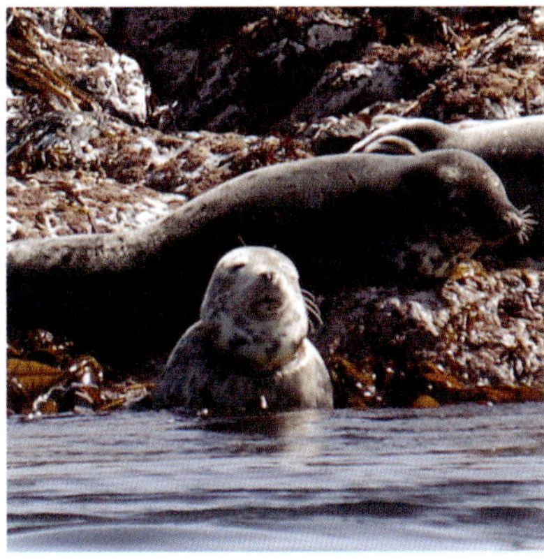

Perhaps one of the most entertaining places to watch Ramsey's seals is on Aber Maharan, on the south-east coast of the island, during the breeding season. This beach has locally been nicknamed 'the bachelor pad', as it tends to be the haunt of those bull seals, both young and old, that have not managed to secure themselves a breeding territory.

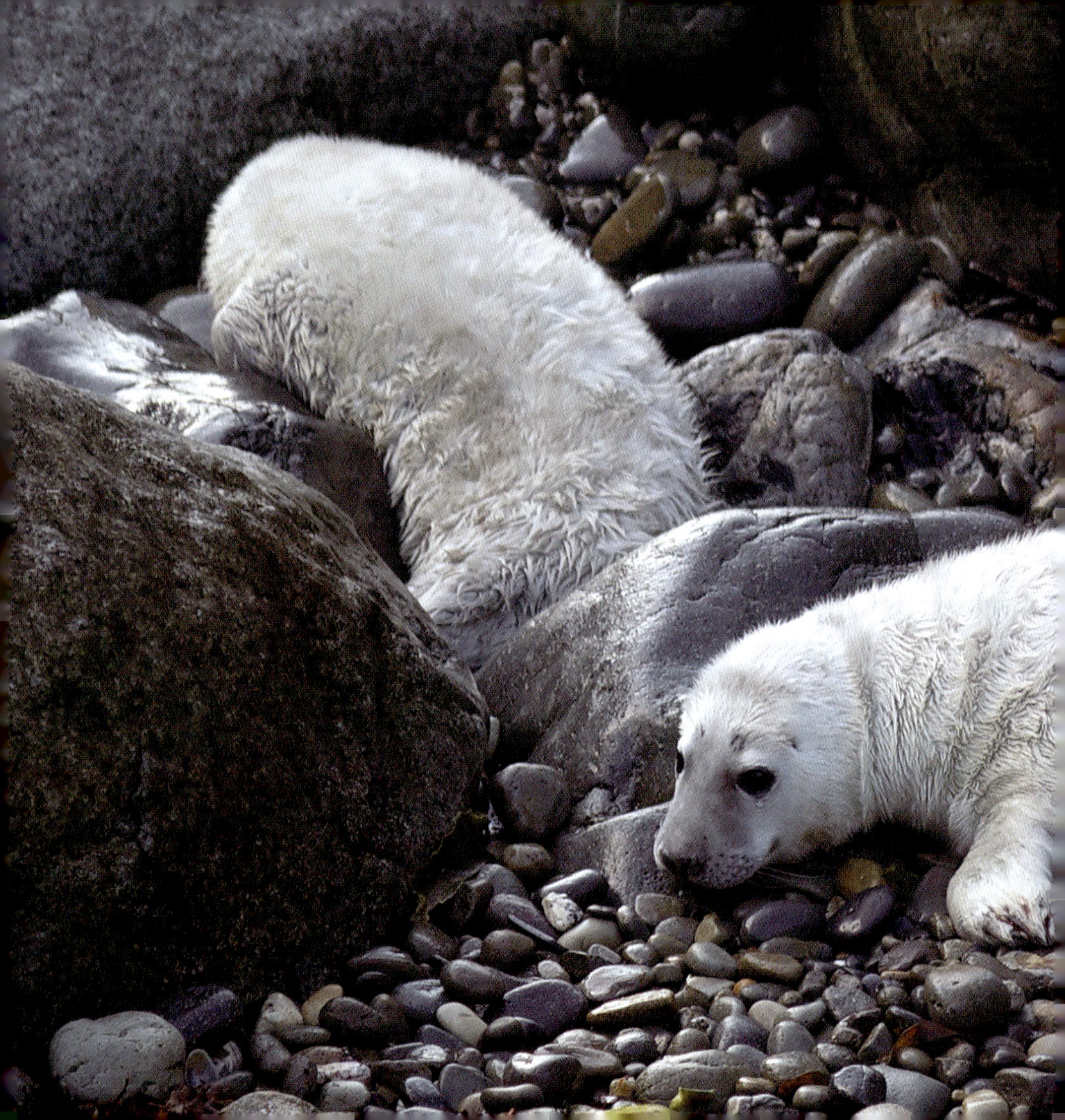

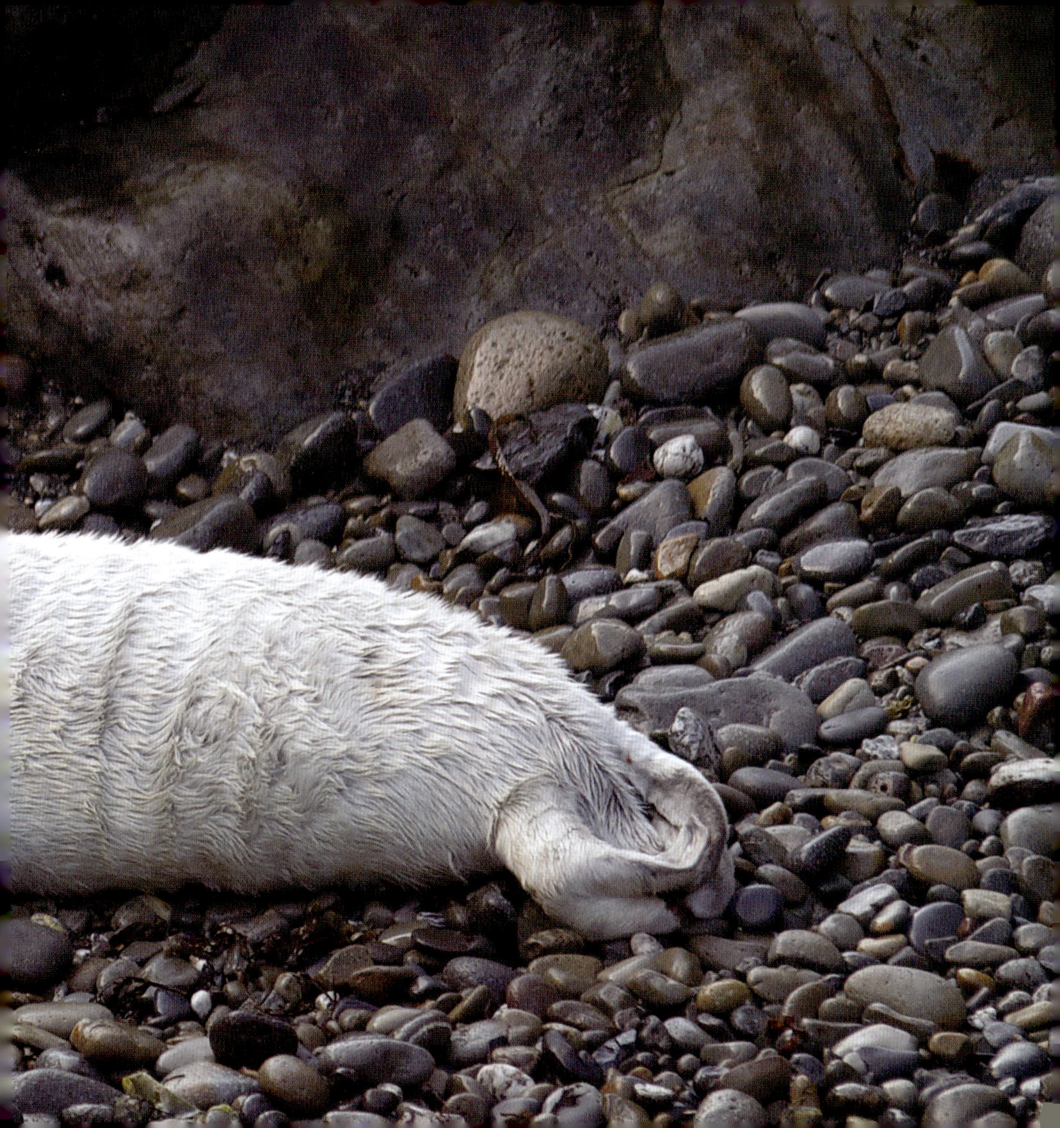

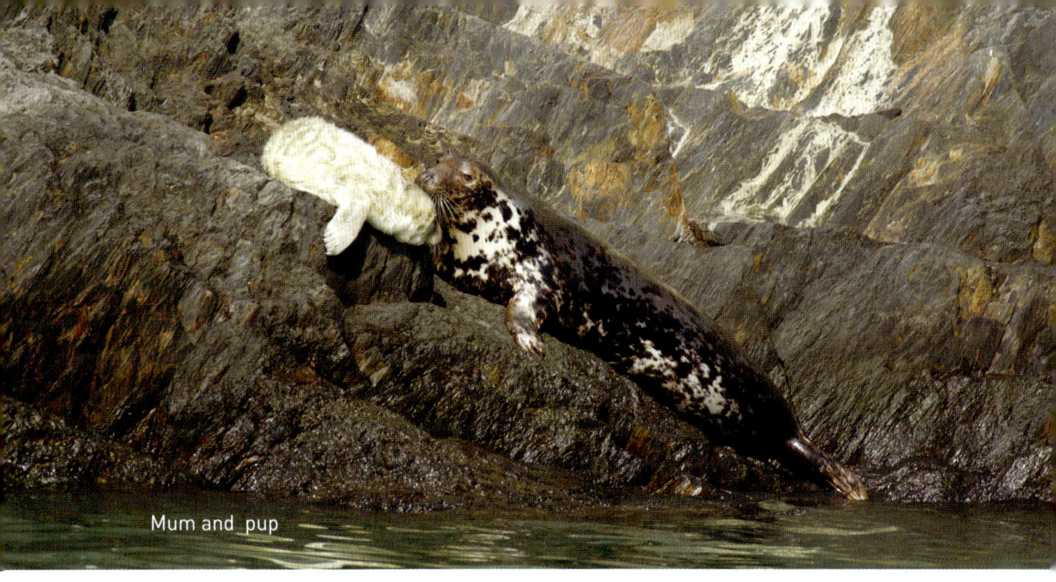



The beach covers at high water, so is unsuitable as a pupping beach, and as a result is the only beach on the island that does not have a resident bull seal during the pupping season. This also makes it the only beach the non-breeding males can hang out without being chased off. With no pups or territories to worry about, the seals here will spend most of their time either snoozing or playing and, despite it being a largely male preserve, some of the young females of below breeding age will also frequent the area for the occasional flirt, so it becomes something akin to the local pub in seal terms!

## Interesting facts

Atlantic greys can stay underwater for five to six minutes at a time, and spend 80% of the time below the surface. This is done by taking down large reserves of oxygen attached to chemicals in the blood and muscles. Their heartbeat also quadruples from 40 beats/min underwater to 120 beats/min on the surface to allow them to quickly take in new supplies of oxygen and get rid of waste carbon dioxide. It is not unusual for them to dive to 70m, and they have been known to reach depths of 300m and stay under for up to twenty minutes, though they usually feed in shallow waters.

They use their super sensitive whiskers to hunt rather than their eyesight, so much so that blind seals have been known to survive. Each whisker has a phenomenal 1500 nerve endings at its base. They do not need to haul out on land to sleep; they can rest in the water by switching on neutral buoyancy and floating with just their noses above the water so they can continue breathing. Seals are also conscious breathers, unlike humans.

## Predator and Prey – an unusual occurrence

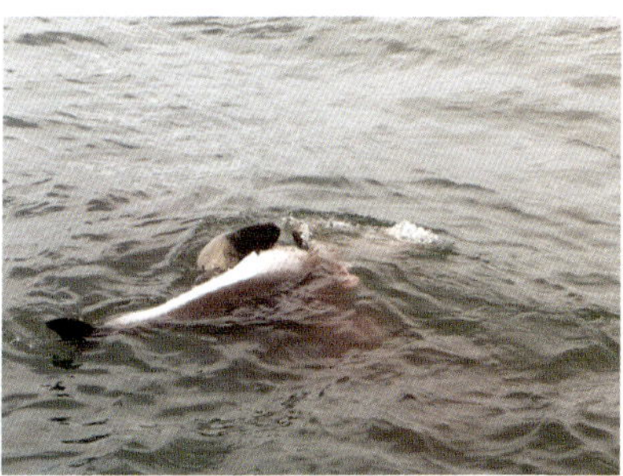

In 2014, we started seeing some very unusual behaviour being demonstrated by what looked to be a single individual bull seal, who was seen catching and eating a porpoise at the south end of Ramsey Sound. Having apparently found the new diet to his liking, he started to frequent the south end of the Sound on the ebb tide, when the porpoise are generally to be found feeding there, and was seen catching and eating porpoise on four separate occasions during June and July of that year. On each occasion he concentrated on eating only the blubber, muscle, stomach and intestines of the porpoise. Now, whilst Atlantic grey seals are very efficient hunters and will eat a wide variety of prey species, including fish, crustaceans, molluscs and cephalopods, even seabirds on occasion, prior to this there had been no recorded sightings of them predating on porpoises in the UK. This despite the fact that they regularly co-occur in our waters, and there is evidence to support that such predation has occurred in Europe. As both the harbour porpoise and the Atlantic grey seal are nationally and internationally protected species, it raises an interesting question in conservation management: when one protected species starts predating on another one! It is possible that it was behaviour that had only been learned by one individual, as on each occasion it was an adult bull seal whose markings would suggest it was the same animal each time, rather than being indicative of a general change in behaviour of the local population. It was such an unusual occurrence that Tom Stringell, a senior marine mammal ecologist for NRW, documented it in a paper.

# Common Dolphin

Common dolphin, spotted on the majority of the offshore trips, are always a delight as they are real crowd pleasers. They will often make a beeline for the boat if they spot us from a distance, flying right out of the water with incredible speed and, if in the mood, will bow ride and play around the boat. As they ride the bow or stern wave or just escort us at the side of the boat, often so close you could reach out and touch them, it is hard not to believe that they do this just for fun. Their grace and agility is mesmerising to watch, like stepping briefly into another world. It is very much on their terms as, if they don't want to play, they can lose us in the blink of an eye, which, as we are visitors in their world, is just how it should be. The reaction of people who are seeing them for the first time is magical, and often results in squeals of delight from young and old alike.

The common dolphin is a pelagic species and as such they are not resident in our waters, despite being frequent visitors, and we know they breed here as we often pick up with groups of females with young. On occasions we have seen them with tiny calves whose dorsal fins are still soft and floppy from when they were curled up in the womb, an indication they may be merely hours old. Another distinguishing feature of the calves, apart from their size, are the pale stripes running vertically around their bodies. These are the foetal folds also resulting from being in the womb. It can take them up to 3 months to completely lose these.

We often pick up with large pods of common dolphins, and very occasionally we are privileged enough to stumble upon what have been called 'super pods', where hundreds of dolphins congregate together and there are dolphins literally as far as the eye can see. Some dolphins may have markings that make them easy to identify, the most obvious being damage to the dorsal fin, and this has enabled us to identify individual animals frequenting our waters in subsequent years. One particularly identifiable dolphin we nicknamed 'Beaky' because of its malformed beak, where the upper part of the beak had grown away from the jaw. This dolphin was spotted in Cornwall a couple of weeks before we saw him in our waters in 2013. Sometimes we find them 'logging' on the surface of the water, which is how cetaceans sleep, floating on the surface, although research suggests they only switch off one side of their brain at a time when they sleep. This is necessary as, like many marine mammals but unlike humans, they have to make a conscious effort to breathe.

Whilst there is a lot we still don't know about dolphins, what we do know suggests they are extremely intelligent, sentient beings. They live in a world of

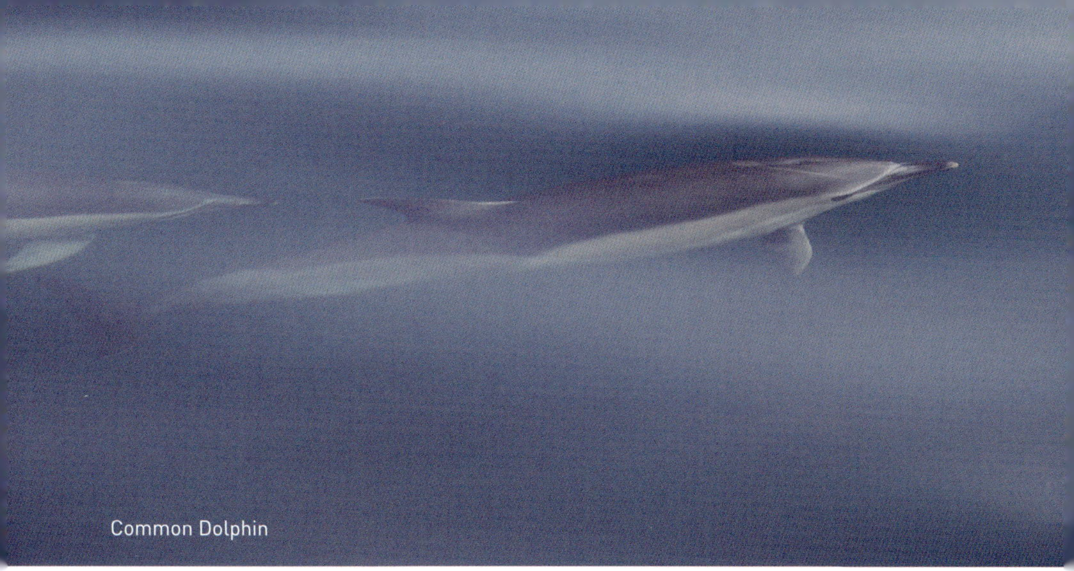

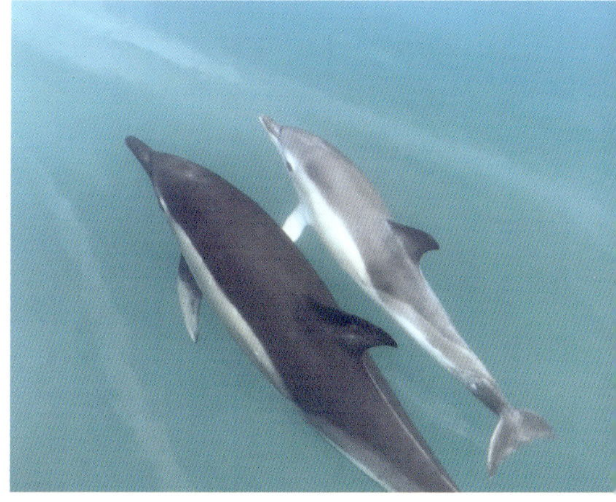

Common Dolphin

sound, using echo location to navigate and find their prey. Sending out a series of clicks and reading the echoes that bounce back, they also use a complex communication system which takes the form of whistles and squeals, which we often hear from the boat when they are bow riding. This enables them to communicate with other individuals in the pod. Some research suggests that they actually have 'names' for each other in the form of a specific whistle. They use this system, coupled with their strong social structure, in order to hunt. This is a team effort and very effective, as they all work together to herd the fish before

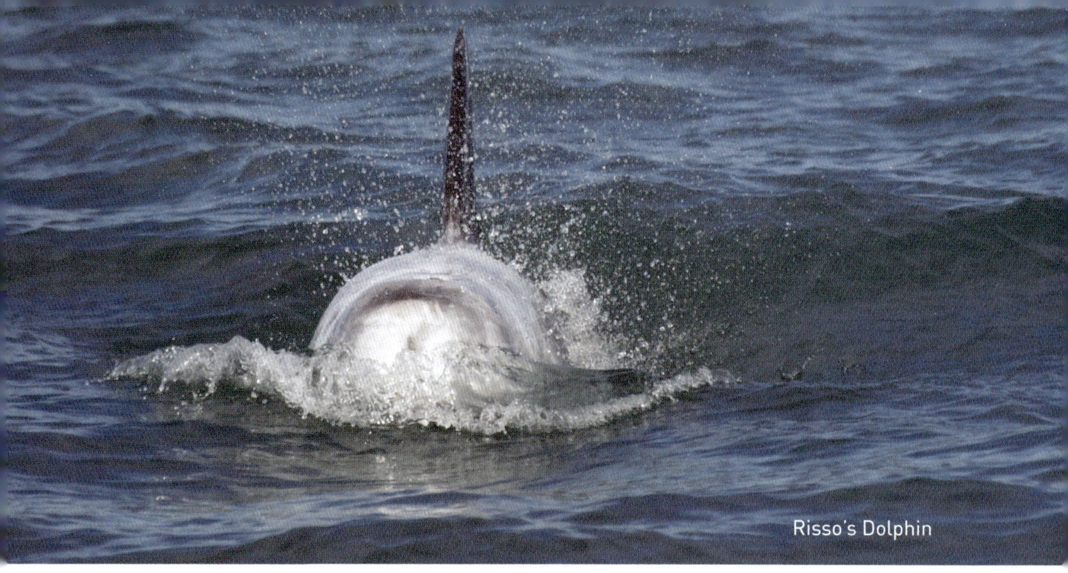

Risso's Dolphin

taking it in turns to dart in and grab a mouthful. They have also been seen emitting a wall of bubbles that serves to confuse the fish.

## Risso's Dolphin

Risso's Dolphin – *Griseus grampus* or 'big grey fish'.

Other species we see regularly in our waters are the somewhat more elusive Risso's dolphins. When I first started offshore trips in search of cetaceans in 2003, we would only see occasional sightings of Risso's dolphins and often only one or two individuals. Over the last few years we have seen a marked increase in the number and frequency of these animals, often seeing pods of up to 30 of them, and regular sightings of young calves. We don't know the reason for this; it could be to do with an abundance of food sources in our area, or a decline in other areas where they have previously hunted.

Relatively little is known about this species. They are considerably larger than the common dolphin, growing to a maximum 3.8m in length. Risso's are thought to mature at thirteen years of age, but we still don't know how long they live. Adults often appear white in colour and this is due to scarring on their bodies, a result of social interaction with each other and from the sharp beaks of the squid on which they feed. They are much shyer than the common dolphin and rarely interact with the boat. Only very occasionally will they bow ride, but we often see them breaching and spy hopping and putting on amazing aerial displays for what seems, again, to be purely for the joy of it, certainly to the outsider. They tend to prefer deeper offshore waters where they will feed almost exclusively on squid, and it is largely due to this that so little is known about them.

Larger cetaceans such as the rorqual whales (fin, minke and sei) and even orca are much more occasional sightings, and are definitely a question of being in the right place at the right time and looking in the right direction! On a couple of occasions I have seen these huge creatures breaching, a sight so spectacular and unexpected that the first time I saw it, both myself and my crew, who happened to be looking in the right direction, were rendered speechless, or at least incoherent when it came to pointing it out to our passengers. That is one of the things that makes working in this environment so special, that even after

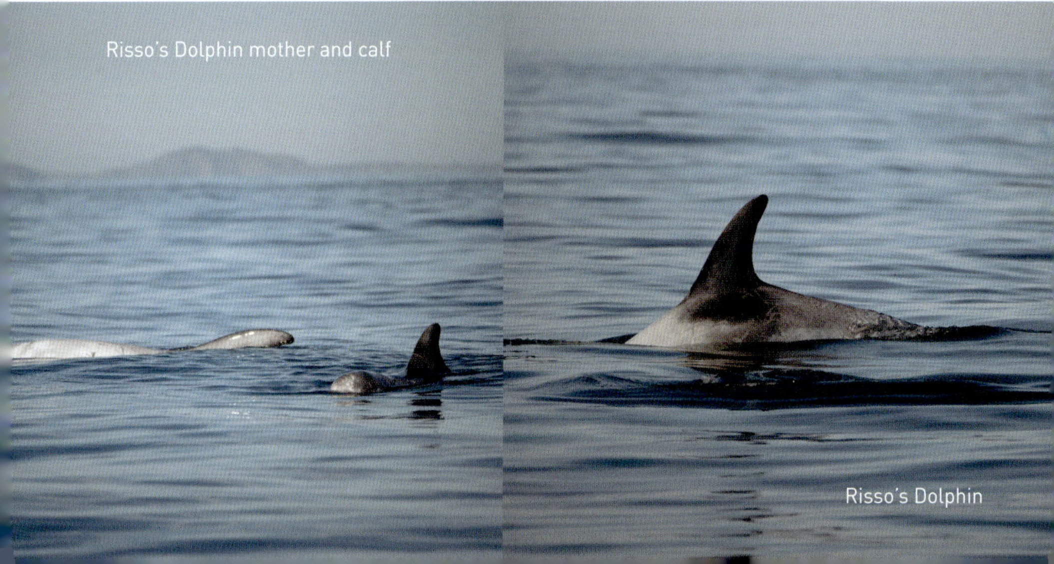

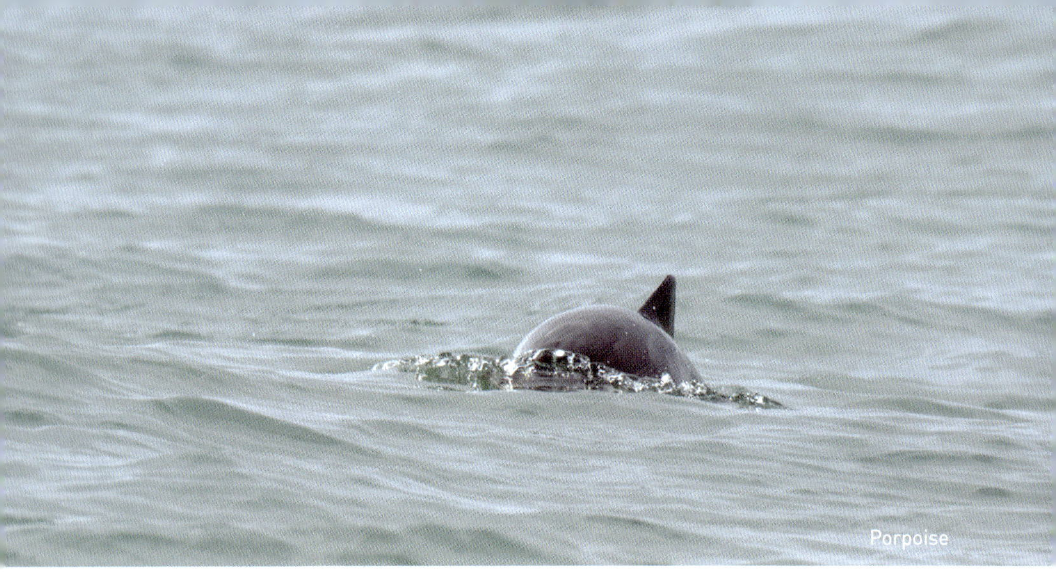



years on the water it still has the ability to deliver small moments of magic and a reminder that we live in a beautiful world.

## Porpoise

Another frequent sighting in the waters of the Sound are the resident pods of harbour porpoise. A small cousin of the dolphin, these are the UK's smallest cetaceans, growing to a maximum 1.8m in length. They are one of only six species of porpoise in the world. They are tidal feeders, and so conditions around Pembrokeshire are ideal foraging ground for them. They can typically be found feeding at the southern end of Ramsey Sound on an ebb tide. Here, the underwater topography and strong south-going tide combine to create ideal feeding conditions. As the tide hits a sharp rise in the seabed, the resultant upwelling brings nutrients to the surface, attracting fish. This, in turn, attracts the larger predators further up the food chain, such as porpoise and gannets, which are often to be found co-feeding with the porpoise.

The porpoise are relatively shy cetaceans and show no interest in the boats at all. They are also not particularly long-lived, ordinarily reaching a maximum twelve to fifteen years of age, though they have been known to reach twenty three.

They differ from dolphins in a number of ways; as well as being smaller, one of the most obvious differences is their blunt, rounded heads, without the beak that is common to most dolphin species. Another difference is that dolphins have cone shaped teeth, whereas those of the porpoise are flat and spade shaped, though this is obviously not easily identifiable unless looking in their mouths.

Porpoise vocalise at a higher frequency than dolphins so, unlike their cousins, we can't hear them. Their behaviour is also unlike that of the dolphin, and you will very rarely see porpoise showing the same sort of exuberant behaviour that is common with dolphins, such as breaching, spyhopping and tail slapping, and their occasional sudden bursts of speed are usually associated with chasing fish. They are relatively solitary, and a pod can be as few as two or three animals, rarely more than eight, although they will congregate in much larger numbers when there is an abundant food source. We occasionally see up to thirty feeding in the Sound, though smaller numbers are more common. We also don't see them working together to herd fish in the same way dolphins do, and consequently they will spend most of their time hunting, showing little inclination for play and

social interaction. A recent paper reports they will forage nearly continuously day and night and attempt to catch up to 550 small fish every hour, with a 90% success rate. This has led to them being referred to as 'aquatic shrews'.

Females mature at three or four years old, gestation takes 10-11 months and they will feed the calf for 8-12 months. As they give birth to a calf every one or two years, they can be pregnant and lactating at the same time. In our waters they will often disappear late May to early June for a couple of weeks, when they seem to go further offshore, possibly where the tidal flows are less ferocious, to give birth to their young. The young calves, when they first appear with mum, are tiny and often seem to find swimming in the strong tides quite hard work, having to give an extra kick of their tail to get their blowholes clear of the surface. Initially mum and calf will swim in unison, coming up to breathe together, until the calf gains in strength and confidence and becomes a bit more independent. They are locally nicknamed the 'puffing pig', due to the distinctive noise they make as they exhale when they surface.

## Jellyfish

During the summer months, as the Gulf Stream sweeps close to our coastline, the water temperature rises and a large

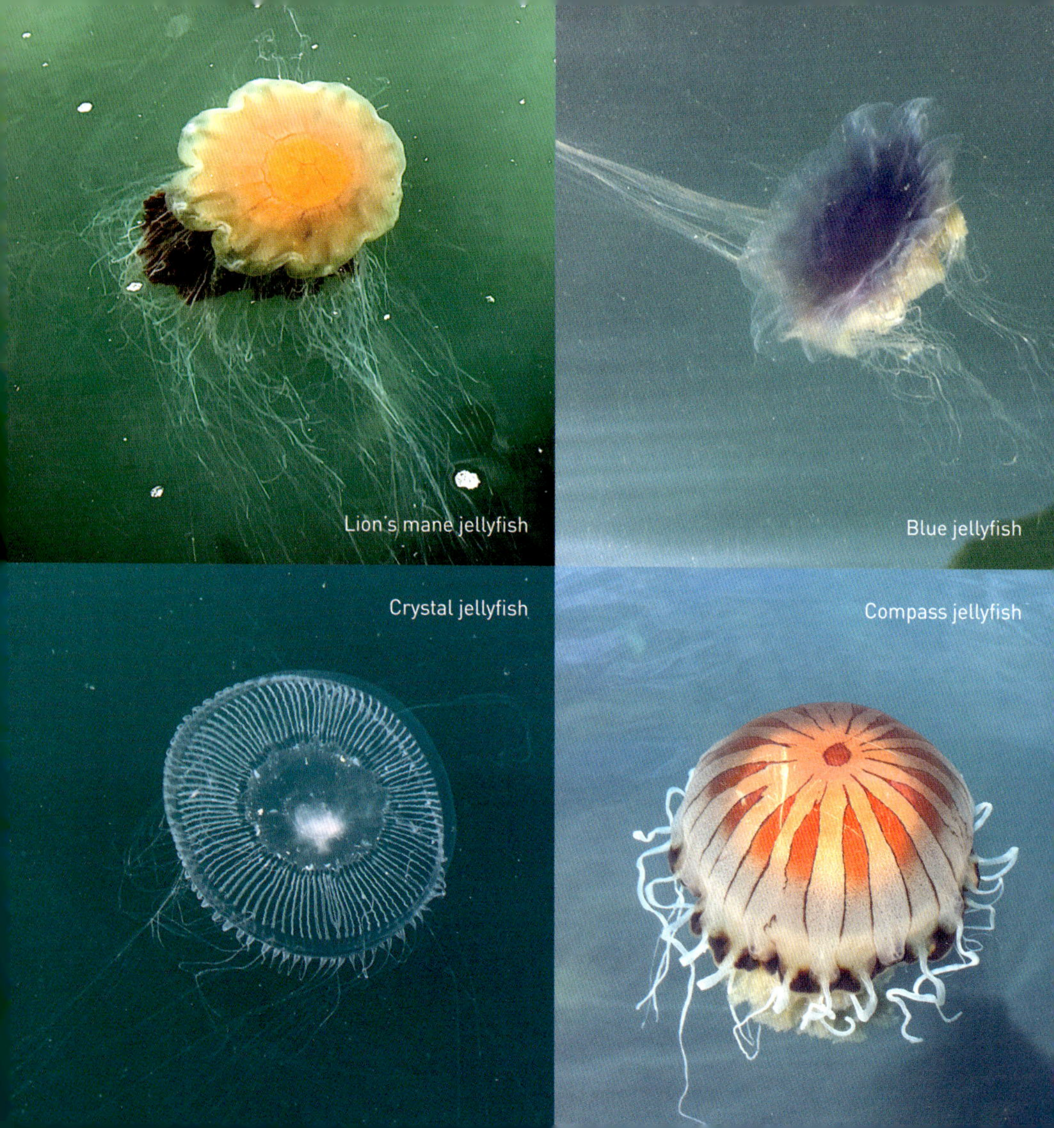

Lion's mane jellyfish
Blue jellyfish
Crystal jellyfish
Compass jellyfish

variety of jellyfish can be found in the waters off the Pembrokeshire coast. Which species we see more of will vary from year to year, and can be anything from the harmless comb jellyfish and sea gooseberries to the rather more ominous looking lion's mane jellyfish. The latter have tentacles that can grow to a phenomenal 120ft long, and have as many as 1,200 tentacles, which emanate from them in delicate, filament-like strands. They are a cold water jellyfish, often found as far north as the Arctic, and feed on zooplankton, small fish, shrimp and other jellies.

Compass jellyfish are also frequent visitors, so named because the markings on the top of the bell are thought to resemble that of a compass rose, not, as we once convinced a new crew member, because they always point north! One of the most beautiful jellyfish, in my opinion, are the sea gooseberries or combs. These are small jellyfish that are almost completely transparent, but due to eight rows of hair-like cilia running down their bodies, which they use to propel themselves and which refract the light, they produce a rainbow effect of colours which looks like bioluminescence. They are, in fact, not jellyfish at all but belong to a different family called ctenophore. We also have moon jellyfish, blue jellyfish, and occasionally By-the-Wind sailors, which tend to turn up in large swarms

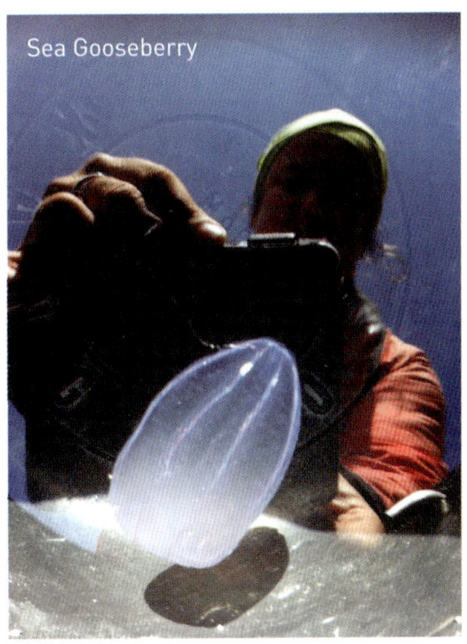


when we have the wind blowing from a certain direction for a prolonged period of time, as the top part of them acts like a sail allowing them to be propelled by the wind. These are actually related to the Portuguese man o' war, which, whilst uncommon, is also occasionally seen in our waters, and definitely to be avoided. I am often asked which jellyfish sting and the answer is all of them, as that is how they catch their prey. Many of them have such a mild sting you wouldn't feel it, but if they are brightly coloured or have long tentacles it is especially worth giving

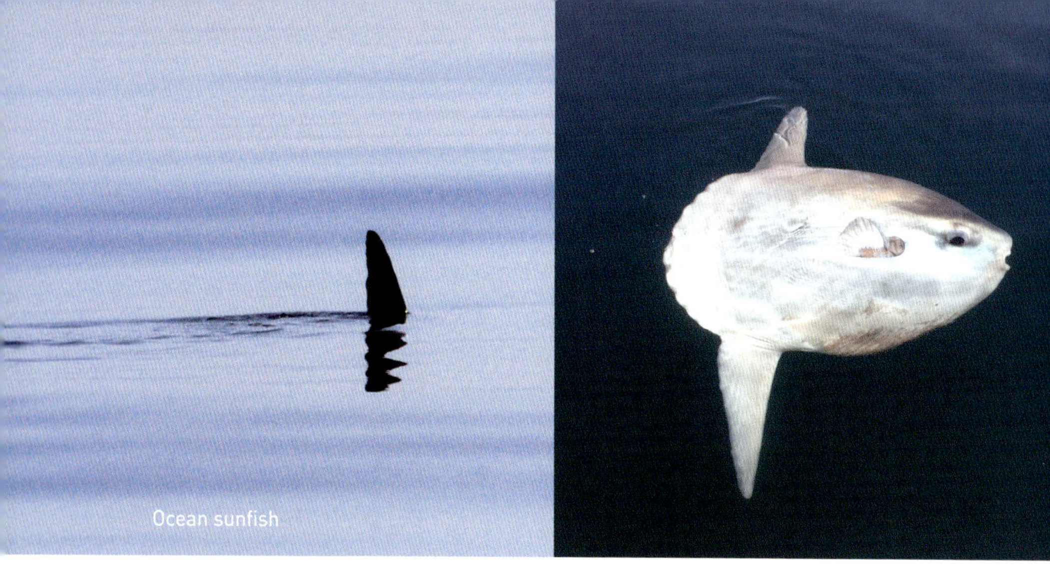
Ocean sunfish

them a wide berth. The largest jellyfish in terms of bell size that we see regularly is the barrel jellyfish, a particular favourite of leatherback turtles which are attracted to our waters by their presence.

## Ocean sunfish

Perhaps one of the more unusual sea creatures to feed on the jellyfish is the Mola Mola, or sunfish. They are the heaviest bony fish in the world, with an average weight of 1 tonne and are 1.8m in length, although the largest recorded one weighed in at 2235kg, and just over 3m in length. They are very strange looking fish, being almost round with a fin top and bottom, and are often to be seen on or near the surface with their upper fin flapping clumsily above the water, making them easy to spot. This bizarre basking behaviour is thought to be an attempt to warm up in the surface layer of water after deep dives. Generally we only see small ones in the waters off Pembrokeshire; the largest I have seen was approximately 1.5m. Our waters are thought to be too cold for them and they often won't survive this far north. They are host to as many as 40 different types of parasite, and they have to recruit the help of small fish to rid themselves of these.

## Goose Barnacles

We often find goose barnacles, *Lepas anatifera*, attached by their stalk to flotsam floating on the water's surface. This can be anything from a piece of driftwood to a fridge and, if it has lots of these marine crustaceans attached to it, it is a sure sign that it has spent several months floating around at sea. They are most common in tropical and subtropical waters, but because of their tendency to attach themselves to floating objects as well as rocks they are sometimes found in colder waters as well. They are hermaphrodite and their eggs hatch into free-swimming larvae, which will then become part of the zooplankton. They will attach themselves to an object in the sea where they will continue to grow, and at one time they were common on the hulls of ships. Their name comes from the bizarre medieval belief that this is how Canada geese started off in life; growing on the planks of ships where they would then gain feathers and emerge to fly off as geese. This is thought to have come about because variously the shell is supposed to resemble the head of a Canada goose and/or the brown feeding tentacles, or cirri, were thought to resemble the down of an unhatched gosling. In addition,

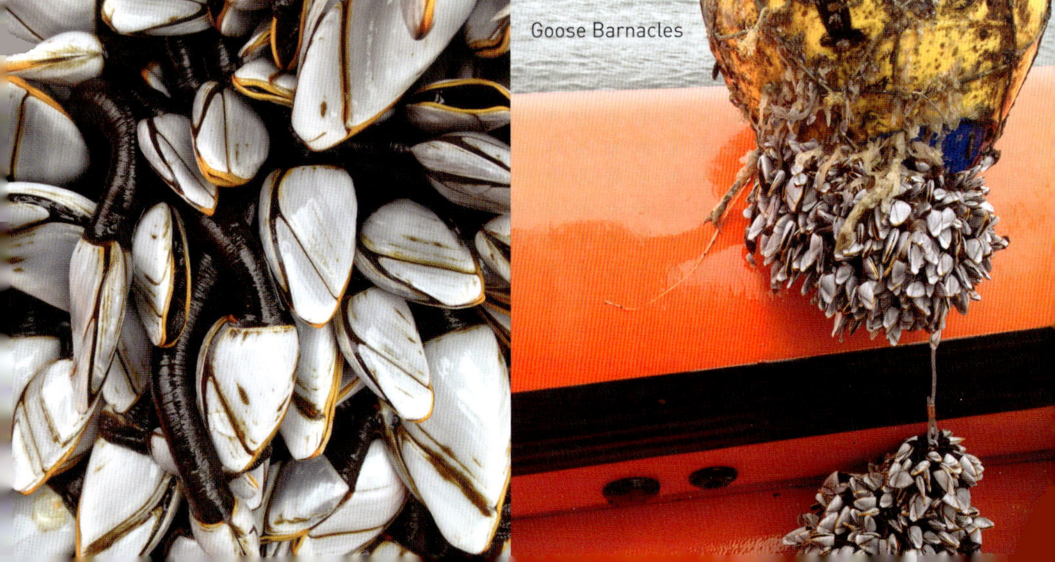

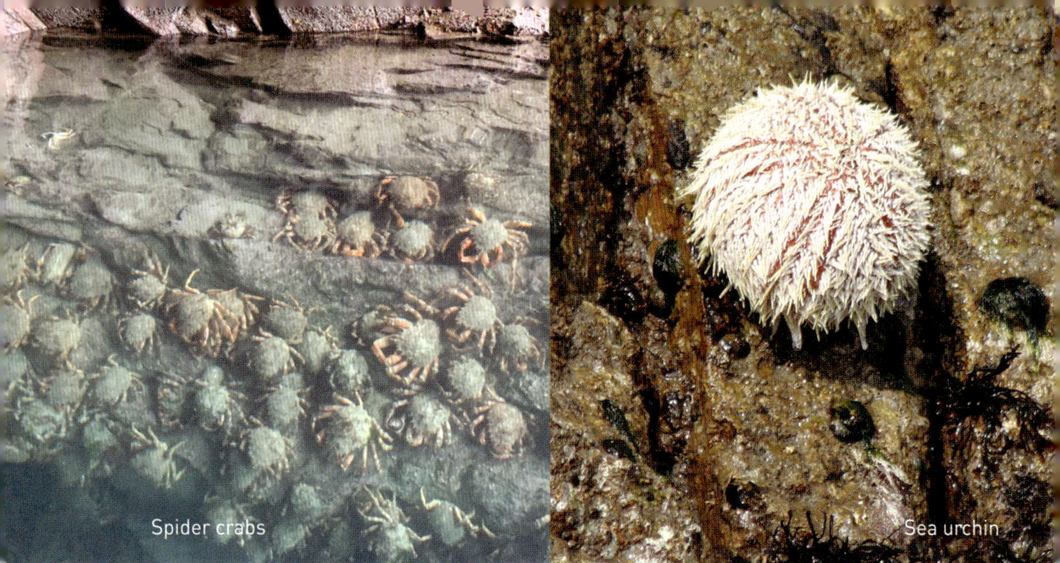



Canada goose eggs and nests had never been seen, as they rarely nest in Britain. Often identified on driftwood, Giraldus Cambrensis in his *Topographia Hiberniae* made the dubious assumption that they were attached to the branches before they fell into the water. This curious belief had an added advantage that, as barnacle geese were not considered to be flesh or 'born of flesh', they could be eaten on Fridays and during Lent when Christians were forbidden to eat meat.

## Other underwater sightings

During the summer months, spider crabs will often frequent caves around the island, as they search for protected spots to breed and to shed their shells in order to grow. The cave by Ogof Capel, known as Ogof Juniper, will frequently have hundreds of them on the seabed and cave walls and, not being very deep, they are often visible from the boat.

Because of the very large tidal range in the area, at low water on particularly big spring tides all sorts of interesting flora and fauna can be spotted, such as cold-water sea sponges and even the occasional sea urchin.

## Occupational hazards

Over the years, being far too soft-hearted for my own good has led me to rescue a number of the islands' inhabitants, among them several birds of prey, a young gannet on the water tangled in fishing line, a guillemot chick that used my sofa for flying practices, and a seal pup that, having quite clearly been abandoned at only a few days old, tried to get into my boat.

The latter turned into something of a mission, as I left it for a couple of hours in the hope that Mum might turn up. By the time it was obvious that she was not around, the pup had managed to get itself onto one of the rocks of the Bitches. Whilst temporarily safe, with deteriorating weather conditions and a rising tide its chances of survival without intervention were slim to none. Unable to do the sensible thing, I fetched our small inflatable dinghy, picked up Greg and Lisa from the island for assistance and we set off on our rescue mission. This involved Greg and Lisa landing on the Bitches from the dinghy whilst I held station just off the rocks in the rhib. Armed with a towel and heavy-duty gloves, Greg wrestled the uncooperative seal pup into the dinghy and they then rowed back out, where we transferred the seal to the rhib. Seal pups may look cute and cuddly, but they are anything but if you have to handle them and are quite likely to bite if given the

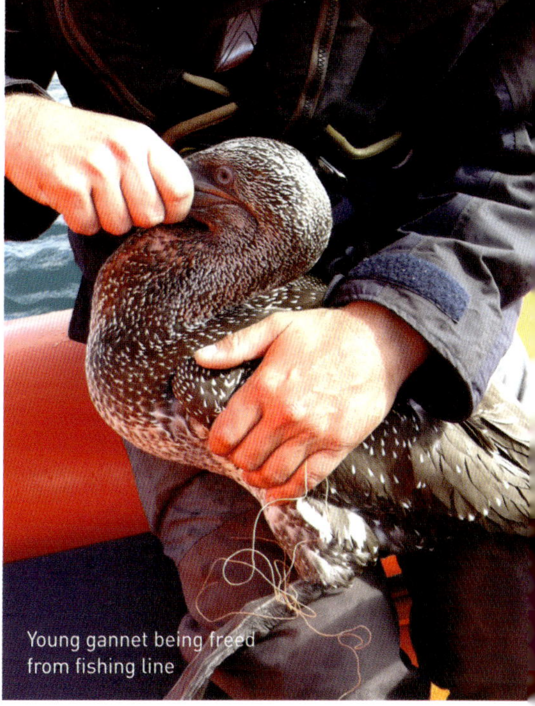

Young gannet being freed from fishing line

opportunity. A seal bite, incidentally, is not to be taken lightly, as they have bacteria in their mouths which doesn't respond to any antibiotics and bites often don't heal.

This particular individual was taken to the seal rescue centre in Milford and, a few weeks later when he was re-released, we found out he was particularly unusual in that when he moulted out he was jet black, and because of this he even made it into the papers.

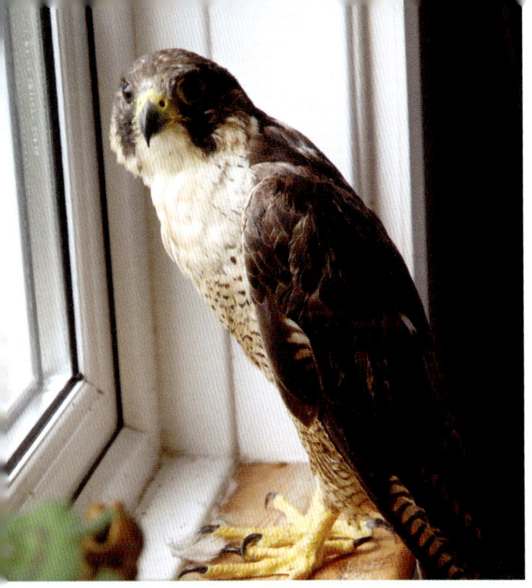

## Hissy's rescue

One of my more recent rescues ended up taking far more of my time and patience than I bargained for. I personally have something of a soft spot for peregrines, particularly after, a few years ago, fate landed one in the water in front of my boat, just off the north end of Ramsey. I had just pointed her out to my passengers as she flew across the bay, but as we watched I could see something wasn't quite right. She flew lower and lower, until eventually she ditched in the water. I scooped her out from where she was drowning, as peregrines don't swim, and little did I realise that this act would result in me committing to eight months of time, patience and a lengthy foray into the world of falconry. This is to say nothing of the accompanying blood, sweat and tears (mostly mine) as I attempted to rehabilitate a wild falcon to the point where she could be released.

When I first took her home she was in a cardboard box. I had gone to the hardware store to get some gauntlets to save my fingers whilst feeding her, and on arriving home I opened the door to find she had eaten her way out of the box and was now somewhere in the house! Looking round a little nervously I discovered her sat on the kitchen windowsill, looking out, having cleared the contents of the windowsill including pot plants to the floor.

Looking back, I think it was probably at this point that she piqued my interest and became a project rather than just another casualty to pass on to someone more skilled than I. I was very fortunate to have the help of a friend and falconer, Rob Davies, who introduced me to some of the basics of falconry. I learnt a lot about a species that has always inspired awe in me and I learnt a lot about a wild thing. I called her Hissy because initially she would show her displeasure by hissing at me. As I spent time with her, eventually training her to fly to the fist as a necessary part of her rehabilitation, she started to tolerate me and grew to trust me. She would even show her impatience

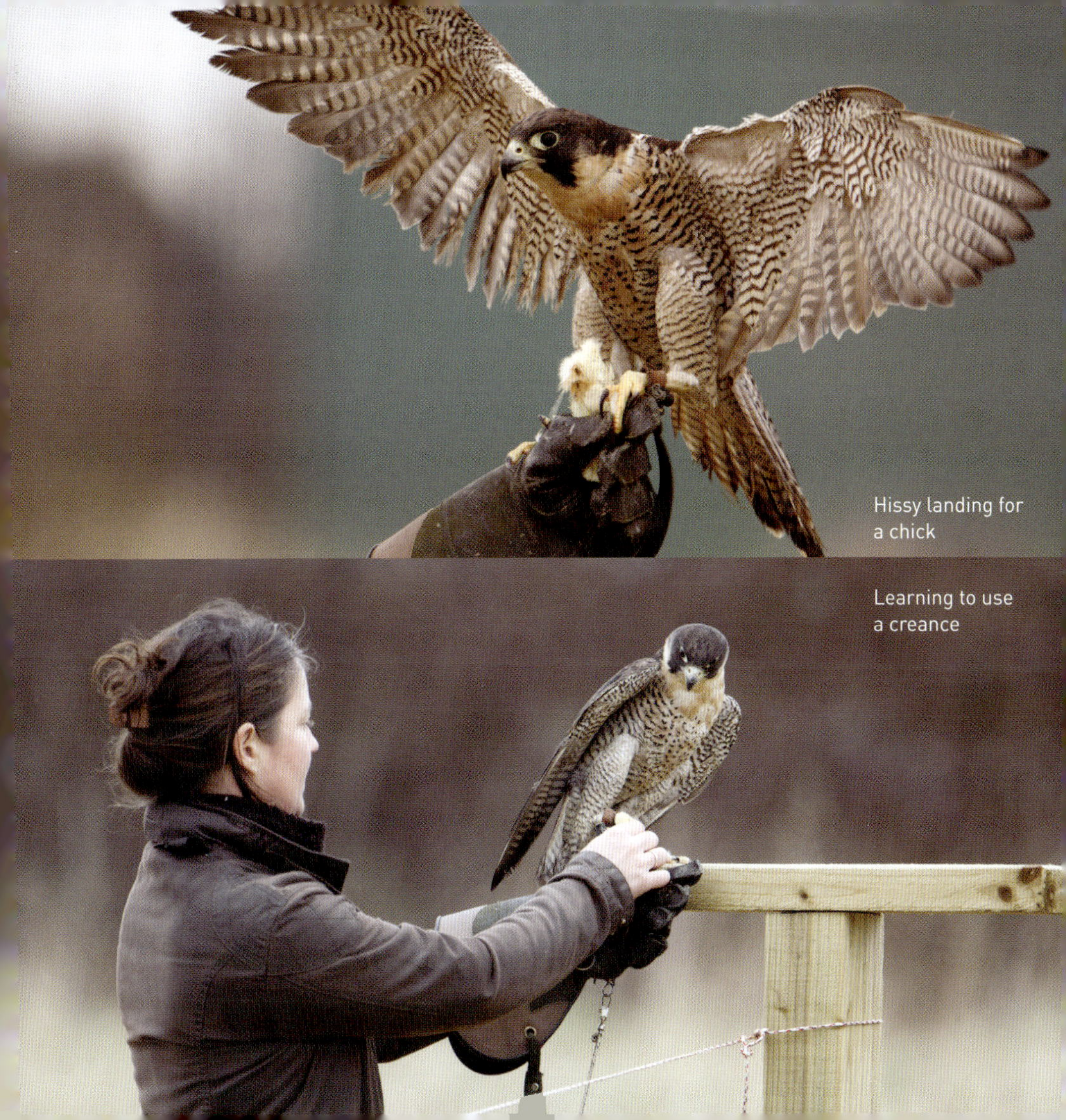
Hissy landing for
a chick

Learning to use
a creance

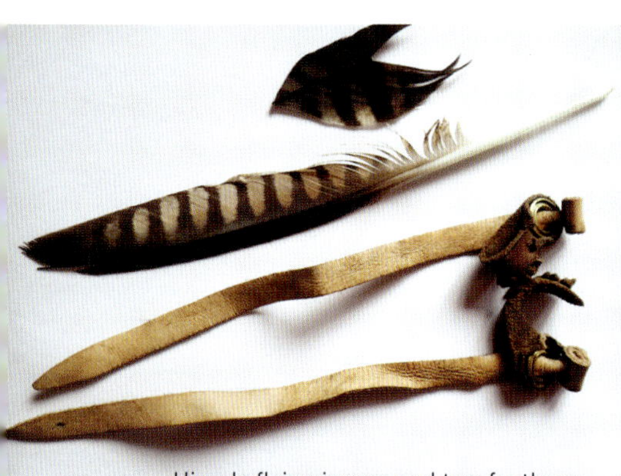

Hissy's flying jesses and two feathers

of my inability to tie falconry knots one handed as she sat on my other fist by 'affectionately' running her beak through my hair, or she would 'gently' peck my head if I was being particularly clumsy and taking too long to give her what she wanted. Despite the bond that slowly grew between us as we both learned to relax in each other's company, she never totally lost her wildness, and this was no bad thing as it had never been my intention to tame her. When the day came to finally let her go, back to where she belonged, I gave her a whole pigeon to see her through the next few days. I put her on the canon in the field where I had been flying her, cut her jesses off and then, having given her her freedom, I retreated to the hedge to observe from a distance. As I sat

and watched in the gathering dusk I was investigated by a young fox whilst Hissy made short work of her pigeon, oblivious to both of us. She then looked around and, without so much as a backward glance, took off and headed straight for the cliffs, and possibly Ramsey. All I was left with were her jesses, a couple of broken feathers, my memories, and the knowledge that I had given a wild thing a second chance.

If you want to know more of the trials and tribulations of training a wild peregrine, Hissy's story is told in another book, *Queen of the Sky* by Jackie Morris. It is worth pointing out that peregrines are a protected species and you can't just pick one up and take it home to rehabilitate. I had to apply for a license from DEFRA in order to be able to do what I did, and then apply for an extension as, inevitably, it took longer than originally planned.

I think one of the most surprising encounters I have had on the water was the day I found a snake on my boat. As you might imagine, given that the boats are moored on swinging moorings at St Justinians, nowhere near the land, this came as something of a shock! It was curled up, perfectly camouflaged on a coil of rope, until I disturbed it. I was driving in to the slip at the start of the day when I nudged the rope with my foot, only to have an angry snake pop its head

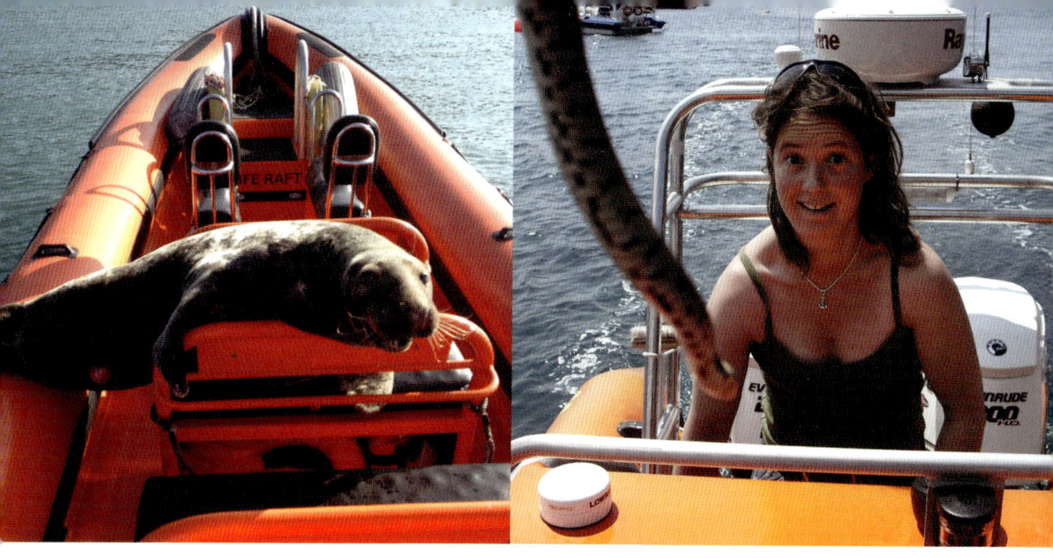

up, ready to strike. I have to confess to stepping sharply away from the helm until I persuaded my crew, Dick Wells, to come and deal with it. How it got there remains a mystery, but I can only surmise that maybe a buzzard dropped it there by accident. This particular stowaway was also put ashore unharmed, if a little disgruntled.

When it comes to evicting grumpy squatters however, the seals win hands down. Over the years there have a been a few seals at St Justinians that have taken to sleeping in the dinghies whilst we are at sea working. They prefer the inflatable dinghies, as these offer a more comfortable bed, and ignore the barricades of fuel cans and oars put there to try and dissuade them. On one occasion, a seal even managed to sink one of the dinghies. And why not? After all, it beats getting washed off rocks whilst caught snoozing on a rising tide. It is not unheard of for them to get into the rhib itself, and one year we had to serve eviction notices before stepping on the boat! The last individual I had to evict was particularly recalcitrant, taking up the entire dinghy. Having found himself a comfy spot wedged underneath the seat, he was not going to give it up without a fight. I tried pushing him out with a broom, tipping him out and banging on the side of the dinghy, all of which he

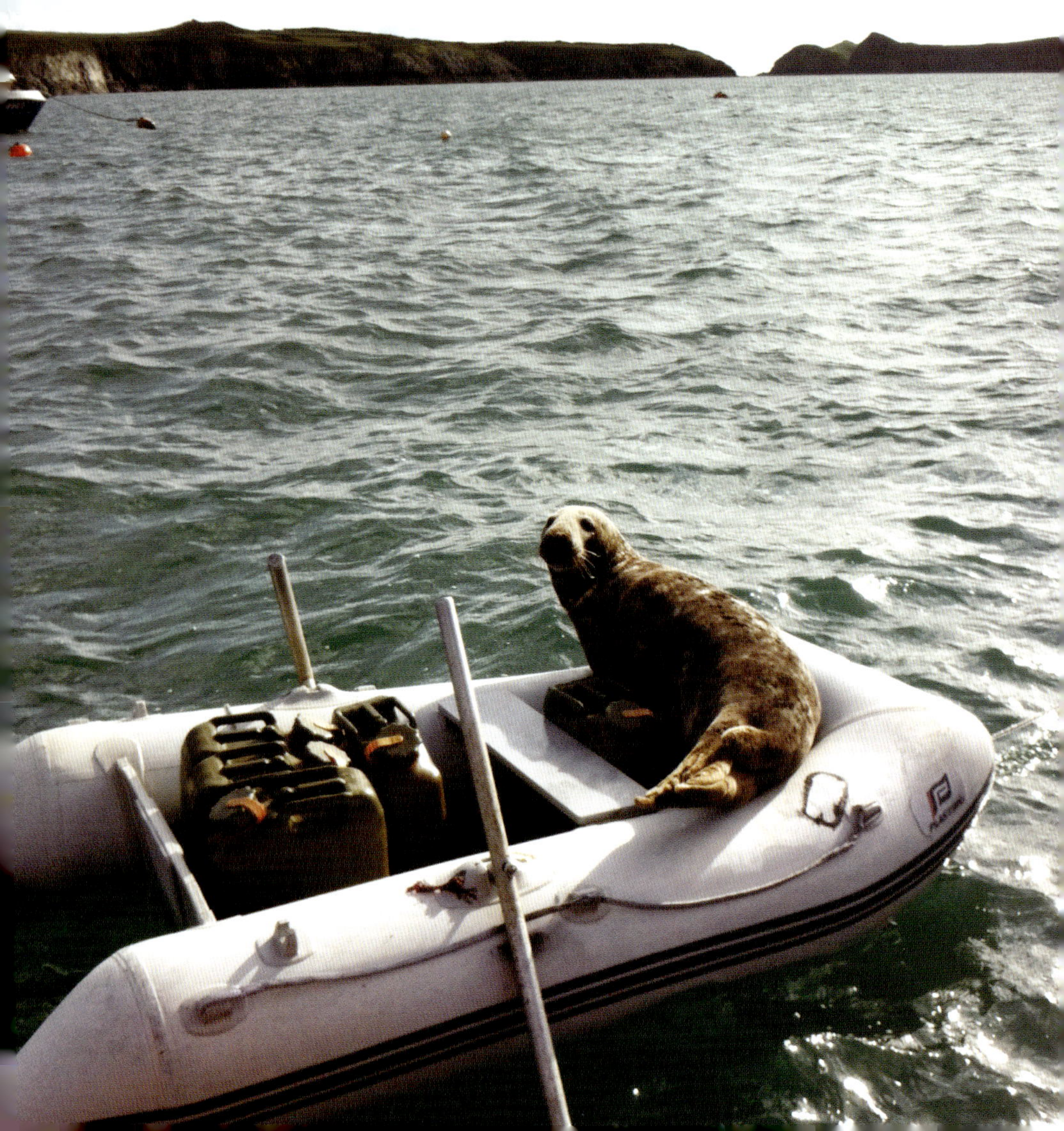

largely ignored, giving the occasional growl and a few half-hearted attempts to bite me. Now, this dinghy was my only transport home, so in the end I had to resort to throwing a bucket of water over his head, at which point he disembarked with disgust, only to get straight into the RNLI's launching boat. The commute to and from work can get a little crowded at times.

I think it's safe to say one never knows what the day will hold in store when working the waters off the coast of Pembrokeshire, and for me this is certainly part of its charm. I would like to end my sojourn around these islands with a quote that was told to a friend by another local, and it sums up beautifully the sense of place and belonging that this world on the water evokes for me.

'I think that you can know a lot of places, or you can know some places in great detail. I think there is a lot of satisfaction to be had, say, there's a half-mile stretch of coast near here and we know all of the rocky coves, and every rock you could jump off, and every rock that you could fish from, and where the caves are and where the seals live... Because you have to be somewhere and know it in great detail to have that sort of intimacy with it. In a sense for me that's as rich an experience as going to lots of far-flung places that you'll only go to once.' – Kate Meopham

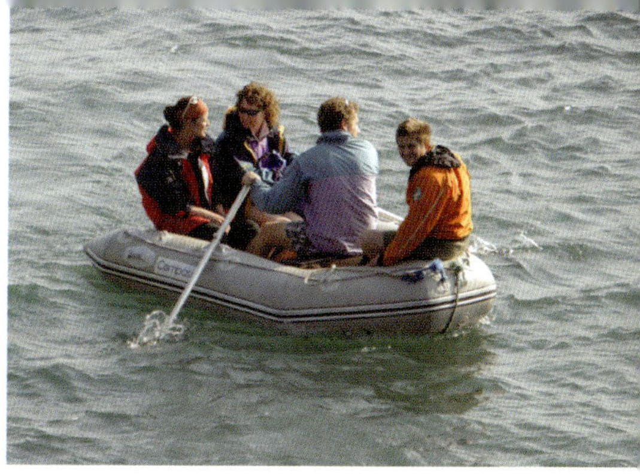

It is this that has ultimately led me to set up my own business, Falcon Boats, running wildlife boat trips round the Pembrokeshire islands, where I get to share my love and passion for the Pembrokeshire coastline and that sense of kinship with our land.

I believe that by introducing people to the natural beauty on our doorstep and helping them learn about the diverse marine life that inhabits this coastal realm, a connection will be fostered that inspires all to preserve and protect. If you would like to find out more about what we do visit **www.falconboats.co.uk**

To quote Sir David Attenborough: 'It seems to me that the natural world is the greatest source of excitement; the greatest source of visual beauty; the greatest source of intellectual interest. It is the greatest source of so much in life that makes life worth living.'

# SEASONAL TIMELINE

|  | Jan | Feb | March | April | May |
|---|---|---|---|---|---|
| **Porpoise** | Resident all year | | | | |
| **Seals** | Moult | | | Resident all year | |
| **Gannets** | | Return to Grassholm | | Lay eggs | |
| **Shearwater** | | | Arrive mid March | | Lay eggs |
| **Puffins** | | | Arrive mid March | Nest building and egg laying | |
| **Razorbills and guilliemot** | | | Arrive back | | Lay eggs |
| **Kittiwake** | | | | Arrive back | Nest building & egg laying |
| **Chough** | | | | Lay eggs | |
| **Peregrine** | | | Lay eggs late March/ early April | | Chicks hatch late April/ early May |
| **Raven** | | Lay eggs | Eggs hatch late March to mid April | Young fledge in mid April, late May | |
| **Spring Flowers** | | | | Flowering | |
| **Heather** | | | | | |

| June | July | August | September | October | November | December |
|---|---|---|---|---|---|---|
| | | | | | | |
| | | Pupping season | | | | |
| Chicks hatch | | | Chicks fledge and start leaving the island | | | |
| Chicks hatch | | Adults leave | Fledgelings leave | | | |
| Chicks hatch begin June | Chick fledge | Adults leave late July/ early August | | | | |
| Chicks hatch | Chicks fledge Adults leave | | | | | |
| Chicks hatch | | Chicks fledge late July early August | | | | |
| Chicks fledge | | | | | | |
| Chicks fledge early June | | | | | | |
| | | | | | | |
| | | | | | | |
| | | Flowering | | | | |

## Ffion Rees

Ffion Rees was born in north Wales but grew up in Pembrokeshire. She spent five years doing an MA Hons degree in German and Celtic Civilisation at the University of Aberdeen, including a year teaching English in Vienna, before moving back to Pembrokeshire. After spending a couple of years alternating between Vienna and Pembrokeshire she settled back in Pembrokeshire where she now lives with her partner, dog and her horse.

After many years of working on boats both locally and abroad, including running specialist powerboat training, in far-flung places such as Bangladesh, Indonesia and Oman, she set up her own wildlife boat-tripping company, Falcon Boats, in 2016. She has also been a crew member on the St Davids lifeboat for 18 years.

In the last few years she has also provided safety boat cover for SY Ranger, a 41m J Class Super yacht, for regattas in Europe and the Caribbean, and in 2015 crewed on her first Atlantic crossing. She now spends her winters working as an expedition guide, zodiac driver and lecturer which has seen her working in the South Pacific, Indian Ocean and Antarctica.

## Landing on Ramsey

If you want to land on Ramsey there is a daily ferry run by Thousand Island Expeditions from Easter to October. Their booking office is on Cross Square in St Davids. www.thousandislands.co.uk Tel 01437 721721

## Boat trips

If you want to explore the islands by boat contact Falcon Boats. www.falconboats.co.uk Tel 07494 141764

## RSPB

Ramsey and Grassholm are National Nature Reserves owned and managed by the Royal Society for the Protection of Birds. The RSPB offer daily landings on Ramsey from April to October but note there are no landings on Grassholm, only round island trips offered by local boat operators. www.rspb.org.uk ramsey.island@rspb.org.uk Tel: 07836 535733

## RNLI – St Davids Lifeboat

St Davids lifeboat station was opened in 1869 and to date has been involved in saving over 360 lives at sea in more than 420 launches. www.stdavids-rnli.org.uk Tel 01437 720215

## Photo credits

The © copyright of photographs is attributed to Ffion Rees other than:
© Bathymetry images courtesy of Dr Paul Evans, Cardiff University, as part of the

Low Carbon Research Institute Marine
Consortium (www.lcrimarine.org)
(WEFO: 80366): page 113
© Crown Copyright and/or database rights.
Reproduced by permission of the Controller
of Her Majesty's Stationery Office and the UK
Hydrographic Office (www.GOV.uk/UKHO).
Not to be used for Navigation: end papers
and page 122
© Lyndon Lomax: pages, 18-19, 21 (top), 26,
32/33, 36, 45, 48/49, 69, 90, 92, 95 (bottom),
105, 116-117, 157.
© Janet Baxter: pages 6-7, 16 (top), 17, 79,
87 (bottom left), 88, 124, 144.
© Rob Davies: pages 39, 73, 90, 93, 94, 156.
© Dafydd Rees: page 139.
© Greg and Lisa Morgan: pages 46 (top), 101
(top), 102 (top), 103 (top).
© Tom Sutton: pages 40, 104.
© Judd Kohler: page 155 (left).
© Dick Wells: page 155 (right).
© Sam Hobson: pages 24 (middle), 25 (top).
© Huw James: page 9 (left)
© Georgina Jeremiah pages 74 (bottom).

## Poem credit

Moore, L., 'Until I Saw The Sea', *The Puffin
Book of Fantastic First Poems*, ed. June
Crebbin, Penguin, 2000, p.64.: page 10.

Every effort has been made to trace
copyright holders of material and
acknowledge permission for this publication.
The publisher apologises for any errors
or omissions to rights holders and would
be grateful for notification of credits and
corrections that should be included in future
reprints or editions of this book.

## Bibliography


Howells, R., *The Sounds Between*, The Five
Arches Press, 1976.

James, H. and T., *The Archaeology Of
Ramsey Island*, Initial Survey, for RSPB
1993-4.

Freeman, E., *The Solva Saga*

Bloom, T., *A History Of Solva*, Trevor Bloom,
1995.

Hague, D.B., *Lighthouses of Wales*,
RCAHMW, 1994.

Voitier, S.C., Bicknell, A., Cox, S.L., Scales,
K.L., Patrick, S.C., *A bird's Eye View of
Discards Reforms:Bird-Borne Cmaeras
RevealSaebird/Fisheries Interactions*, March
6th 20, 3, DOI: 10. 137/journal.pone.0057376

*Aquatic Mammals* 2015, 41(2), 188-191, DOI
10.1578/AM.41.2.2015.188

Stringell, T., Rees D. and F., Morgan, G. and
L.Hill, D.,Morris, C., *Predation of Harbour
Porpoises (Phocoena phocoena)by Grey
Seals (Halichoerus grypus) in Wales*, Aquatic
Mammals 2015, 41(2), 188-191, DOI 10.1578/
AM.41.2.2015.188

Hampson, D.G., Middleton, G.W., *The Story of
the St Davids Lifeboats*, booklet

2012 Field Report Ramsey Island Manx
Shearwater Geolocation Study
Kirk, H, Morgan,G.D, Guildford, T
(Joint initiative, RSPB and Oxford Naz
Research Group, Oxford Uni)

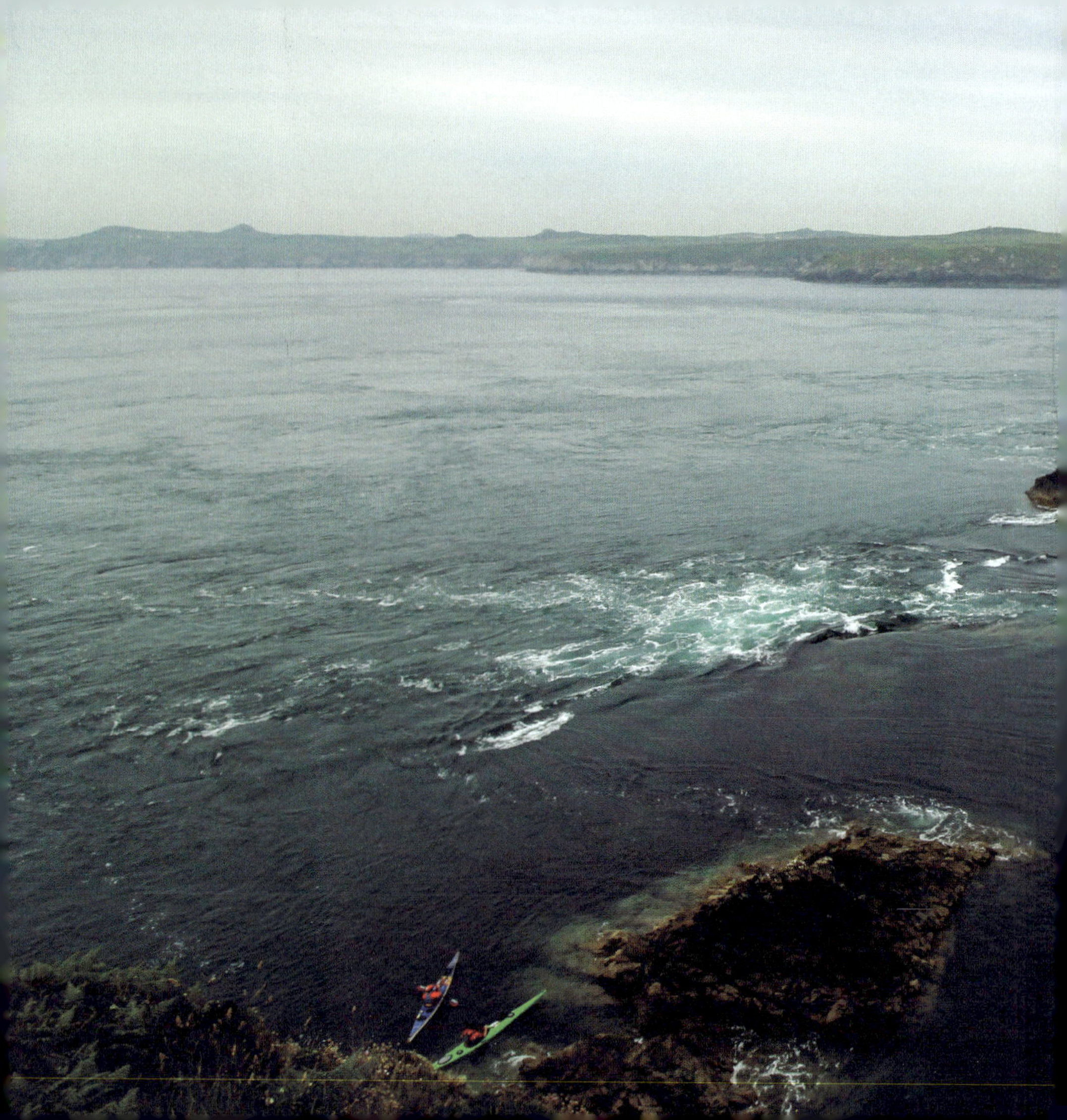